# TREBLE WINNERS

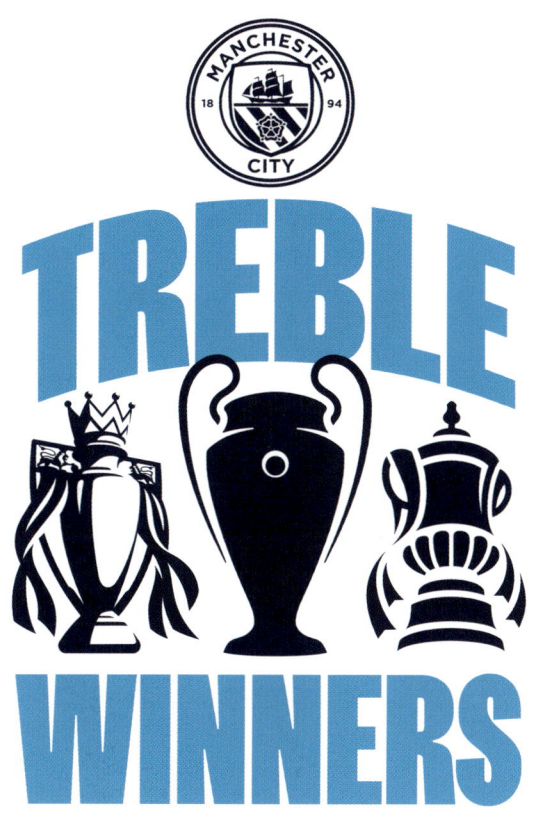

2022/23

# TREBLE WINNERS

2022/23

TREBLE

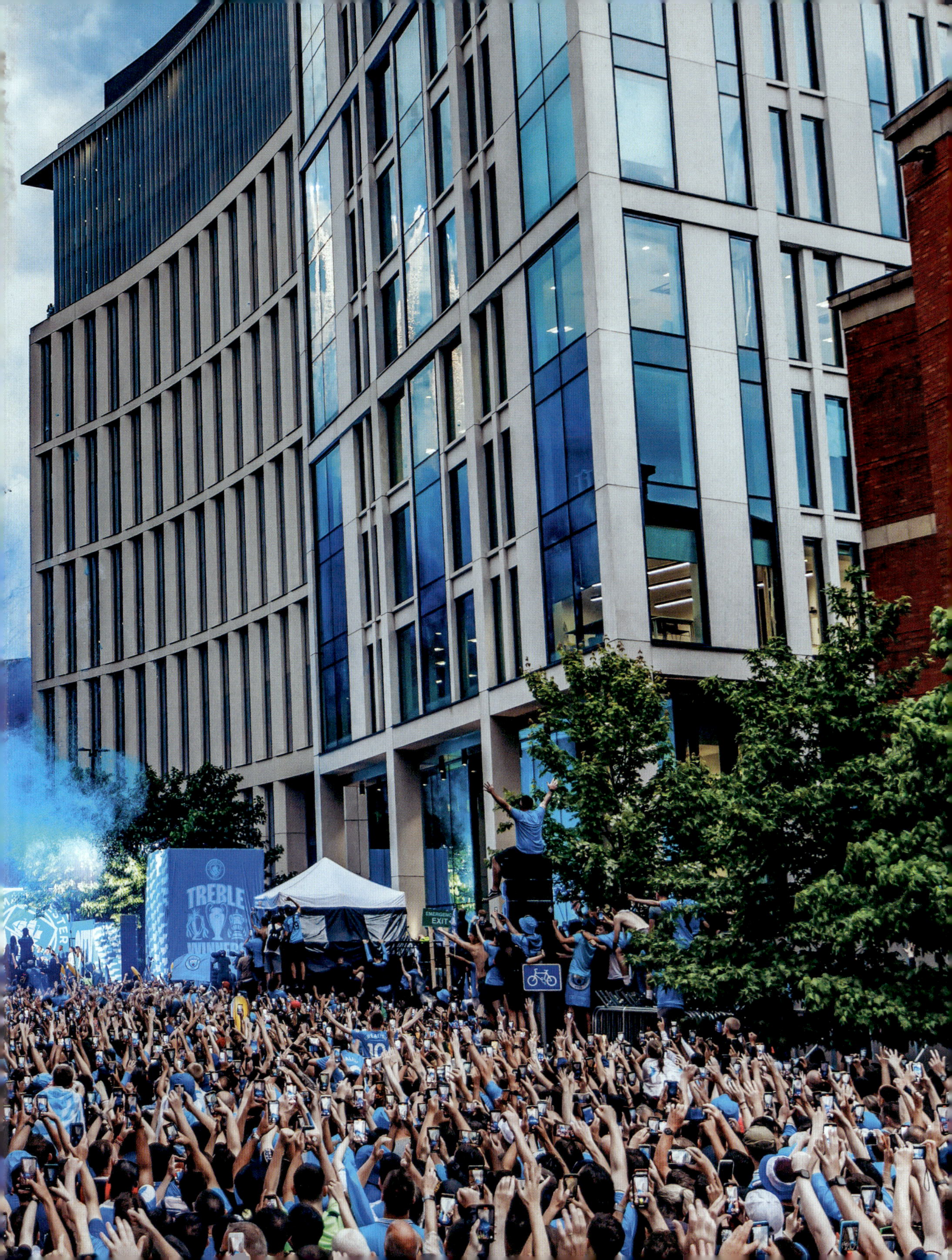
TREBLE
EXIT

Copyright © Manchester City Football Club

The right of Manchester City Football Club to be identified as the owner of this work has been asserted in accordance with the Copyright, Designs and Patents Act, 1988.

All Rights Reserved. No part of this publication may be reproduced, stored in a retrieval system, or transmitted in any form, or by any means, electronic, mechanical, photocopying, recording or otherwise without the prior permission in writing of the copyright holders, nor be otherwise circulated in any form of binding or cover other than in which it is published and without a similar condition being imposed on the subsequent publisher.

ISBN: 9781914197925

Writers: Rob Pollard, Paul Brown, David Clayton, Jonathan Smith, Neil Leigh, George Kelsey, Sam Cox, Jack Mumford and Holly Percival
Photo Editor: Declan Lloyd
Photography: Tom Flathers, Lexy Ilsley, Isaac Parkin, Harriet Jones and Alex Cuschieri
Additional imagery with thanks to Getty Images and PA Images
Production Editor: Nick Moreton
Executive Art Editor: Rick Cooke
Senior Designer: Neil Haines
Additional production: Harri Aston
Cover Design: Manchester City FC

First published in Great Britain and Ireland in 2023
by Reach Sport, a part of Reach PLC Ltd

www.reachsport.com

Printed by Bell & Bain

MIX
Paper | Supporting responsible forestry
FSC® C007785

# CONTENTS

**FOREWORD**
By Rob Pollard — 10

**CHAPTER 1: STAYING STRONG TO RETAIN OUR CROWN**
The Story of the Premier League — 14

**CHAPTER 2: THE HISTORY MAKERS**
Pep Guardiola — 56
Kyle Walker — 60
Ruben Dias — 64
Kalvin Phillips — 68
John Stones — 72
Nathan Ake — 76
Joao Cancelo — 80
Ilkay Gundogan — 84
Erling Haaland — 88
Jack Grealish — 92
Aymeric Laporte — 96
Rodrigo — 100
Kevin De Bruyne — 104
Stefan Ortega Moreno — 108
Julian Alvarez — 112
Bernardo Silva — 116
Sergio Gomez — 120
Manuel Akanji — 124
Riyad Mahrez — 128
Ederson — 132
Maximo Perrone — 136
Scott Carson — 140
Phil Foden — 144
Cole Palmer — 148
Rico Lewis — 152

**CHAPTER 3: WEMBLEY WONDERS DELIVER THE DOUBLE**
The Story of the FA Cup — 156

**CHAPTER 4: TREBLE DREAMS COME TRUE IN ISTANBUL**
The Story of the Champions League — 184

**CHAPTER 5: 48 HOURS IN ISTANBUL**
A fan's eye view of the greatest weekend in our history — 224

**CHAPTER 6: TREBLE TREBLE**
Re-writing the record books with our Academy — 234

**CHAPTER 7: BEHIND THE SCENES**
A unique perspective from our first team film unit — 242

**CHAPTER 8: RECORDS AND MILESTONES**
The standout stats from an incredible campaign — 272

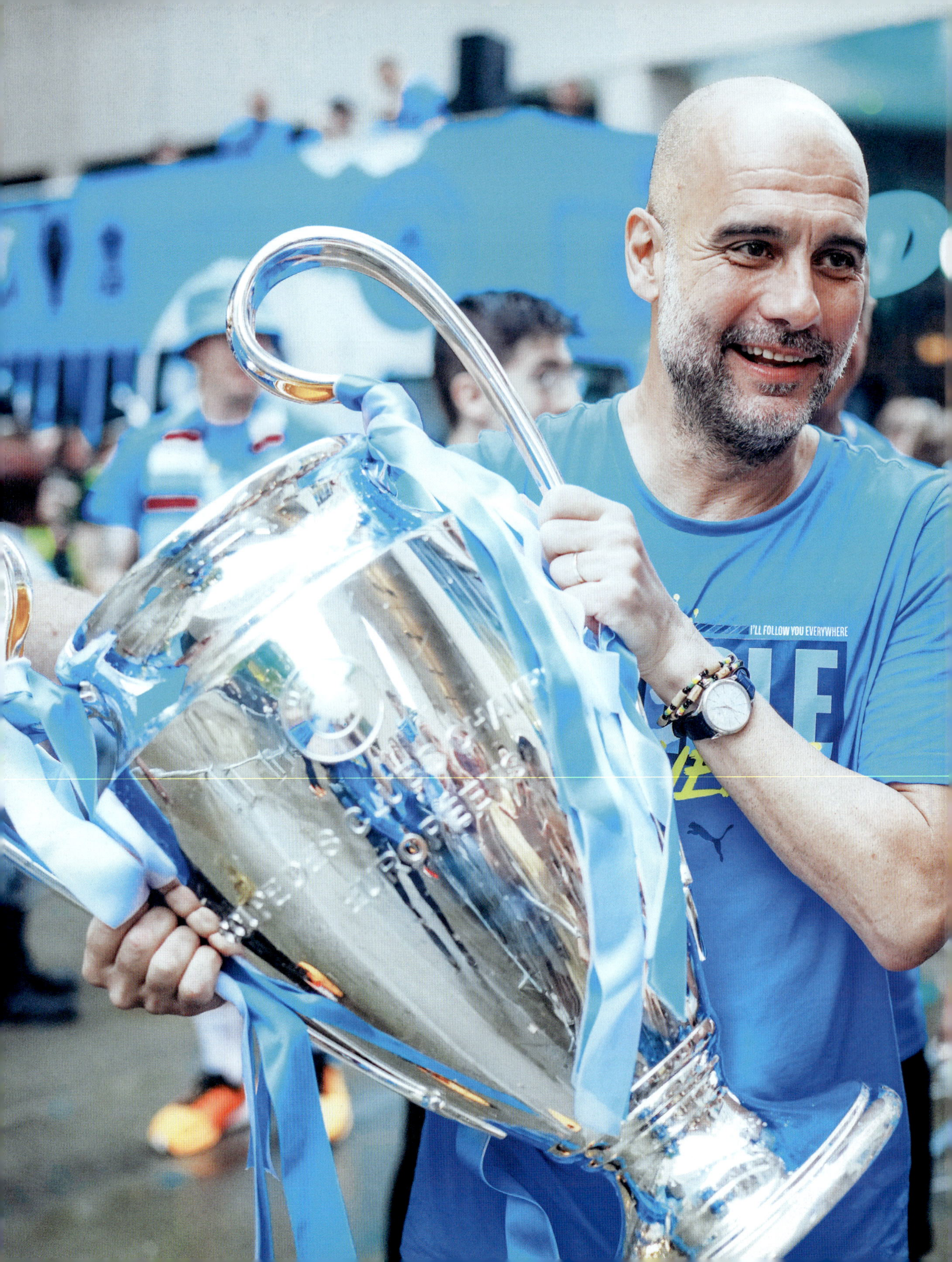
I'LL FOLLOW YOU EVERYWHERE

'IT WAS WRITTEN IN THE STARS'

PEP GUARDIOLA

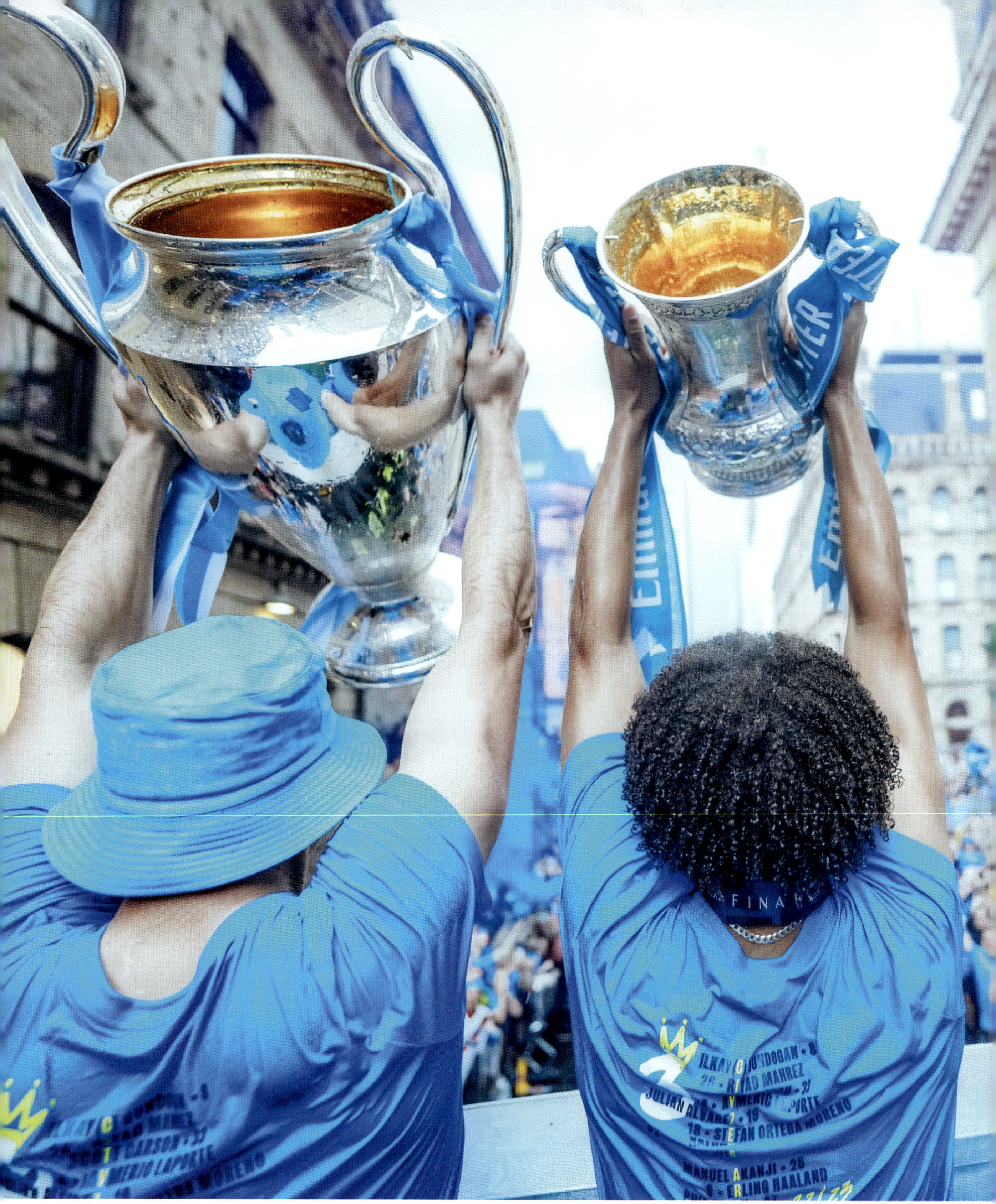
18 - STEFAN ORTEGA MORENO
MANUEL AKANJI - 25

## FOREWORD

**The 2002/23 season was the best in Manchester City's 129-year history.**

The Treble of Premier League, Champions League and FA Cup is the holy grail for any English football club – and City, led by the expert management of Pep Guardiola, delivered this historic achievement in style.

When we lost 1-0 away at Tottenham on 5 February in the Premier League, Guardiola's side were five points behind Arsenal having played a game more than the North Londoners. But an inspired run of 13 wins from our next 14 Premier League matches saw us secure a third title in succession with three matches to spare. Arsenal, who won admirers throughout the season for their style and determination, were ultimately powerless to stop the City juggernaut.

In the FA Cup, City didn't concede a goal en route to the final, dispatching Chelsea, Arsenal, Bristol City, Burnley and Sheffield United in the process (aggregate score 17-0), before defeating Manchester United 2-1 at Wembley in the first ever Manchester derby in a major final.

That FA Cup win, the seventh in our history, means we extended the record for the longest time between a club's first FA Cup win and most recent – 119 years – with our first success in the competition coming back in 1904.

But arguably the most glorious chapter was the final one, our 1-0 win over Inter in Istanbul that sealed our first-ever UEFA Champions League success, ending

**TREBLE WINNERS**

our quest for success in Europe's elite competition and completing a magical Treble.

It may not have been a classic, with City struggling to conjure the kind of beautiful football we have all become so used to against a well-drilled and tenacious Inter side. However, unlike two years earlier when we lost 1-0 to Chelsea in Porto when not at our best, this time we got the job done thanks to Rodrigo's winner with 22 minutes remaining.

It's only the tenth occasion a European side has won a Treble, with City joining Celtic (1967), Ajax (1972), PSV Eindhoven (1988), Manchester United (1999), Barcelona (2009 and 2015), Inter (2010) and Bayern Munich (2013 and 2020).

Guardiola has now won 14 major trophies since joining the club in 2016 – a collection comprising five Premier League titles, two FA Cups, four League Cups, one Champions League and two Community Shields – and is the first manager to win two European Trebles (Barcelona 2009 and City 2023).

This book is a celebration of City's greatest season. In it you will find wonderful imagery telling the story of our season, captured by our embedded team of photographers. There are reviews of key matches and profiles of every single player who contributed along the way. And there's a celebration too, of our amazing Academy success, which has seen us win the Premier League 2 and Under-18s Premier League titles for the third consecutive year.

This is the most comprehensive look back at the greatest season in Manchester City's history.

Enjoy the book.
CITY!

**Rob Pollard**

www.mancity.com 13

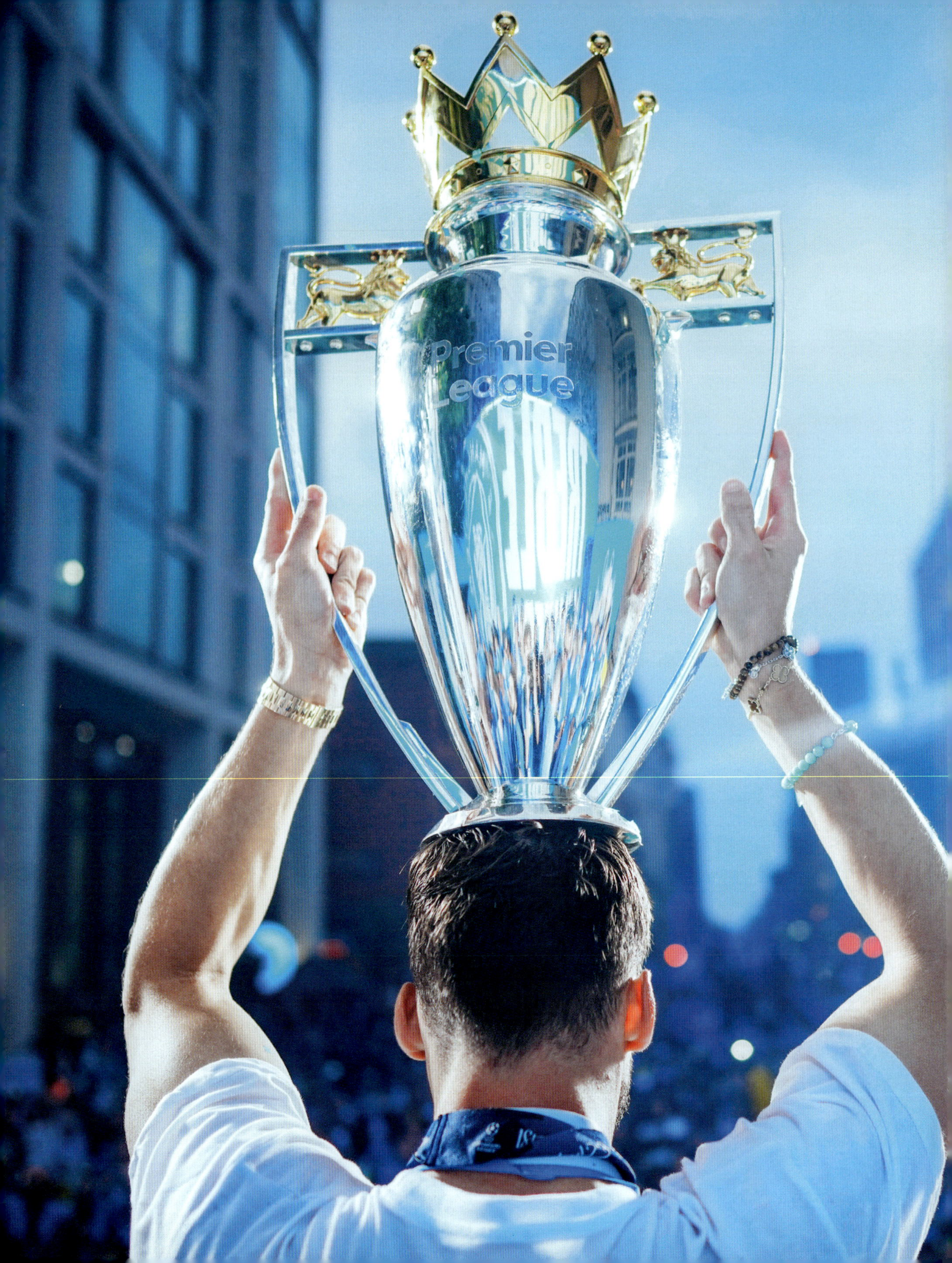
Premier
League

# 1

### THE STORY OF THE PREMIER LEAGUE

# STAYING STRONG TO RETAIN OUR CROWN

TREBLE WINNERS

# AUGUST: HAALAND'S EXPLOSIVE START

**Prior to the 2022/23 season, there was an electrically-charged crackle in the air among City fans, thanks in no small part to the arrival of Erling Haaland.**

Arguably the most coveted striker in world football had chosen his boyhood club for the next chapter of his career and, in doing so, providing an already potent Manchester City squad with a natural goal-scorer.

The previous campaign had seen Pep Guardiola utilise his squad to fill the void left by Sergio Aguero's departure with false No.9s and Gabriel Jesus.

Jesus, along with Oleksandr Zinchenko, both left the Blues to join Arsenal in the summer of 2022, while Haaland and Julian Alvarez significantly boosted our striking options.

Goalkeeper Stefan Ortega Moreno, midfielder Kalvin Phillips and, a little later, Manuel Akanji also joined City for the new campaign.

Many wondered how City would adapt to having an out-and-out striker, given the intricate build-up play that had become a trademark during the Guardiola era – many suggested the Blues would have to change the brand of football that had already resulted in so many trophies.

In the eyes of many City fans and pundits, Haaland was the missing piece of the jigsaw – only time would tell whether that would prove true.

There were other questions to answer, too.

How would a World Cup tournament in the middle of the campaign affect a team who always seem to click into top gear in the weeks before and months after Christmas?

And with 16 players heading for Qatar, how would that affect their rhythm and momentum?

The opening fixture for the Blues was against the team that had been our biggest challengers in recent years – Liverpool.

The FA Community Shield clash at Leicester City's King Power Stadium offered the chance for an early glimpse at Haaland, but it would be Liverpool's big summer signing – Darwin Nunez – who would steal the headlines in a 3-1 win for the Merseysiders.

Haaland was the subject of an expected but unfair spotlight after his first game in City colours, but he would answer those critics quickly – and how!

A week later, the Premier League schedule kicked off with a tricky-looking game away to West Ham United.

The Hammers had been the surprise package of the previous campaign, finishing seventh in the table, and had also held title-chasing City 2-2 at the London Stadium just a few months before.

It would turn out to be a Premier League debut to remember for Haaland, who won and then converted a

> "He was really calm, he trained really well but the way he took the ball for the penalty I said, 'I like it'. I think if someone is taking the ball, he would punch them in the face even though they are his mates! And that is a pretty good sign. To be so confident, I like it"
>
> - Pep Guardiola on Erling Haaland

penalty kick on 36 minutes to put City ahead and then, in what would become a lethal understanding, he raced onto a precise through-ball from Kevin De Bruyne to expertly sweep home his second after the break and secure a 2-0 opening-day win.

"I know how he handled a lot of criticism this week," said Guardiola.

"He was really calm, he trained really well but the way he took the ball for the penalty, I said, 'I like it.'

"So direct and I think if someone is taking the ball, he would punch them in the face even though they are his mates! And that is a pretty good sign. To be so confident, I like it."

The defending Premier League champions were off and running and Haaland's finishing had been the difference on the day.

A week later, City cruised home 4-0 against Bournemouth at the Etihad Stadium, with the only surprise being Haaland wasn't among the scorers – Ilkay Gundogan, De Bruyne, Phil Foden and Jefferson Lermer, with an own goal, did find the net, however.

If West Ham had been a difficult trip to begin the title defence, the next fixture on the road looked even tougher against a revitalised Newcastle United.

A fixture City had rarely failed to win over the past decade, the hosts recovered from an early Gundogan

TREBLE WINNERS

goal to lead 3-1 at an ecstatic St James' Park with only 54 minutes played.

Were Eddie Howe's side about to deliver an early blow to the Blues' title aspirations?

The answer would be no, as we responded as a tiger having its tail pulled and within 10 minutes the scores were level at 3-3 thanks to Haaland and Bernardo Silva, and a precious point was rescued.

Guardiola's men hadn't been at their best, but we had demonstrated we could shift up a gear when needed.

"When you take these type of players with this quality, it can happen. It's the beginning of the season and I think it's really, really good for us to live this kind of experience," said the boss.

"We spoke about that at half-time, 'we need to live this, 2-1 down, we'll see what happens now, how we are as a team, let's go'.

"That's what we have to do, we have to live these kind of situations.

"That's why the Premier League is so difficult. Everyone is going to drop points and we have dropped the first two, but considering how we behaved from 2-1 down..."

Remarkably for this side, a week later City again trailed by two goals, this time at the hands of bogey team Crystal Palace, who opened up a 2-0 lead inside 21 minutes at the Etihad.

Again, the response was impressive as Bernardo began the fightback eight minutes after the break and then it was the Erling Haaland show as the Norwegian struck three times in 19 minutes to give his team a 4-2 victory.

The Blues were turning on the style when needed, but there had been uncharacteristic defensive lapses in the early weeks of the season that concerned Guardiola and Manuel Akanji was signed to give the boss further options.

City ended the month with a 6-0 home win over newly-promoted Nottingham Forest and Haaland's incredible start to life in sky blue continued with another hat-trick, taking his tally to nine in his first five league games - Cancelo and Alvarez (2) were also on the scoresheet.

City ended the month in second place, with Arsenal top with a 100% record from their first five matches.

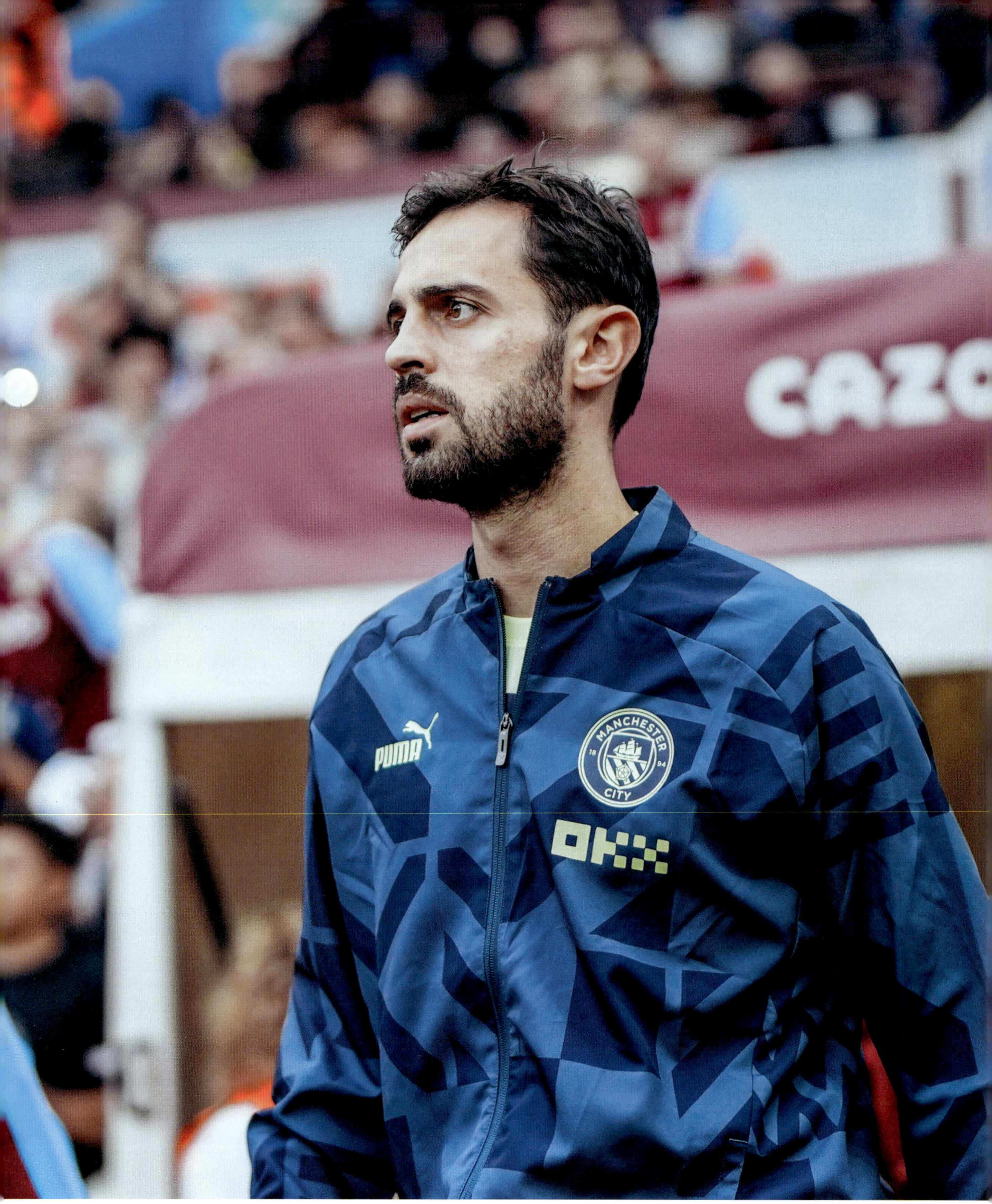
CAZO
PUMA
MANCHESTER
CITY
18
94

THE STORY OF THE PREMIER LEAGUE

## SEPTEMBER: ONCE UPON A TIME IN THE MIDLANDS

**Due to an international break, September featured just two Premier League games.**

Struggling Aston Villa were not expected to cause too many problems for City, but at a vibrant Villa Park, Steven Gerrard's side proved a tough obstacle.

After a goalless first period, the Blues broke the deadlock five minutes into the second-half, with a wonderful De Bruyne cross picking out Haaland at the back post to volley home his 10th of the season.

But Villa clawed their way back into the game through Leon Bailey's leveller and the 1-1 draw felt like two points dropped for City.

"It was a good game, we conceded just one goal to one shot on target," said Guardiola.

"We were not precise enough on our final touches. The game was in our hands. They defended really well, so we drew. We were better after our goal. They were well organised, but for the way they defended, we created enough chances to score goals. Every game is difficult."

The Blues returned to the Midlands a week later to take on Wolves and the Blues were two goals ahead inside 16 minutes at Molineux.

Jack Grealish scored after just 55 seconds and Haaland – inevitably – added a second with a low drive from 20 yards.

Nathan Collins saw red for a bad challenge on Grealish 33 minutes in and Foden killed off 10-man Wolves with a third on 69 minutes.

Guardiola's men headed into the international break unbeaten in any of the nine games played and were one point behind leaders Arsenal.

www.mancity.com 21

TREBLE WINNERS

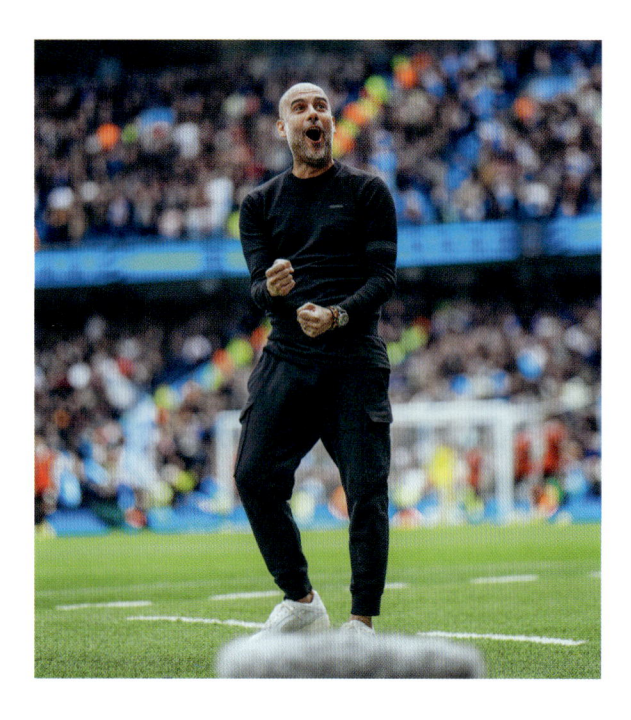

# OCTOBER: DEMOLITION DERBY

**City could not have started October any better, beginning with a blistering display against Manchester United.**

Haaland and Foden both scored twice as the Blues went in 4-0 up at the break – with the Etihad in raptures – and it looked as if it could be a record victory over our neighbours.

Antony pulled one back after the re-start, but further goals from Haaland and Foden, who both completed their hat-tricks, made it 6-1 with 20 minutes or so remaining.

Two Anthony Martial goals in the dying moments gave the final 6-3 scoreline a flattering look for the Reds, but nobody was complaining (at least on the blue side of Manchester).

Incredibly, it was Haaland's third successive home Premier League treble, with the Norwegian looking unstoppable.

www.mancity.com 23

24 www.mancity.com

## THE STORY OF THE PREMIER LEAGUE

For boyhood Blue Foden, it was an ambition realised.

"It's a dream come true playing in a derby being a City fan as well," he said. "It's been a pleasure to be a part of this team.

"Our determination was there from the kick-off and we finished our chances."

Given the goals scored so far, you'd have got terrific odds on the Blues failing to score in the next three games – yet that's exactly what happened with a 1-0 defeat to Liverpool sandwiched between two goalless Champions League draws with Copenhagen and Dortmund which secured passage to the Round of 16.

Normal service was resumed in the final two games of October with a 3-1 win over Brighton (Haaland scoring twice and De Bruyne getting a decisive third) and De Bruyne's stunning free-kick away to Leicester was enough to edge a 1-0 win over the struggling Foxes.

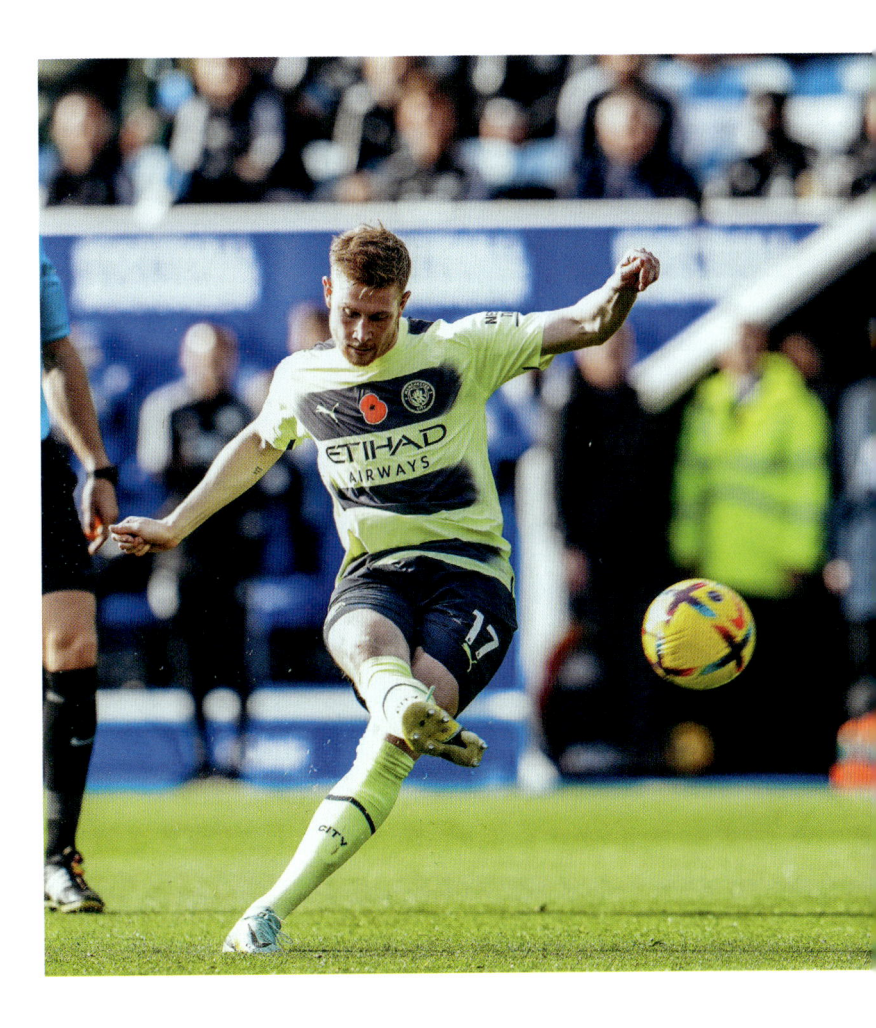

www.mancity.com 25

TREBLE WINNERS

# NOVEMBER: ADVANTAGE ARSENAL

**With the World Cup on the horizon, City looked to end the first part of the campaign as strongly as possible, but it would turn out to be a stuttering rather than barnstorming few weeks.**

First up, Fulham proved dogged opposition and despite going behind to an early Alvarez goal, when Cancelo was red carded on 26 minutes and Andreas Pereira converted the resulting penalty, it looked like being a long afternoon for the 10-man Blues.

Then, deep into added time, De Bruyne won a penalty that Haaland just about tucked home to give the Blues a dramatic last-gasp 2-1 win.

The celebrations at the end from the players, fans and the City boss suggested this had been a much bigger victory than it might have looked on paper.

"We didn't win the Premier League today, but this moment makes sense for our job," Guardiola declared.

"Everyone was exceptional, playing for 65 minutes v Fulham with 10 men, the way we played, the moment and my period here in Manchester celebrating with the fans…

"Seeing the faces in the crowds, the run round the pitch – it was very good.

"It was so exciting, the emotion as a manager. After seven years here, you have doubts, thousands of training sessions and matches and travel, but still they are alive and want to do it. It makes me so, so proud."

Next, Chelsea were beaten 2-0 in the Carabao Cup thanks to goals from Mahrez and Alvarez before the final

26 www.mancity.com

> "After seven years here, you have doubts, thousands of training sessions and matches and travel, but still they are alive and want to do it. It makes me so, so proud"
>
> - Pep Guardiola

game ahead of the World Cup against Brentford.

Few believed the Blues wouldn't recover from Ivan Toney's 16th-minute header and when Foden thumped home the equaliser in first-half added time, Guardiola's men were expected to go on and win the game.

But Brentford's game plan and an off-colour City meant that Toney's second three minutes into additional time gave the Bees a shock 2-1 win at the Etihad – a sting in the tail if ever there was one, but Guardiola simply said afterwards: "The better team won."

It was Mikel Arteta's Arsenal who went into the domestic break five points clear at the top – there would be work to do when the season resumed, with the Gunners looking confident and comfortable out in front.

www.mancity.com 27

TREBLE WINNERS

# DECEMBER: WORLD CUP HANGOVER?

As City fans watched proudly as Julian Alvarez became a World Cup winner, the domestic campaign in England began again.

The Blues began with a rip-roaring 3-2 Carabao Cup win over Liverpool, with many of our World Cup stars back in action against the Reds.

In a game that ebbed and flowed, Haaland and Mahrez saw goals quickly cancelled out by levellers from Fabio Carvalho and Mohamed Salah before Nathan Ake grabbed a decisive fifth goal of the contest to put City in the quarter-finals of a competition that had been nicknamed 'the Man City Cup' after Guardiola's side had dominated the tournament in recent years.

But despite a 3-1 win at Leeds as the title race kicked back into life – Rodrigo and Haaland, whose two goals made him the fastest player to reach 20 Premier League goals, on target – the Blues ended 2022 with a hugely disappointing 1-1 draw with struggling Everton at the Etihad.

Haaland scored again, but Demarai Gray's stunning equaliser meant two more points had been dropped and Arsenal took full advantage, beating Wolves 4-2 to move seven points clear.

"They made a fantastic goal with the first shot on target they had, so we played a really good game," said Guardiola.

"Of course the result was not expected but that is football, it is not the first time it happened. We did everything to win. They played really well.

"In general, we did everything and unfortunately could not win."

Retaining the title for a third successive year was suddenly looking increasingly difficult.

www.mancity.com 29

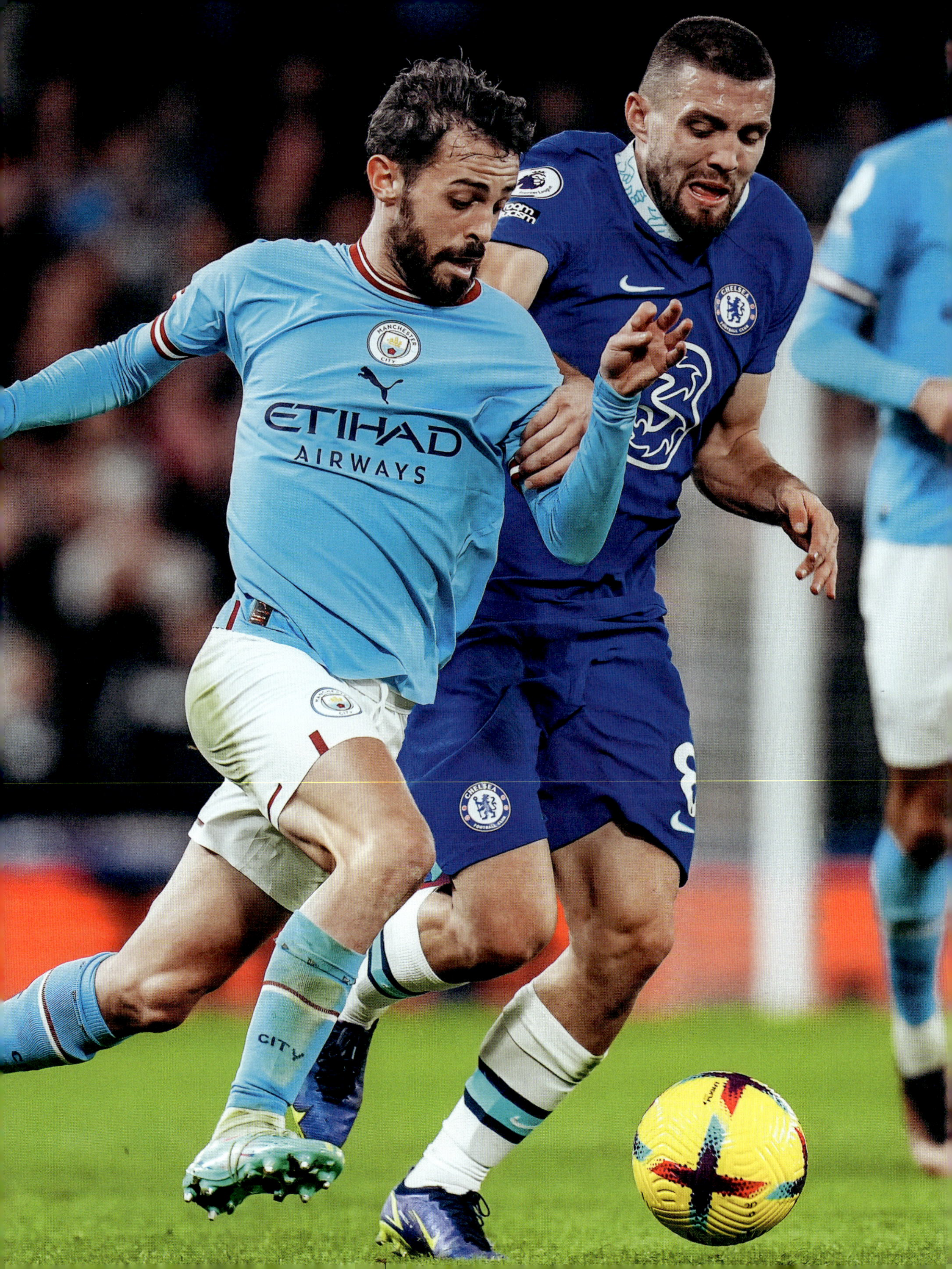
ETIHAD
AIRWAYS
CITY

THE STORY OF THE PREMIER LEAGUE

# JANUARY: RHYTHM HARD TO COME BY

**The start of the New Year proved something of an up and down month.**

Mahrez's goal midway through the second half was enough for City to edge a hard-fought 1-0 win over Chelsea at Stamford Bridge – never an easy venue to collect points from.

City then travelled to the south coast to face relegation-threatened Southampton in the Carabao Cup quarter-finals, but the Blues turned in easily the worst display of the campaign with a deserved 2-0 defeat to Nathan Jones' side.

Worse still, a 2-1 Manchester derby defeat to United followed despite City taking the lead through a Grealish header.

A bizarre VAR decision then allowed a Bruno Fernandes equaliser to stand on 78 minutes after an offside Marcus Rashford had initially chased a through ball and then Rashford himself scored the winner four minutes later.

The Blues felt hard done by – and no wonder.

Guardiola commented: "Marcus Rashford is offside, Bruno Fernandes is not. Rashford distracted our keeper and centre defenders. It is what it is."

Something wasn't quite clicking for the Blues, and at home to Spurs next, with 45 minutes played, many wondered if the title race was effectively over.

The North London side silenced the Etihad with two goals in two minutes just before the break to go in 2-0 up.

At that point, it looked like the gap between City and Arsenal would increase to eight points plus the Gunners had played one game less – that would be a significant advantage, even with less than half the season played.

What followed was arguably the most important 45 minutes of City's season – and Guardiola's men rose to the challenge, turning a two-goal deficit into a 3-2 lead within 18 exhilarating minutes courtesy of goals from Alvarez, Mahrez and Haaland – a late fourth from the excellent Mahrez completed a 4-2 win and it was the third time that season the Blues had recovered from two goals down.

But Guardiola was furious with the way things seemed to be panning out.

Memorably, he said after the game: "I don't recognise my team. Everything is so comfortable, but opponents

www.mancity.com 31

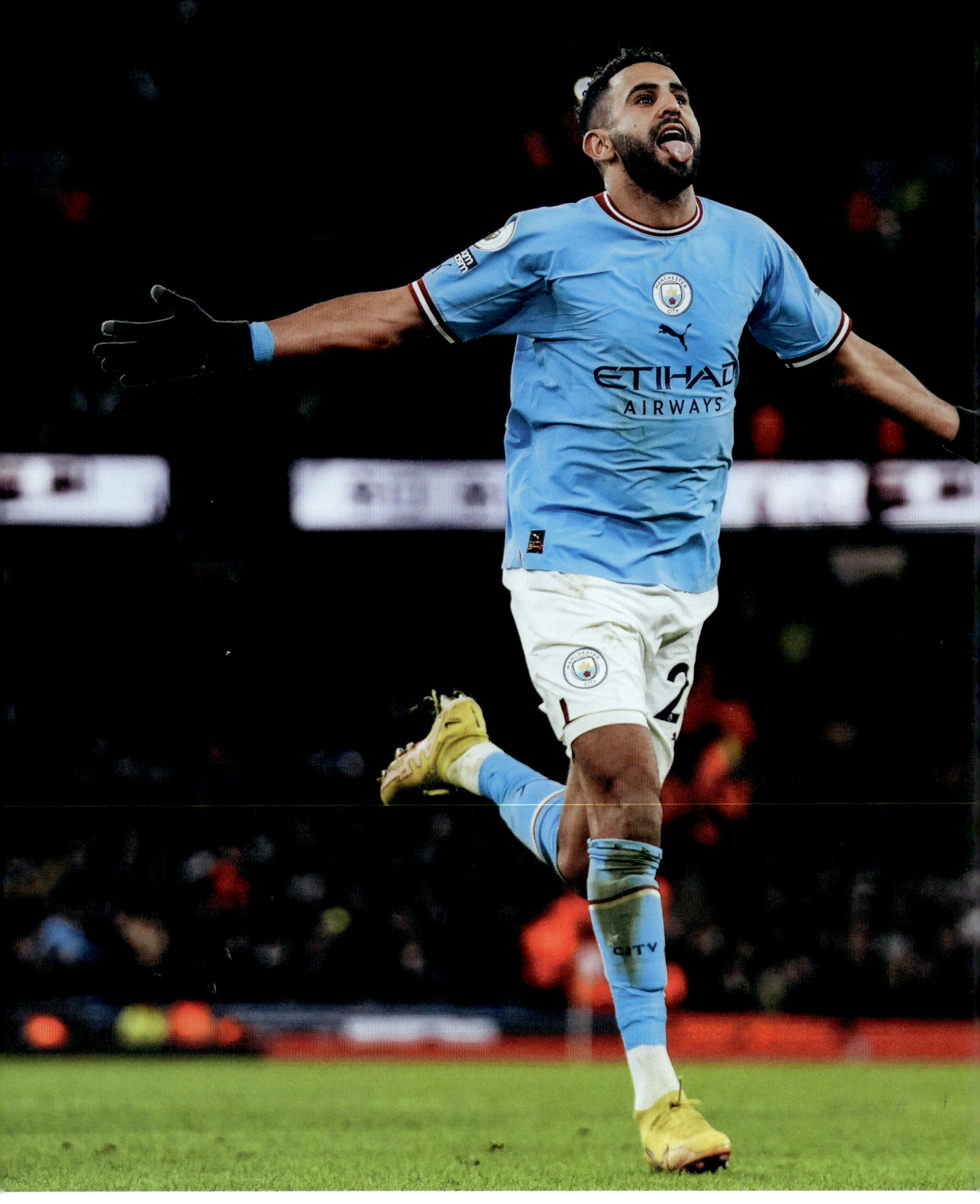
ETIHAD
AIRWAYS

## THE STORY OF THE PREMIER LEAGUE

don't wait. There's nothing from the stomach, from the guts. The same with the fans, they are silent for 45 minutes. I want my fans back.

"I want a reaction, from the whole club, everyone. We're a happy flowers team. I don't want to be happy flowers. I want to beat Arsenal. If we play that way, Arsenal will beat us."

It was an emotional and inspirational speech that was perhaps the wake-up call everyone needed – City weren't going to succeed playing at 70-80% of their ability – it needed to be all or nothing.

The response was immediate and a 3-0 win over Wolves three days later, with Haaland scoring yet another hat-trick and taking his tally to 31 in all competitions, might have been tempered by a last-gasp Arsenal winner over Manchester United later in the day, but the focus had been reset and everyone was on the same page again.

And January ended with a first meeting between the Premier League's top two teams as City looked to strike a psychological blow over the Gunners in the FA Cup – and Nathan Ake's 64th-minute goal proved the difference between two evenly-matched sides.

www.mancity.com

TREBLE WINNERS

# FEBRUARY: BLUES SHIFT UP A GEAR

**Though Arsenal still had a game in hand, their shock 1-0 loss away to Everton gave City the chance to move within touching distance of the league leaders.**

That meant doing something the Blues had never done away at Tottenham's new stadium – score a goal and avoid defeat.

Incredibly, for the fifth time in succession, City left the North London venue having failed to score and Harry Kane's 15th minute goal ensured a 1-0 loss and a chance definitely had been missed to close the gap at the top.

"One day we are going to score in this stadium," said Guardiola afterwards.

"We are a team that scores goals, but I could not expect against Tottenham to create a lot of chances. We created in the beginning, but they defended with nine players really well, well organised, the squad is fantastic that they have."

Some pundits and journalists suggested that perhaps the title race was as good as over, with the Blues far from their best and an ever-increasing feeling that this might be Arsenal's year given the nature of some of their late victories and definite rub of the green in a number of games.

What nobody could have predicted was what was to come next, and those who doubted this group of Manchester City players would eventually have to eat their words as the sky blue juggernaut finally began to pick up speed.

The City players knew we hadn't been firing on all cylinders and needed to up the ante – the doubters merely fuelled the fire in the bellies of the defending champions and the fight was very much on.

City made light work of Aston Villa, with three first-half goals from Rodrigo, Gundogan and Mahrez putting the Blues on the way to a 3-1 home victory ahead of the biggest game of the campaign yet – a trip to face Arsenal in a game many felt would play a major role in the title race.

The Gunners had hit a sticky patch at precisely the wrong time and hosting a resurgent City was probably the last thing Arteta's side wanted – but a home win and the destiny was very much in Arsenal's own hands.

With the Emirates Stadium a cacophony of nervous energy, the best two teams in the country went to battle.

A superb De Bruyne lob gave the Blues the advantage before a generous penalty award allowed Bukayo Saka to level before the break.

34 www.mancity.com

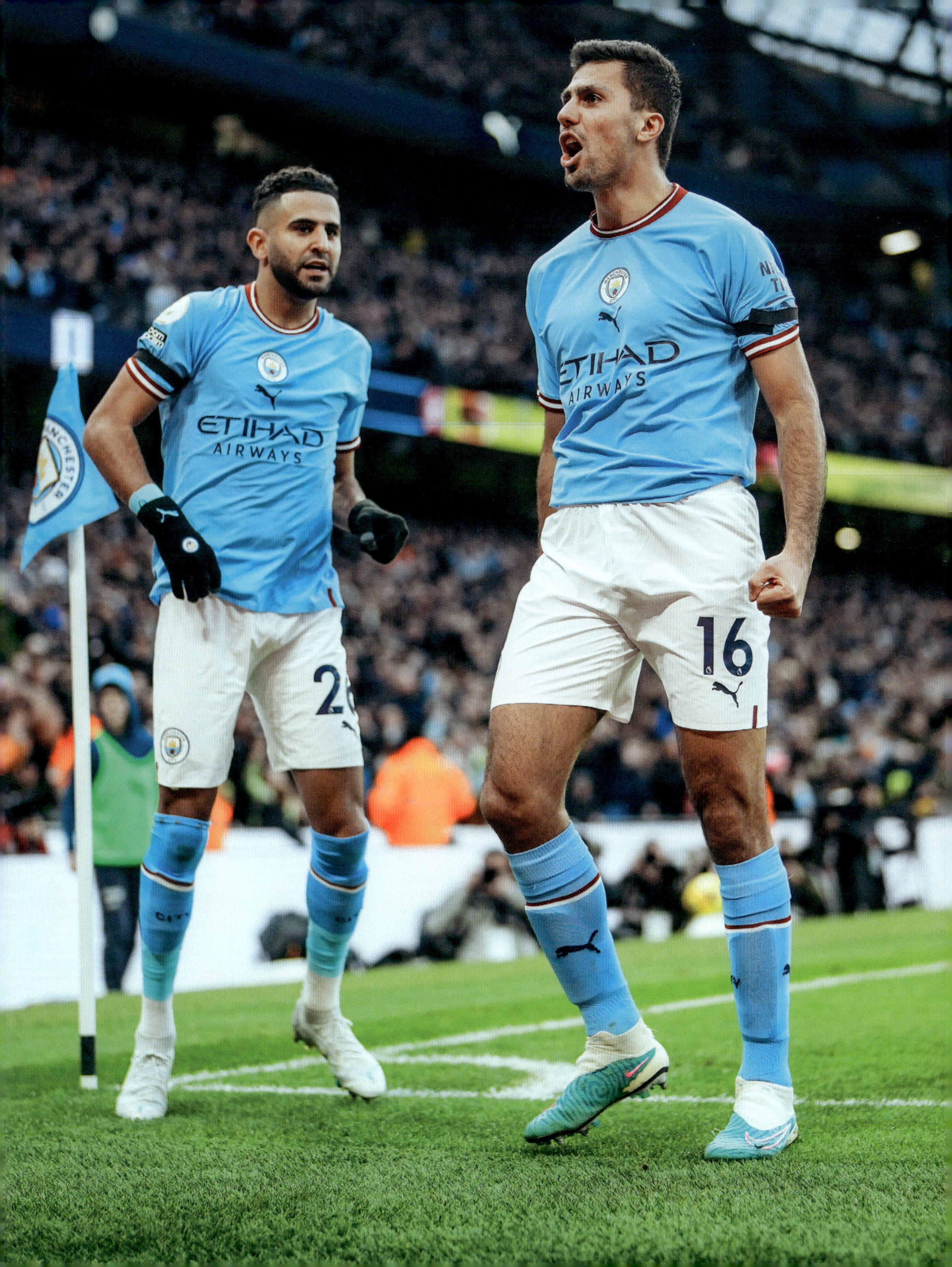
ETIHAD
AIRWAYS
ETIHAD
AIRWAYS
16

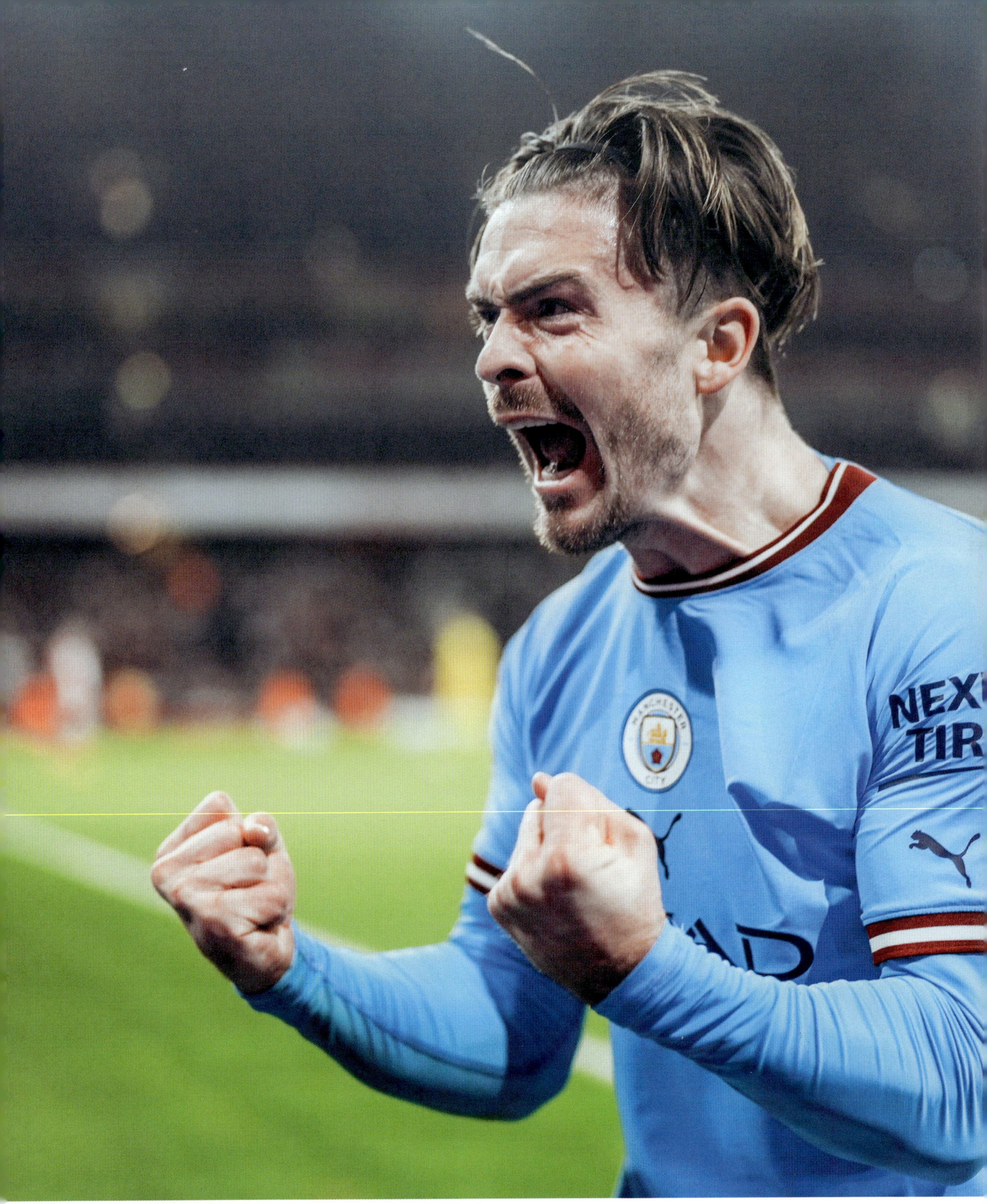
NEXT
TIR

### THE STORY OF THE PREMIER LEAGUE

The game was teetering one way, then the other, but a deflected Grealish goal on 72 minutes, followed by an instinctive Haaland finish 10 minutes later, gave Guardiola's side a crucial 3-1 victory – and finally the Blues were top of the table once again, albeit briefly.

"When you come to these moments against your rival, it just means everything," Ruben Dias said afterwards.

"For our team that's the way to live it. One game at a time but leave it all there in that one game and make sure you have nothing left to give. We know how talented our team is so in the end it's about giving the best of ourselves because if we get that then it will be very difficult for teams to beat us.

"We're taking it one step at a time and there's still a long way to go. It's in our mind to just keep getting better and better. We're getting into the deep of the season, a lot to play, this is the moment to be here and be present. Important day for the team and I hope we keep doing like this."

It felt as though the pendulum had swung our way, but in the next game City were made to pay for a host of missed chances as Nottingham Forest snatched a late equaliser at the City Ground through Chris Wood after Bernardo had opened the scoring.

Arsenal's 4-2 win at Aston Villa put them back top, two points clear with a game in hand, and the Blues had to go again.

www.mancity.com 37

TREBLE WINNERS

# MARCH: RELENTLESS CITY POWER ON

**There was hardly time to catch breath as the games came thick and fast.**

City were gradually moving into top gear and a hard-earned 2-0 win over Newcastle United at the Etihad – Foden and Bernardo on target – ticked off another difficult fixture.

"You know when you play Newcastle how good they are this season," said Bernardo.

"They went for it because they need points. We knew they would press more and create more chances, so the second goal was important for us.

"There is a good team spirit at the moment. We have had tough moments this season, but we want to compete and do our best. It won't be easy, but we will fight for all of the titles we are still in.

"We'll see, we can only focus on ourselves now, we cannot focus on Arsenal. We need to do our job because if we don't it will not matter what Arsenal does or not."

It was full steam ahead for the Blues.

Next up, Crystal Palace away.

In a tough, physical, and tactical battle with Palace, it looked as though the Eagles might hold out for a 0-0 draw, until clever work from Gundogan drew a foul in the box and the referee pointed to the spot.

Haaland kept his cool and slotted home to give the Blues a vital 1-0 win at Selhurst Park.

And City continued to progress in both other competitions with a quarter-final booked in the Champions League and a FA Cup semi-final berth guaranteed.

38 www.mancity.com

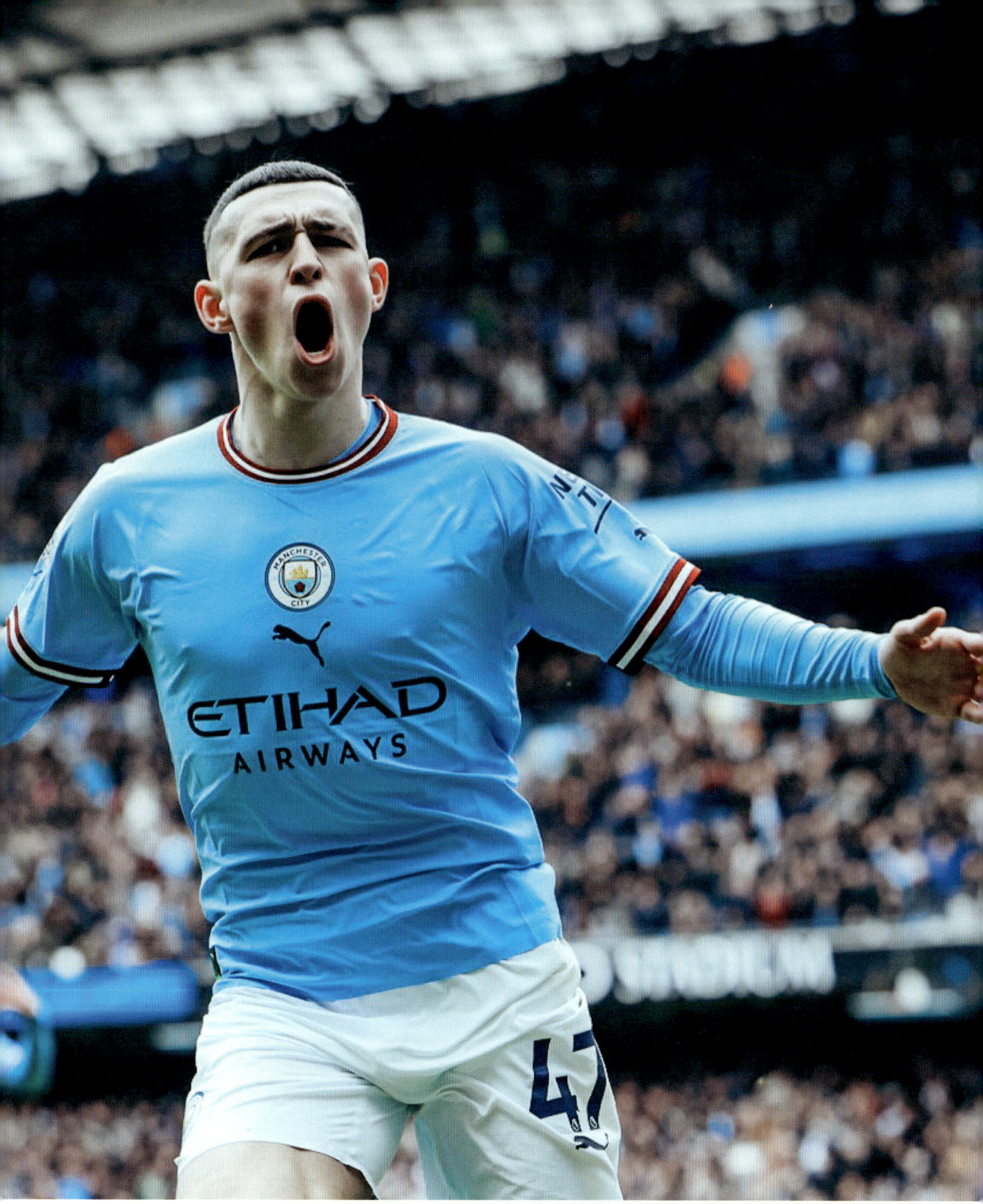
ETIHAD
AIRWAYS

TREBLE WINNERS

# APRIL: ADVANTAGE CITY

**City began April in superb style, coming from behind to thrash a misfiring Liverpool 4-1 at the Etihad.**

Goals from Alvarez, De Bruyne, Gundogan and the outstanding Grealish, cancelled out Salah's early strike as our biggest rivals for the past five years were easily brushed aside.

"I was in the toilet, and I felt sick all morning, but I was buzzing in the end. I love football and I love playing," said Grealish.

"I love training, and when it's going well and stuff like this there's nothing better. I'm back to my normal self now, back to full fitness, I'm feeling confident, and scoring today and getting the assist is perfect."

The title race was still swinging one way and another, with City's cup involvement meaning Arsenal led the table by eight points but having played one game more.

Destiny remained in the Gunners' hands with a meeting at the Etihad still to come.

Southampton were no match for the Blues who avenged the Carabao Cup defeat in January with a 4-1 win – Haaland on target twice, Grealish and Alvarez from the spot being the scorers.

The Blues were purring, playing devastating football and blowing teams away, and Leicester City were the next side to feel the blast, beaten 3-1 at the Etihad, with the prolific Haaland finding the net twice and Stones also on the scoresheet.

Intriguingly, with Arsenal again dropping points unexpectedly, it left City three points adrift of the leaders and with a superior goal difference.

The title destiny was now in City's hands and next up was one of the most eagerly-awaited Premier League games for many years as City hosted Arsenal in a summit meeting watched by millions around the globe.

Victory for Guardiola's men and it was surely City's title to lose – an Arsenal win and it would be hard to see Arteta's men not sprinting on confidently to the finish line.

The Etihad was a sea of noise and colour, with the Blues' supporters well aware of the part they had to play in proceedings and, like their team, they were magnificent.

The Blues, inspired by an incredible atmosphere and sense of occasion, were irresistible, taking the game to the Gunners from the kick-off and going ahead with only seven minutes played thanks to a superb individual goal by the masterful De Bruyne.

Arsenal looked bewildered as City bossed the game

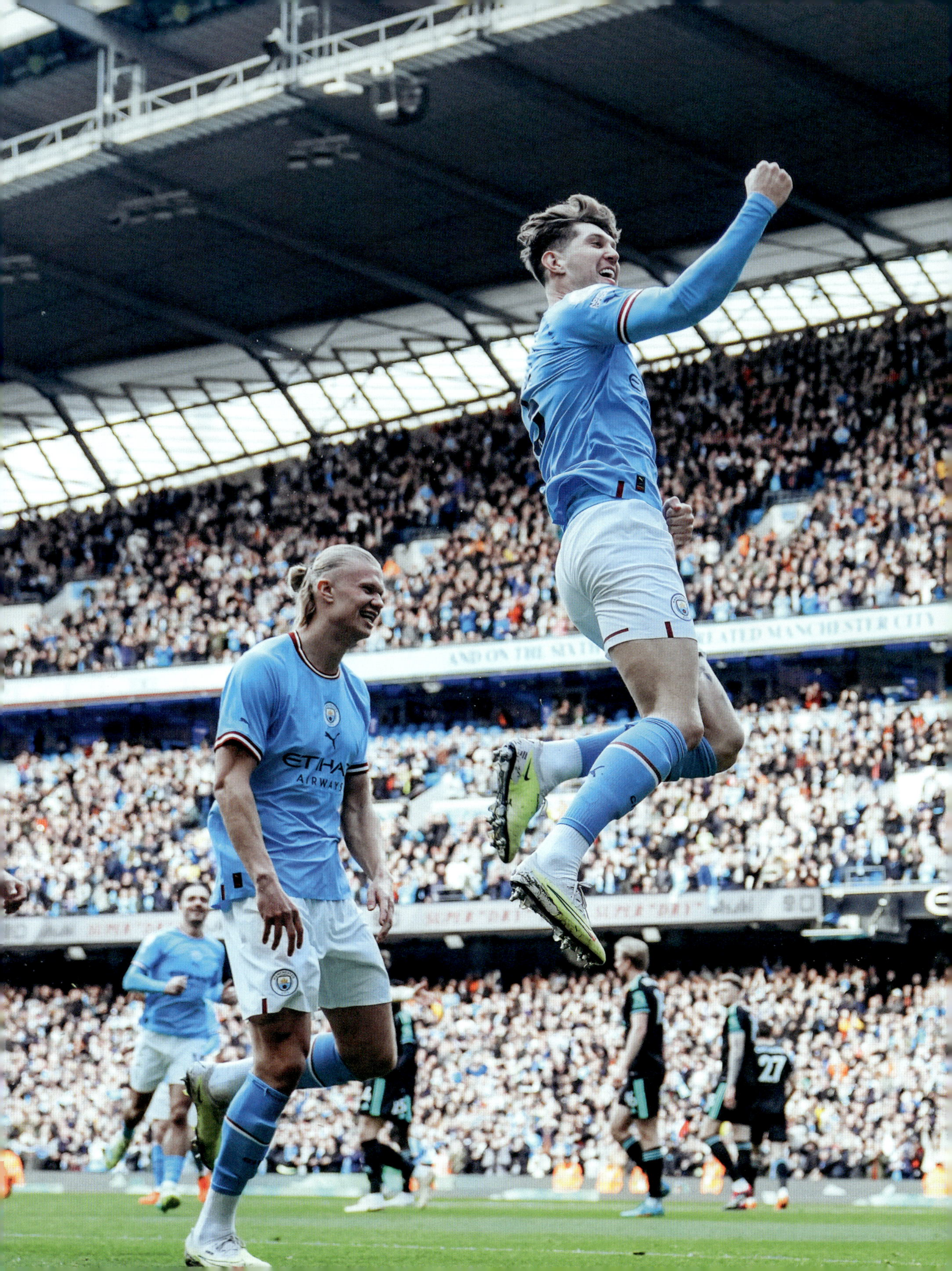
AIRWAYS
AND ON THE SIXTH

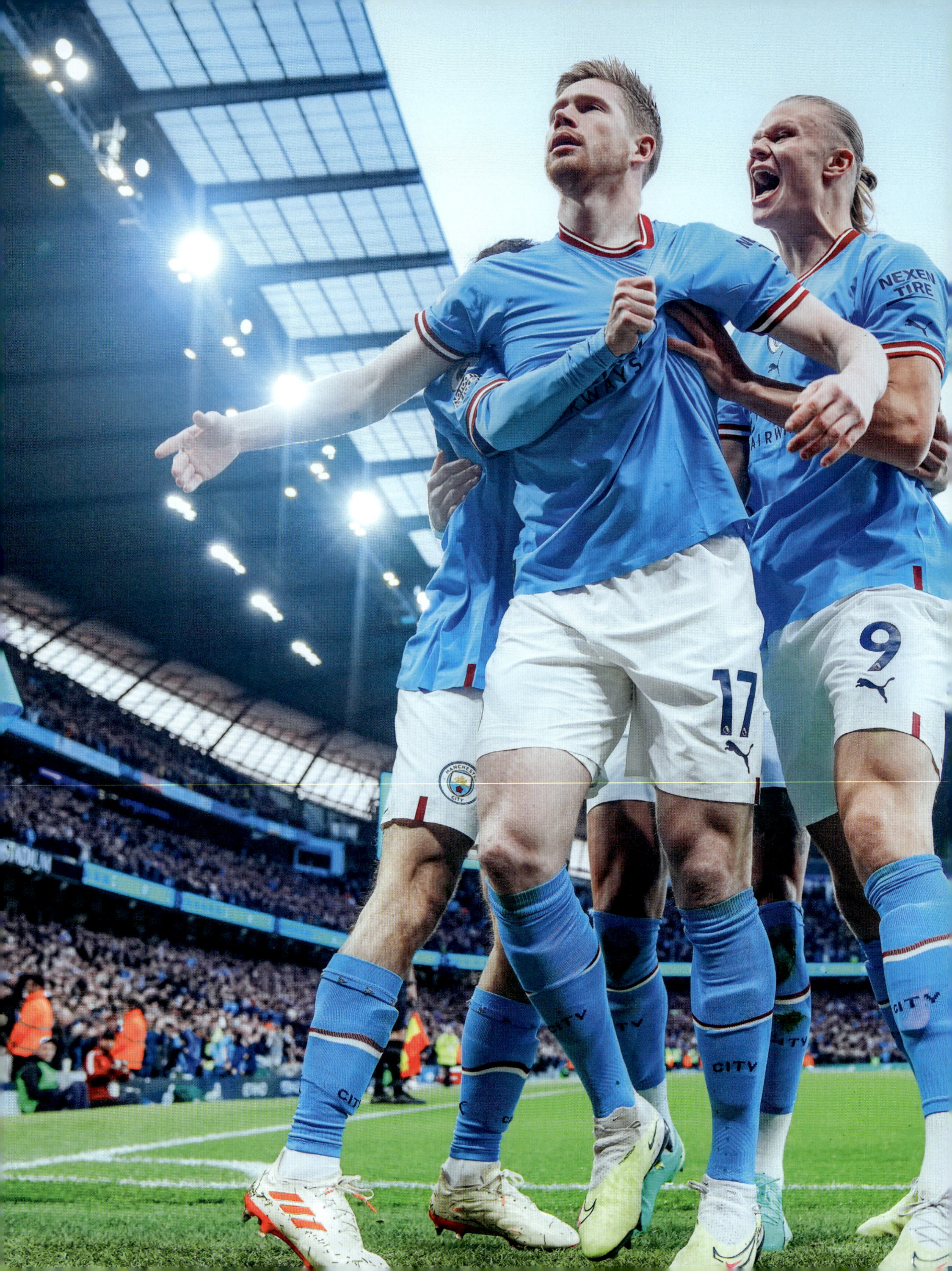
NEXEN
TIRE
17
9
CITY

**THE STORY OF THE PREMIER LEAGUE**

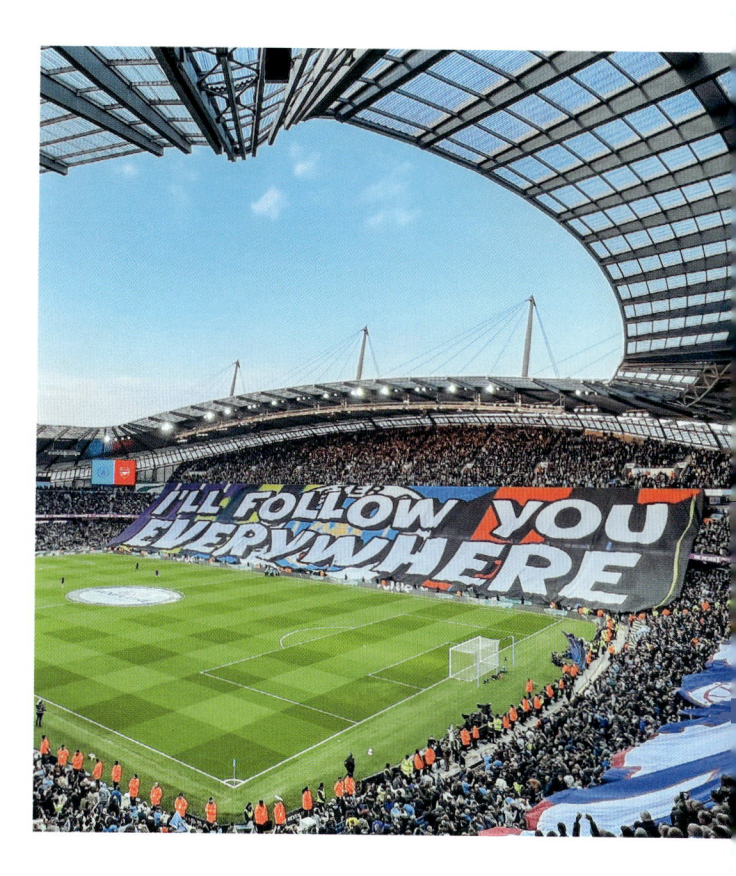

and totally dominated the first 45 minutes.

A single goal lead for City, if anything, flattered the visitors but then, on the stroke of half-time, Stones' soaring header – initially disallowed for offside – was overruled by VAR after a lengthy check and City had a priceless 2-0 lead.

Another sublime De Bruyne finish on 54 minutes all-but settled the game as the Blues went 3-0 up, and though Rob Holding pulled one back late on, Haaland – his blond locks released like a Nordic god - added a fourth in stoppage time to send the Etihad wild.

"When they played man to man we had to go a bit longer because there was no place for short passes," opined De Bruyne.

"The first half was really good. We could have scored more. The second half was 50-50 but we didn't give much away. They're a class team and hard to play against. We had to be at our best today – and we were."

The Blues ended April with another tense victory – a 2-1 win away to Fulham – with Haaland scoring goal No.50 in all competitions from the penalty spot and Alvarez hitting a stunner from 20 yards, to move back to the top of the Premier League by one point, but crucially, City had a game in hand over Arsenal.

www.mancity.com 43

TREBLE WINNERS

# MAY: THE FORCE IS WITH US

**City were relentless. Like a champion Olympic distance runner, the Blues had stayed on Arsenal's shoulder before easing past in the home straight.**

There was to be no let-up from hereon in and West Ham (3-0) and Leeds United (2-1) were both dispatched at the Etihad as expected to send City four points clear with four games remaining.

Arsenal's excellent campaign was disintegrating as they continued to ship points, their excellent season stalling at the worst possible time and the confidence of their young squad shot.

Any hope the Gunners fans had held that the Blues would lose focus with the Champions League dream, so strong and within touching distance, proved fruitless. If, anything, the opposite was true, with the possibility of the Treble a driving force to fully focus on all three fronts with the FA Cup final to come and an epic Champions League semi-final date on the horizon.

But a third successive Premier League title was the first and most cherished trophy that could be secured, and on the day a Gundogan-inspired City beat Everton 3-0 at Goodison Park, Arsenal's title dream was effectively ended by the same scoreline as they were beaten at home by Brighton.

City could even be crowned champions without playing should Arteta's side lose their penultimate game at Nottingham Forest the following weekend.

And so it came to pass.

The first part of the Treble was completed a few days after booking our second Champions League final spot and ironically without kicking a ball – as Forest did indeed beat Arsenal to officially end a thrilling title race at the City Ground.

The crowning of the Premier League champions took place the day after, with a 1-0 win over Chelsea not quite the title-clinching occasion the Blues had perhaps craved and deserved, but it mattered little – City were champions of England once again.

"It is unreal. I don't know what to say. I am so happy," said Haaland post-match.

"These are the memories I will remember for the rest of my life. I don't know what to say.

"It is special. I am going to enjoy this day. It is amazing. Debut season, 36 goals, Premier League trophy and two more finals to come. Not bad."

Grealish added: "It is different for me personally, I have played more of a part. I feel back to my normal self. Last season was nice because it was the first one but

44 www.mancity.com

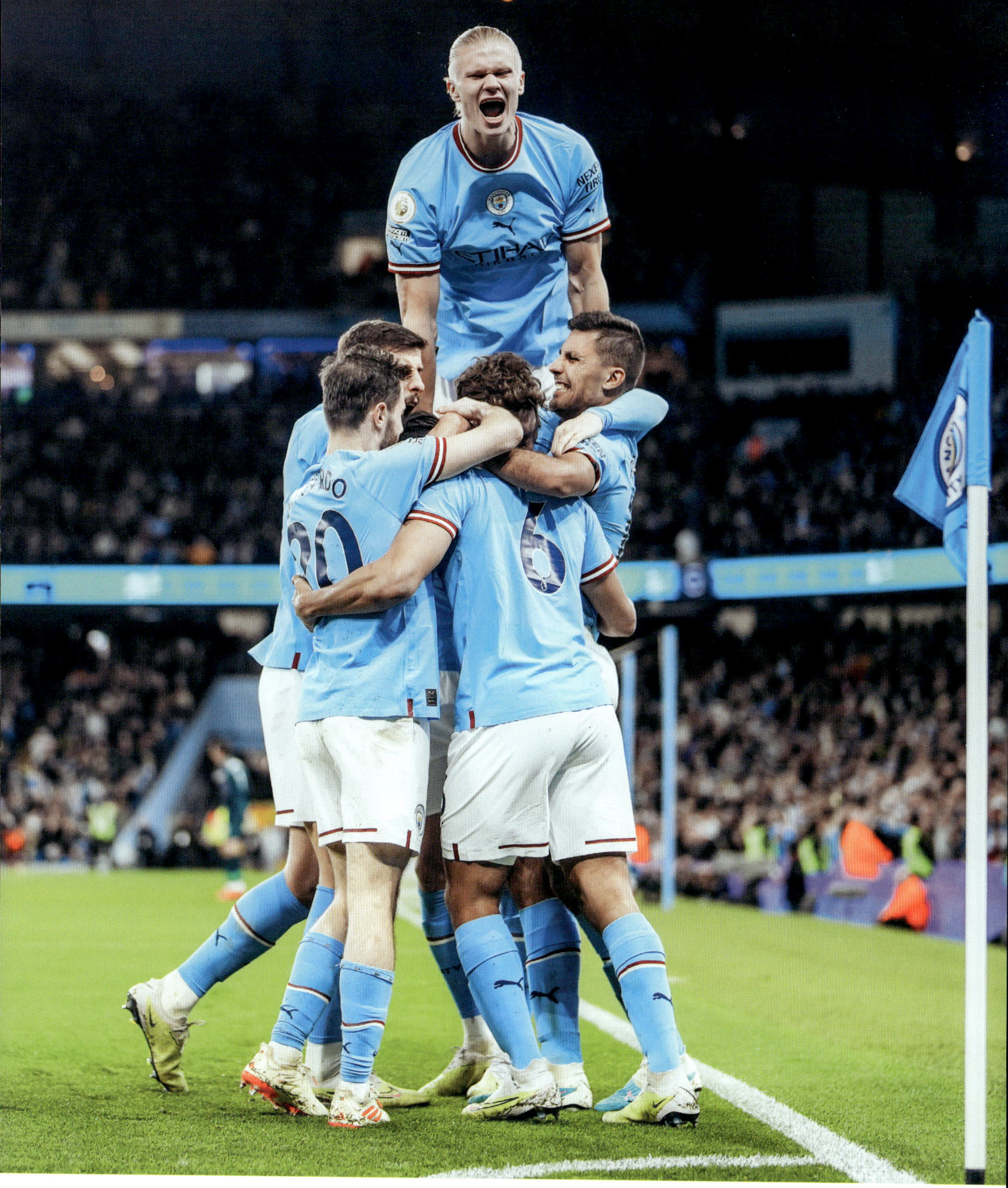

46 www.mancity.com

THE STORY OF THE PREMIER LEAGUE

this year it is so nice as I feel I have played more of a part.

"It is mad. I spoke to some of the lads a while ago and said imagine you have to win 12 games in a row to win the league. We have so much talent and we feel unstoppable.

"I feel so much more confident in this team. I feel fitter and back to what I know, what I can do. This is why Man City bought me and I have so much to offer.

"It doesn't stop yet, we still have some massive games left.

"Especially since the last international break, we feel unstoppable, and we have been unbelievable."

The boss was equally delighted, saying it was an "extraordinary achievement" to win the title for a third straight season and a fifth time in six seasons.

After a titanic struggle with Mikel Arteta's men, City had clinched the title with three games to spare.

There were still two league games to play ahead of an epic end to the campaign, with the FA Cup final against Manchester United to come and a Champions League final against Inter in Istanbul.

A much-changed City saw out the league programme with a 1-1 draw at a buoyant Brighton & Hove Albion and our long unbeaten run of 25 games was ended with a final-day 1-0 loss to Brentford.

It had been an epic, exhausting and enthralling Premier League campaign and yet again, the champions had chased down our quarry and crossed the finish line in the final strait.

Manchester City – champions of England yet again.

www.mancity.com 47

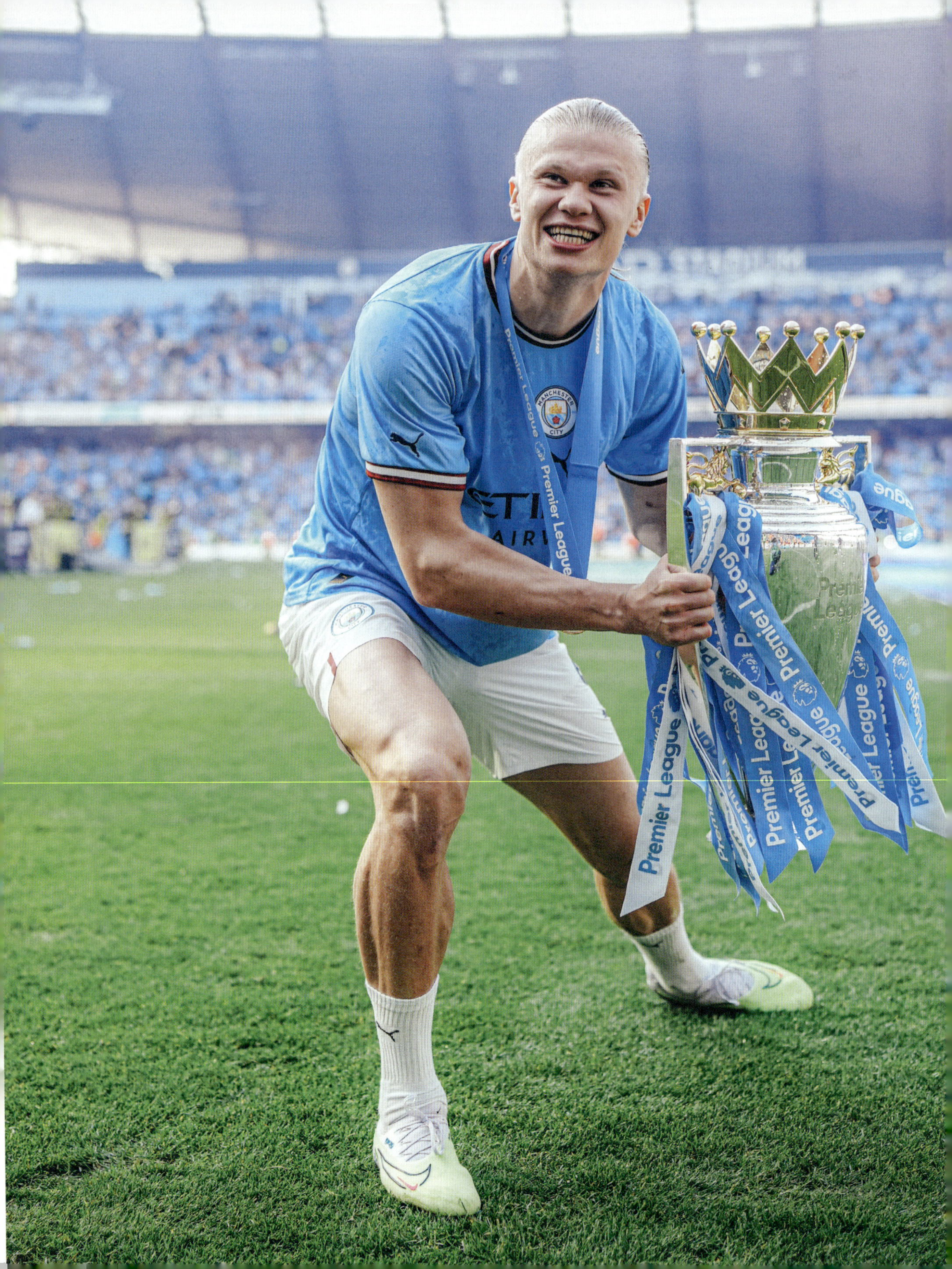
Premier League

THE STORY OF THE PREMIER LEAGUE

www.mancity.com 49

# TREBLE HEROES

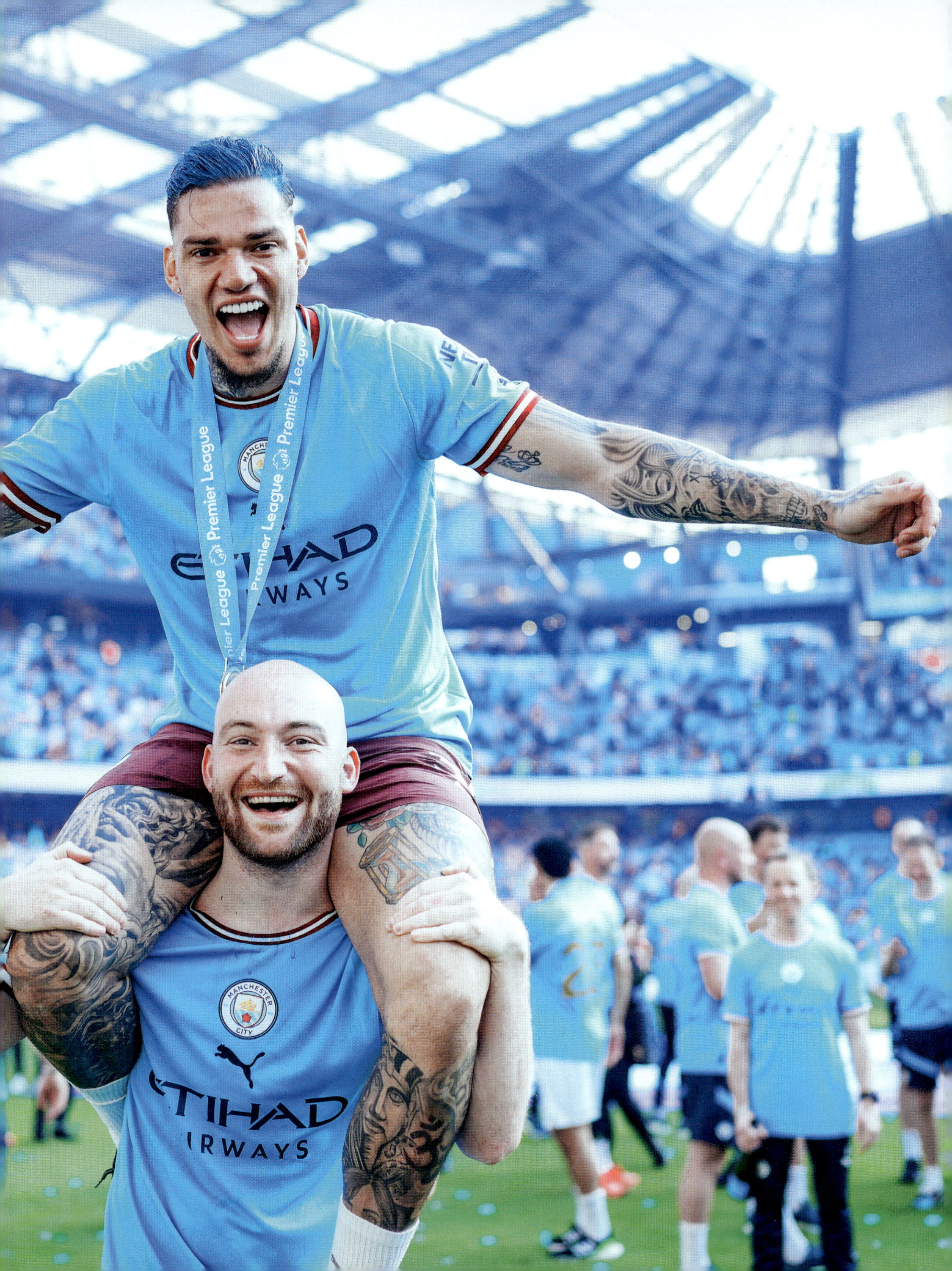
Premier League
ETIHAD
IRWAYS

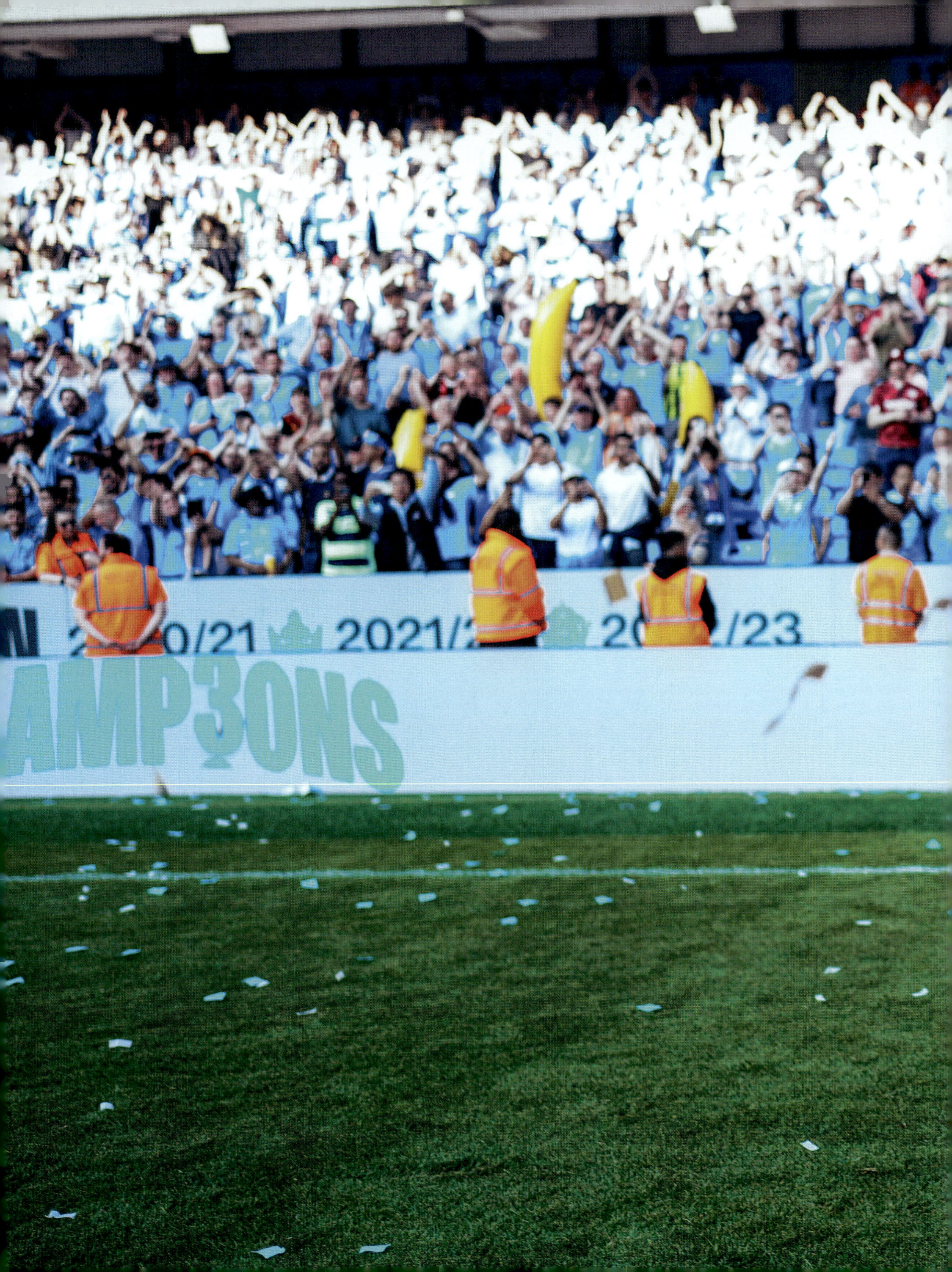
0/21
2021/
/23
AMP3ONS

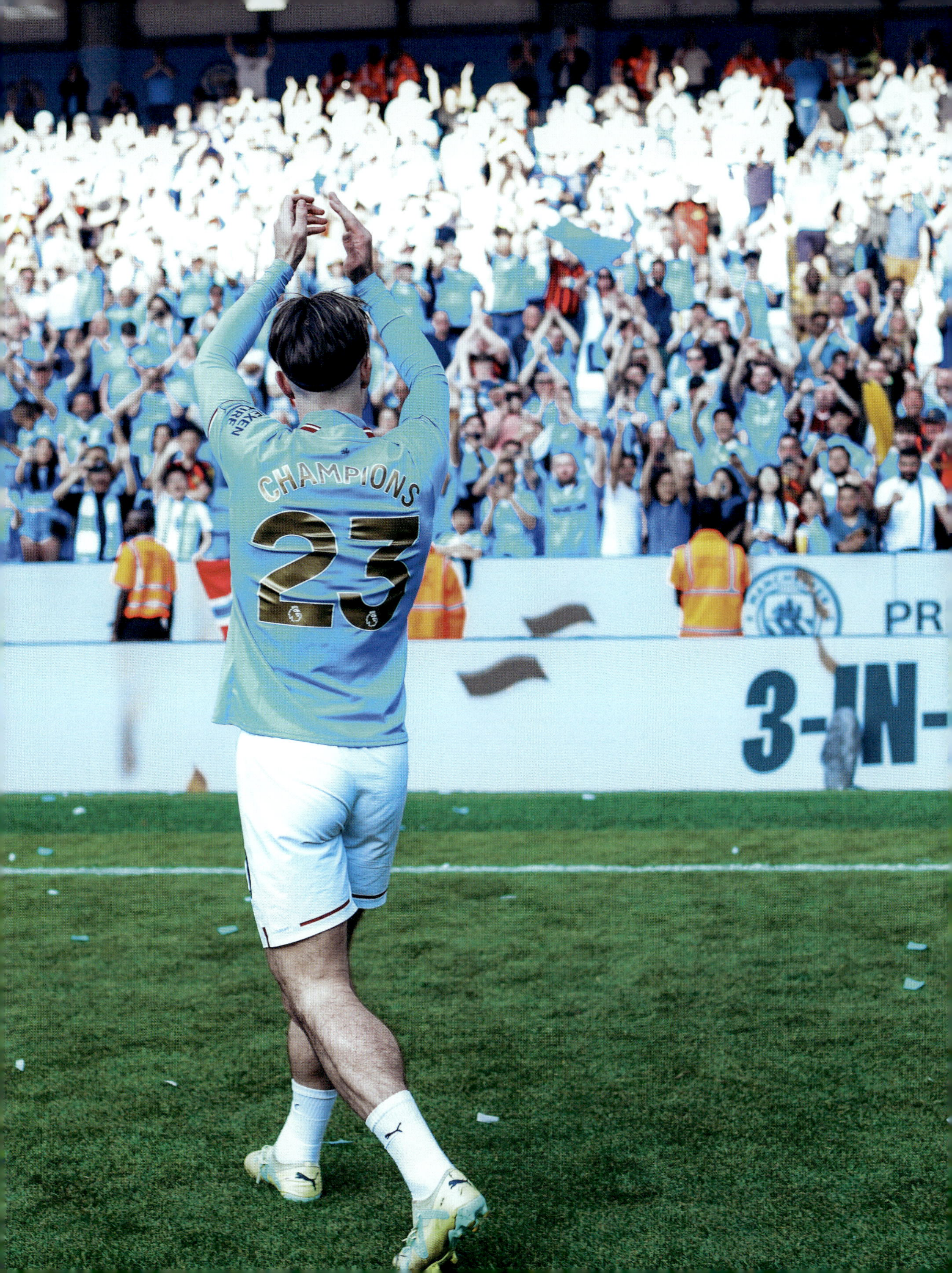
CHAMPIONS
23
3-IN-

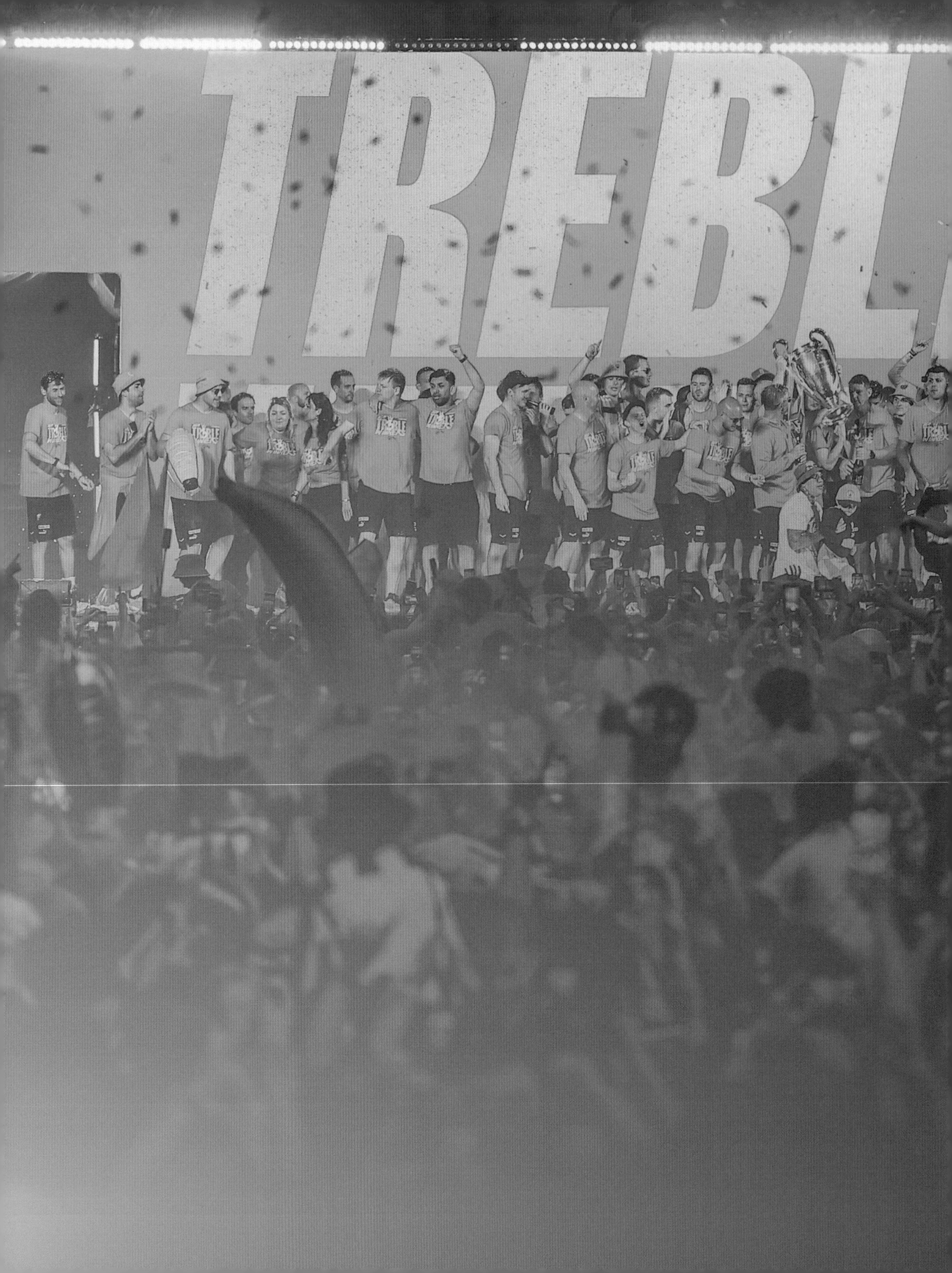
TREBL

# 2

## THE MANAGER AND THE PLAYERS

# HISTORY
# MAKERS

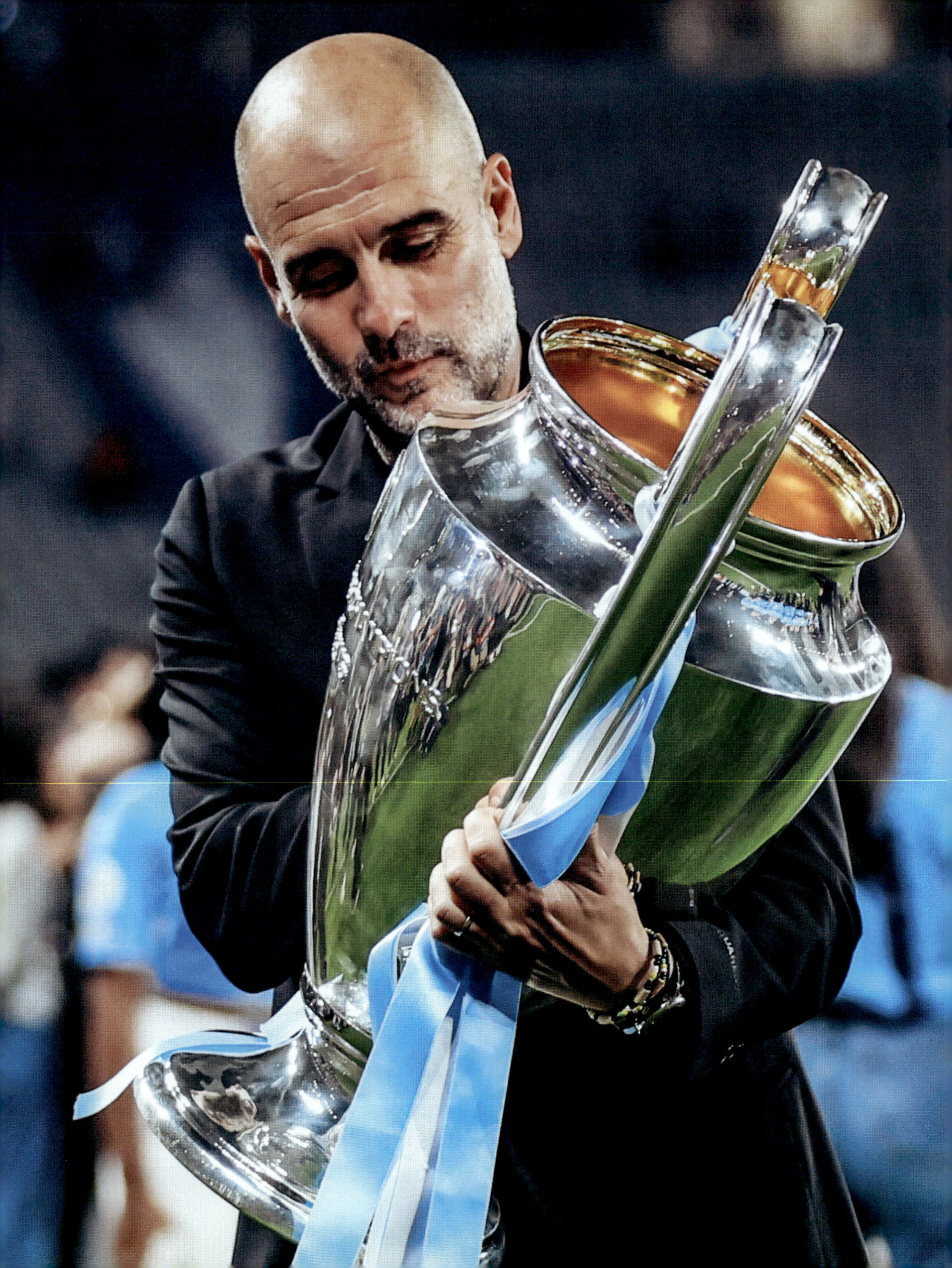

## THE MANAGER

## MANAGER

# PEP GUARDIOLA

**Already rightfully acclaimed as one of football's greatest-ever managers, Pep Guardiola further cemented his standing amongst the pantheon of the game's true elite thanks to Manchester City's record-breaking 2022/23 campaign.**

The Catalan, who has overseen the greatest period in City's proud 129-year history since taking charge in 2016, proved an inspirational figurehead once more by overseeing the club's iconic Treble season.

In the process, Guardiola again carved his name into history by becoming the first manager to win two European Trebles in the men's game.

The City boss achieved the astounding feat following June's dramatic 1-0 win over Inter in the UEFA Champions League final in Istanbul.

Rodrigo's second-half piledriver at the Atatürk Olympic Stadium confirmed our status as champions of Europe for the first time – and also meant City secured the coveted Treble of Premier League, FA Cup and Champions League.

The achievement saw Guardiola secure a unique place amongst the game's all-time managerial ranks, with Pep having now surpassed the eight other bosses who have won one European men's Treble.

That notable list includes fabled figures such as Jock Stein, who achieved the feat with Celtic in the 1966/67 season, Stefan Kovacs of Ajax (1971/72), Guus Hiddink with PSV (1987/88), Sir Alex Ferguson with Manchester United (1998/99), Jose Mourinho with Inter (2009/10), Jupp Heynckes of Bayern Munich (2012/13), Luis Enrique of Barcelona (2014/15) and Hansi Flick of Bayern Munich (2019/20).

City's historic Treble success saw Guardiola repeat the iconic feat he first achieved as Barcelona manager during the 2008/09 campaign, when a 2-0 win over Manchester United in the Champions League final followed Barca's success in lifting the La Liga trophy and Copa del Rey.

Across the 2022/23 domestic season, Pep guided City to a third successive Premier League crown – and fifth title in six years – overseeing a dramatic fightback from an eight-point deficit on Arsenal at the beginning of April to win the title with three matches to spare.

Guardiola then led City to our seventh FA Cup crown, secured thanks to an enthralling 2-1 victory against Manchester United at Wembley.

That subsequent dramatic Champions League triumph over Inter saw City complete the Treble and so set the seal on the most extraordinary season in our history.

Fittingly, the Istanbul triumph also saw the Catalan clock up his 300th City victory in just his 413th match as boss, smashing the previous record set by Mourinho, who took 493 games to reach that landmark.

Our 44 victories registered across all competitions in 2022/23 was the fourth time Guardiola has led City to at least that many wins in a single season.

Liverpool's 2021/22 team and Manchester United's 2008/09 side are the only others to win at least 44 games across a single campaign.

Lifting the Champions League also took Guardiola's tally of major honours secured during his seven-year tenure at the Etihad Stadium to an incredible 14.

THE MANAGER

Those trophies secured since 2016 also make him the most successful manager in Europe's major leagues during that period.

When his magnificent stints in charge of Barcelona and Bayern Munich are also included, Guardiola has now claimed 36 major honours as a manager. Another quite astonishing statistic.

Alongside the sheer volume of silverware accumulated by Pep, arguably the beguiling, bewitching style of football Guardiola has helped oversee has been just as significant.

With his total and steadfast commitment to a beautiful, bold, attacking brand of possession-based football, it's no exaggeration to say that the Catalan has revolutionised the way football is thought about and played – both in this country and beyond.

Many respected observers have hailed the 51-year-old as the most transformational manager the game has ever seen.

Guardiola's unique coaching acumen has also seen the boss time and again demonstrate how he and his staff have helped make already great players even better in the way they play and approach the game.

Meanwhile, just as in his stellar playing career, Guardiola's hunger and relentless drive on both a personal and collective basis has also underpinned his remarkable Etihad tenure.

It all makes for an astounding catalogue of success, with 2022/23 standing proud as the greatest season in what has been a period like no other for City.

## STATS

**DOB:**
18 JANUARY 1971

**Nationality:**
SPANISH

**From:**
SANTPEDOR, CATALONIA

**Joined:**
1 JULY 2016

# 2

## DEFENDER

# KYLE WALKER

**Few full-backs in world football can match the devastating speed and physical power of Kyle Walker.**

The 2022/23 season marked Walker's sixth in a Manchester City shirt, and he once again showed why he is still one of the best around in his position.

Since his record-breaking move from Tottenham Hotspur in July 2017, Walker has been a mainstay in City's starting XI – a challenge in itself for any top player in this team of stellar talent – clocking up a total of 254 appearances by the end of the Treble-winning campaign.

Following a strong start to the season, Walker suffered a groin injury during the first half of the 6-3 Manchester derby victory in October, and that would be his last involvement for City in 2022.

Despite making three appearances for England during the Qatar World Cup, Walker would face another injury setback following his return to City training in December, with Pep Guardiola being forced to adapt his defence due to the absence of his first choice right-back.

John Stones regularly deputised for his England colleague, with a remit to advance into midfield as often as possible.

Walker effectively had to fight to win his spot in a newer system, with Guardiola stating that every player in his squad "has to earn" their place in the starting XI.

But as seen throughout his City career, Walker showed thorough resilience and dedication to regain his place in the team and rose to the challenge.

When he did return to the side, it was clear that Walker was determined

TREBLE WINNERS

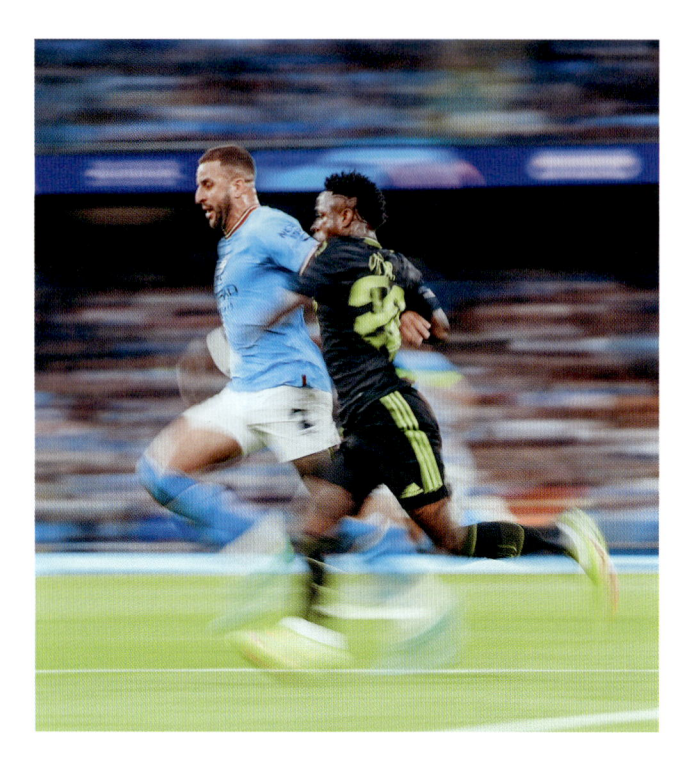

not to lose his place, turning in a series of superb performances that were a mixture of athleticism, speed and power.

Most notably, ahead of City's heavily anticipated UEFA Champions League semi-final fixture with Real Madrid, plenty of pre-match talk surrounded Walker and how he would deal with the Spanish giants' talented winger – and equally pacy – Vinicius Júnior.

It proved to be a one-sided duel, as Walker came away from the two legs having only been dribbled past once from an attempted eight opposition take-ons, while dispossessing the Brazilian seven times. It was a display so impressive, it was labelled "exceptional" by Guardiola.

More statistics would highlight Walker's impressive end to the campaign, including his 37.31km/h sprint during the win at Everton in May being the highest recorded top speed of any player in the Premier League in the 2022/23 season.

In comparison to other full-backs in the Premier League with a minimum of 1,000 minutes, Walker had the highest pass completion rate from open play (88.2%), as well as completing the most passes per 90 minutes (71.2) of any other player.

For Kyle, having overcome so many setbacks during the 2022/23 season, there was no better way to bring it to an end than completing the Treble.

Winning the Champions League now means he has won every trophy he has competed in with City, and along with this season's Premier League and FA Cup triumphs, he now has 14 winners' medals in his decorated collection since joining the club six years ago.

Undoubtedly one of the world's best right-backs.

## STATS

**DOB:**
28 MAY 1990

**From:**
SHEFFIELD, ENGLAND

**Nationality:**
ENGLISH

**Joined:**
14 JULY 2017

www.mancity.com 63

# 3

THE PLAYERS

## DEFENDER

# RUBEN DIAS

**A colossus in a City shirt since his 2020 arrival, Ruben Dias rubber-stamped his position as one of the world's best defenders in 2022/23.**

Since signing for the club from Benfica, the centre back had already enjoyed a trophy-laden spell at the Etihad Stadium, but two major honours had just evaded his grasp – the FA Cup and Champions League.

That was until the curtain fell on last term.

Having made 41 and 50 appearances respectively across the previous two seasons, the Portuguese defender's importance to Pep Guardiola was clear for all to see.

And that was once again reflected from the first kick of the ball last term as he was a vital figure in the heart of our defence – making a further 43 outings.

A player who likes to dominantly defend first and foremost, Dias also showcased his exceptional ability in all departments as City iconically completed the Treble.

In all competitions, the 26-year-old completed the second highest number of passes in a sky blue shirt (bettered only by Rodrigo) with 3,180.

This also saw him record the second highest in the Premier League (1,921) and Champions League (907), as again only the Spanish midfielder recorded more.

Dias also didn't have to wait long in the season for a landmark goal in his City career to arrive, as he netted his maiden Champions League strike in sky blue in a group game with Sevilla.

Thanks to goals from Erling Haaland (two) and Phil Foden, we already had

## TREBLE WINNERS

a strong lead going into second-half injury time, but a neat move saw Joao Cancelo drill a ball across the face of goal, where Dias had ghosted into the six-yard area and tapped home.

But his excellent defending across the campaign was what grabbed the headlines.

And alongside John Stones, Manuel Akanji, Nathan Ake and Kyle Walker, he was a member of the toughest defence at home domestically and against European powerhouses.

In the Champions League specifically, he recorded our second highest number of tackles and the most blocks in all competitions, highlighting his immense capability of spotting and nullifying danger.

As the season reached fever pitch, Dias formed a tremendous partnership with Stones – allowing the England international to maraud into midfield.

Following our pulsating 4-1 victory over Arsenal at the Etihad in April, the duo played eight of the next nine games together – with Dias sitting out our 1-0 win over Chelsea after the Premier League title was already secured.

This included our exhilarating 4-0 Champions League second-leg win over Real Madrid which booked our place in the competition's showpiece in Istanbul.

After the seismic success over Los Blancos, City were placed even further under the microscope as claiming the Treble came into full focus.

THE PLAYERS

Dias, though, was relishing the added eyeballs on our performances, stating after our FA Cup final win – and his first triumph in the competition: "We love the pressure. Since a long time, the pressure has been on and we love it."

This, of course, proved to be true as we lifted the famous European trophy for the first time in the club's illustrious history thanks to Rodrigo's iconic second-half piledriver.

As the shutters fell on the 2022/23 campaign, Dias' sparkling trophy cabinet in sky blue was complete.

However, with his immense mentality, he will only look to add more to his honours list after cementing his place in football's elite roster and as an irreplaceable player in City's ranks.

## STATS

**DOB:**
14 MAY 1997

**Nationality:**
PORTUGUESE

**From:**
AMADORA, LISBON, PORTUGAL

**Joined:**
29 SEPTEMBER 2020

#4

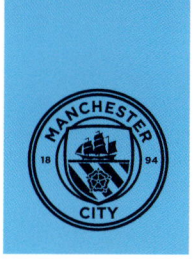

## MIDFIELDER

# KALVIN PHILLIPS

**Competition for places is absolutely key in any successful side – and City were certainly that across 2022/23.**

The sky blues completed a memorable campaign in Turkey's Ataturk Olympic Stadium as Champions League winners, adding Europe's biggest prize to our Premier League and FA Cup honours.

The goalscorer in that historic UCL victory was Rodrigo, a powerhouse in the middle of the park and the lynchpin for Pep Guardiola's all-conquering Treble winners.

His level of performance across the campaign made it incredibly difficult for his central colleague, Kalvin Phillips, to force his way into the team, although when he did play he more than contributed.

Phillips joined City in July 2022 on a six-year contract, having earned the move courtesy of his displays for his hometown club, Leeds, and England.

He'd made 234 appearances over the course of eight seasons for the Elland Road outfit, scoring 14 goals and assisting 14.

His performances for the Three Lions had also not gone unnoticed by the City hierarchy, the midfielder proving to be a key cog in the England wheel during both Euro 2020 and World Cup 2022.

City swooped to capture the combative and competitive young star as he looked to battle Rodrigo for a place in that energetic engine room.

What seemingly happened was that the arrival of Phillips spurred Rodrigo on to new heights and the Spanish star was a standout in sky blue throughout the campaign.

Phillips made his debut for City on the opening day of the 2022/23 season, coming on for Rodrigo in the 89th minute of the 2-0 victory over West Ham, with fellow summer signing Erling Haaland bagging both goals.

He came on once again against Sevilla, as we beat the Spanish outfit 4-0 in the Champions League group game at the Ramon Sanchez Pizjuan Stadium, and then again late on in the home 2-1 win over Borussia Dortmund.

But, in the aftermath of that victory, it was announced that Phillips was to have surgery on his shoulder, an issue that had been troubling him for some time.

Two months later, he returned to action as a 50th-minute substitute in the 2-0 League Cup win over Chelsea, before an anxious wait overnight to see if he had made the Three Lions squad for the winter World Cup in Qatar.

It was good news from the England camp as Phillips – alongside Jack Grealish, Phil Foden, Kyle Walker and John Stones – made the 26-man party.

He didn't see action in either of the first two group games – a 6-2 win over Iran and a 0-0 draw with USA – but came on for Declan Rice in the 57th minute of the 3-0 victory over Wales and then for Jordan Henderson in the 82nd minute in the 3-0 win over Senegal in the Round of 16.

# THE PLAYERS

England were knocked out at the quarter-final stage by France, with Phillips not seeing action in that concluding clash.

He returned to the CFA for the second half of the 2022/23 campaign and hoped to have more of an impact as the season came to a conclusion.

Having featured off the bench in City's Premier League and FA Cup victories over Chelsea on his return from Qatar, Phillips made his first start in the Carabao Cup quarter-final at Southampton.

Sadly, it was a night to forget as we went down 2-0 to the Saints in an undoubted low point in a season that eventually offered so many highs.

Phillips continued to make appearances from the bench as the term continued and eventually made his first Premier League start in the 1-0 win over Chelsea at the Etihad, an afternoon of unbridled joy as we celebrated winning the title, the outcome of a long, hard battle with Arsenal being decided the night before as the Gunners went down to Nottingham Forest at the City Ground.

He started again in the 1-0 defeat to Brentford as the manager rotated his team on the final day of the top-flight season, with two big cup finals on the horizon against Manchester United and Inter.

He stayed on the bench for both of those showpieces as the FA Cup and Champions League were secured in a delightful denouement for City.

It may not have been a vintage campaign for Phillips personally but, as a team player, he'll have been overjoyed with the Treble outcome and very happy to have walked away with three gold medals.

## STATS

**DOB:**
2 DECEMBER 1995

**Nationality:**
ENGLISH

**From:**
LEEDS, ENGLAND

**Joined:**
4 JULY 2022

# #5

## THE PLAYERS

### DEFENDER

# JOHN STONES

**John Stones has always been a bit more than your average English centre-back.**

Ball-playing, stylish and confident, the 'Barnsley Beckenbauer' as he's affectionately known is different from the no-nonsense defenders associated with the English game.

Some pundits have wanted him to revert to the stereotype, but Pep Guardiola has always encouraged his brave and instinctive way, and to paraphrase an infamous comment, the City boss said he had more 'courage' than all the journalists at a news conference.

Joining City in Guardiola's first season in 2016, there have been some difficult moments for Stones during his time at the Etihad Stadium, but he has steadily evolved into becoming one of the finest footballers in the world.

The Yorkshireman played a significant role in the five Premier League titles won under the Catalan, but perhaps never more so than in the 2022/23 campaign.

Stones reached new heights as he transferred his skills to a new hybrid defender/midfielder role that was transformative to City's season.

His ability to step between the back four and into an advanced role was spectacular and helped unlock a new level of creativity throughout the City side.

Starting at either right-back or in the centre of defence, Stones displayed a remarkable footballing intelligence to complement his technical prowess.

He wasn't afraid to push forward from deep positions and was more than comfortable to find himself the furthest attacking player, even on the biggest stage such as a seismic Champions League semi-final against Real Madrid.

During the 1-0 Champions League final victory over Inter, he completed all seven of his dribble attempts.

To put that into context, he was the first to do that in the showpiece European occasion since Lionel Messi, and only Cristiano Ronaldo and Ronaldinho have equalled the statistic.

His display in the 7-0 Champions League victory over RB Leipzig in March, when he completed 100% of passes while also moving into a 'number eight' role, was when the dynamic really started to come to fruition.

Being further forward also led to important goals against Leicester and Arsenal in the title run-in, and he revelled in a greater influence in the final weeks of the season as he strived to improve his impact.

"I'm watching a lot of footage back after the games and seeing what I can improve on. I want to go out there and play as best as I can," he explained.

"I want to get the ball moving for the team and getting into positions – it's worked quite well so far, and I hope it keeps getting better.

"It only does me good as well – adding these qualities and understanding of the game in different positions on the pitch. I'm really enjoying it and it's paying off I think."

One memorable moment in the FA Cup final against Manchester United showcased his brilliance as he received a ball from Stefan Ortega Moreno on the edge of the box, turned away from two challenges and started yet another attack.

It was a breathtaking moment of bravery and brilliance, and coming against their bitter rivals only endeared him more to the City fans.

THE PLAYERS

"Johnny, Johnny Stones" to the tune of Boney M's Daddy Cool became one of the anthems of the season, sung wildly around the Etihad and stadiums across Europe.

He admitted to being touched by the love he felt from the supporters after collecting his Premier League winners' medal following the 1-0 victory over Chelsea.

"It was so special – something that will live with me forever," he said.

"The fans singing the song when I was walking up to get my medal, honestly it touched my heart and it touched my family's heart. I can't thank them enough. I am just so glad we could share it with everyone in the stadium."

There were two more magical moments to share and Stones was at the heart of both triumphs.

Whether at centre-back, full-back or in midfield, he consistently proved his value to Guardiola's side in a season that will forever be etched in football history.

## STATS

**DOB:**
28 MAY 1994

**Nationality:**
ENGLISH

**From:**
HEMSWORTH, ENGLAND

**Joined:**
9 AUGUST 2016

#6

THE PLAYERS

## DEFENDER

# NATHAN AKE

**The debate about who was City's standout performer of the club's historic 2022/23 season is a conundrum that could well run into next year and beyond.**

For across the course of our Treble-winning campaign, a host of players offered compelling evidence to be considered for that notable accolade.

However, if there was a gong for the most admired and appreciated, there's no doubt Nathan Ake would be a strong contender for top billing.

Throughout a physically and emotionally draining 11-month campaign, the Dutch defender was the very personification of class and composure in City's assured backline.

From the moment he arrived at the Etihad in the summer of 2020, there was no doubting the enormous quality of the 28-year-old.

Armed with a wealth of experience from his time at Chelsea and Bournemouth, it was clear that Ake possessed all the ingredients to bear comparison with the game's finest defensive talents.

However, a combination of injuries plus the fierce competition for places in the City backline meant he hadn't truly been able to give full rein to his vast repertoire of talent in his first two seasons at the Etihad.

All that was to change over the course of what proved a stellar 2022/23 campaign.

With Oleks Zinchenko having moved on to a new challenge at Arsenal in the summer of 2022, it meant more opportunities would inevitably come up at left back as well as in central defence – and the flexible Ake demonstrated he was more than ready to seize the moment.

All told, Ake started 33 games in all competitions for City across the 2022/23 campaign, which was three more starts than in his previous two seasons at the club combined.

A tall and physically imposing player blessed with a fine turn of pace, Ake marries that athleticism with supreme technique allied to a wealth of intelligence and excellent vision that, combined, makes him a superb reader of the game.

Admiring City manager Pep Guardiola, for one, was in no doubt as to precisely what Ake had brought to the side when he reflected on the Dutchman's enormous impact on the Treble-winning term.

"He has been fundamental," was Pep's verdict after City had collected a third straight Premier League title and fifth in six years.

"I learned this season when you play against (Bukayo) Saka, Vinicius (Jnr), (Gabriel) Martinelli, (Mohamed) Salah or (Sadio) Mane in the past, you need a proper defender to win duels one v one.

"Or, in the Champions League, at that level, they need one action to beat you and Nathan gave us that boost that I didn't have in the past."

Ake's impact was also felt at the opposite end of the field on a number of key occasions.

And it was no coincidence that in several instances, his inspired link-up play with Jack Grealish helped bring the very best out of the left-sided attacking winger.

It was a relationship that paid dividends both ways too.

It was the Dutchman's precise finish from Grealish's assist that proved the difference in a tight and hard-fought FA Cup fourth round win against then Premier League leaders Arsenal at the Etihad back in January.

Meanwhile, Ake was on the mark once more to make a crucial second-half

THE PLAYERS

breakthrough with a fine header against a stubborn West Ham in what was a vital Premier League home clash in early May.

A hamstring injury meant he was sidelined for several of the final few games of the campaign – and that also saw him forced to settle for a place on the bench in June's FA Cup final against Manchester United.

However, it was telling that having fully recovered, Guardiola had no hesitation in bringing Ake back into the fold for the biggest game of the season – and arguably City's history – the 2023 Champions League final against Inter.

Once again Ake more than repaid his manager's faith, producing a performance of the utmost quality when the stakes were at their very highest, helping the club to be not only crowned European champions for the first time but also to secure the Treble.

The very definition of a team player, our very own flying Dutchman was the bedrock behind so much of what was good about City in 2022/23.

## STATS

**DOB:**
18 FEBRUARY 1995

**Nationality:**
DUTCH

**From:**
THE HAGUE, NETHERLANDS

**Joined:**
5 AUGUST 2020

#7

## THE PLAYERS

# DEFENDER

# JOAO CANCELO

**Istanbul was, of course, the final destination on what was a truly remarkable campaign for Manchester City.**

And although Joao Cancelo wasn't there to celebrate the historic achievement, he'd more than played his part in that journey.

The Portuguese defender was a key figure for Pep Guardiola's men in the opening months of the season, before a loan move to Bayern Munich in January 2023.

With two successive PFA Premier League Team of the Season inclusions to his name ahead of 2022/23, it would be fair to say that the 29-year-old was playing some of the best football of his career under Guardiola.

City's fluid system, which allows our full-backs to drift into central areas and influence our build-up play in advanced positions, suited Cancelo's remarkable technical ability to a T.

Despite being a defender by trade, it's the Portuguese international's creative prowess which has often made the headlines. No wonder there were few eyebrows raised when he was handed the No7 shirt – traditionally reserved for attacking players – before the campaign.

And those qualities were on show in the opening weeks of the season, with Cancelo opening his 2022/23 account with a sensational curling drive against Nottingham Forest in late August.

He would also continue to provide for his team-mates from deep, grabbing four assists in City's opening three Champions League group stage victories over Sevilla, Borussia Dortmund and FC Copenhagen.

His assist against Dortmund was the jewel in the crown, with Cancelo

## TREBLE WINNERS

finding Erling Haaland with a trademark trivela pass to complete a dramatic late turnaround.

It was a remarkable, acrobatic finish from the Norwegian, but the ball into his path from the Portuguese international was equally deserving of the plaudits it received.

The full-back continued to play his part in City's impressive start to the campaign, which saw us taste defeat on just two occasions in the Premier League ahead of the mid-season break, instigated by the Qatar World Cup.

Another standout display would follow in October against Southampton, with Cancelo grabbing his second Premier League goal of the season at the Etihad Stadium in style.

It might not happen often, but whenever the Portuguese international gets his name on the scoresheet, it's sure to be a strike to remember.

That was certainly the case against the Saints, with the defender picking up play just inside the visitors' half, feinting away from opposing captain James Ward-Prowse and firing an unstoppable low drive into the far corner of the net.

Having opened the scoring at the Etihad Stadium, he would also have a huge say in the final goal of a 4-0 win, providing the spark for Haaland's 20th of the season by playing a neat one-two with Kevin De Bruyne before cutting the ball back into the Norwegian's path.

Cancelo would start each of City's games up until the World Cup break from that point, helping Portugal reach the quarter-finals in Qatar.

Regular game time would be more difficult to come by following the season's restart, with Academy graduate Rico Lewis in particular capturing the eye with a string of hugely impressive performances.

The defender would still feature five times between late December and into the new year but, by the end of January, his aforementioned loan switch to Bayern Munich was complete.

Speaking in February, Guardiola cited a desire for more regular playing time as the reason behind the move, and insisted he departed with the very best wishes.

Indeed, Cancelo had made a significant contribution to City's success in the previous three campaigns and had played an important role in setting the foundations for what would prove our greatest season.

The Portuguese international would return to the Etihad Stadium in April 2023, coming off the bench for Bayern in the Champions League quarter-finals, but could do nothing to prevent his parent club from securing a dominant 3-0 first leg victory.

However, he would help the Bavarians secure their latest league triumph on the final day to round off the season, featuring in all but one fixture during his brief stint in Germany.

## STATS

**DOB:**
27 MAY 1994

**Nationality:**
PORTUGUESE

**From:**
BARREIRO, PORTUGAL

**Joined:**
7 AUGUST 2019

#8

THE PLAYERS

## MIDFIELDER

# ILKAY GUNDOGAN

**New captains might feel fortunate to lift one trophy in their first season wearing the armband, but to be presented with the three biggest pieces of silverware available would be beyond anyone's wildest dreams.**

But that's exactly what happened to the influential and inspirational Ilkay Gundogan after taking over as skipper from Manchester City legend Fernandinho.

Gundogan's own place alongside the Brazilian in City's list of heroes was already secured long before his incredible contribution in the 2022/23 season.

Pep Guardiola's first signing after being announced as City boss in 2016, his maiden campaign was devastated by a serious knee injury that kept him out of the side for nearly nine months.

Returning the following season, Gundogan would go on to become an integral part of City's success, never more than on the final day of the 2021/22 Premier League title race when his double against Aston Villa turned a two-goal deficit into a 3-2 victory in a dramatic climax.

Throughout that campaign, the German was an important figure in the dressing room and was seen as the ideal man to take over as the leader by his team-mates, something which he saw as a huge compliment.

As well as off it, Gundogan set the tone on the pitch with a string of big performances and a selfless work ethic, particularly in the latter stages of the season when City faced a punishing schedule as they attacked the league, FA Cup and Champions League.

## TREBLE WINNERS

His total minutes of 3,854 in all competitions and 45 starts was the third-highest of any outfield player (only less than Rodrigo and Erling Haaland) as he amassed 11 goals and six assists.

But his experience and intelligence made him a crucial contributor, whether making advanced runs to support the attack, helping to break through low-blocking defences or dropping deep to free up team-mates.

And there were some big goals on the way to the Premier League title, including both in a 2-1 victory over Leeds United at the beginning of May and another double in a 3-0 away win against relegation candidates Everton the following weekend, when he scored an outrageous flicked opener and a wonderful free-kick.

But possibly his greatest contribution was in the FA Cup final at the beginning of June when City beat neighbours United in the first-ever all-Manchester final.

Gundogan took just 12 seconds to score a brilliant volley to fire City ahead with the quickest goal ever scored in the final of the competition's 151-year history.

He then repeated the trick with a second-half volley to secure a 2-1 win and a chance to climb the Wembley steps and receive the famous old trophy.

A Treble was now one game away but the Champions League had been a heart-breaking competition for Gundogan, who had lost two finals – one with City and the other with Borussia Dortmund.

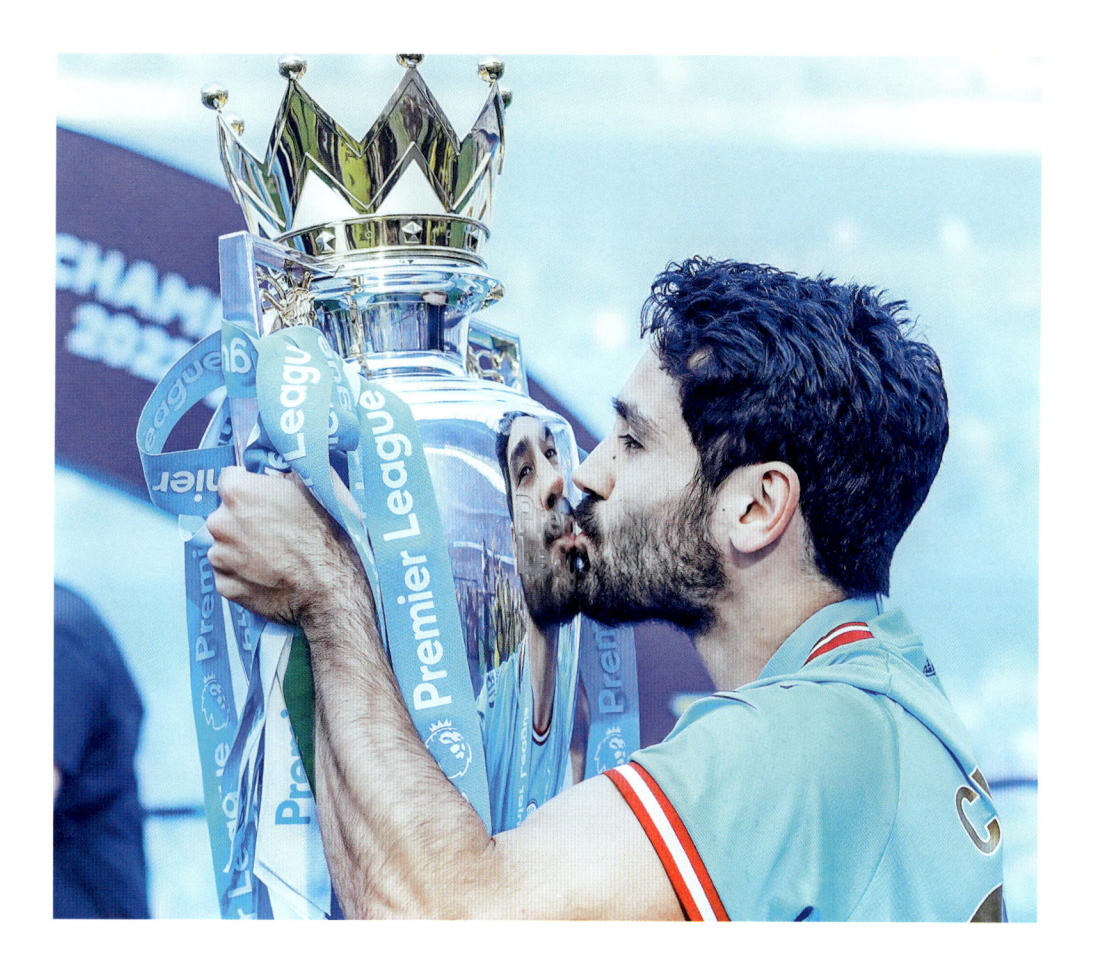

It was a proud moment for the skipper when he finally got his hands on the trophy following the 1-0 win over Inter, particularly being on Turkish soil, land of his father.

But his team-mates, supporters and Guardiola were just as thankful for his contribution.

"He's so intelligent, Gundo, so clever and competitive," the City boss said. "Under pressure he handles it without a problem.

"He's one of the best players I ever trained in my career in terms of the whole package. He's top, top class."

## STATS

**DOB:**
24 OCTOBER 1990

**Nationality:**
GERMAN

**From:**
GELSENKIRCHEN, GERMANY

**Joined:**
1 JULY 2016

#9

## FORWARD

# ERLING HAALAND

**Start as you mean to go on. Not only has Erling Haaland already won the three biggest trophies a City player can, he spent his first season at the Etihad Stadium relentlessly breaking records.**

The Premier League Player of the Year, Young Player of the Year, Golden Boot winner and Football Writers' Footballer of the Year scored 36 on the way to his first major honour in English football.

That was two better than the previous best set by Andrew Cole (1993/94) and Alan Shearer (1994/95) when the division comprised of 42 matches.

The 22-year-old also led the way in the Champions League, winning the tournament's Golden Boot and equalling Ruud van Nistelrooy's single-campaign record of 12 goals in the competition for an English club.

In total, his 52 goals is the most a player has ever managed for a club in the Premier League era, eclipsing van Nistelrooy and Salah, who previously shared the accolade with 44 strikes. It could hardly have gone better.

Arriving from Borussia Dortmund last summer, there was much discussion around the Norwegian's ability to integrate into a team that play the possession-based football that Pep Guardiola has all but perfected.

Having played without a recognised striker for much of the previous two campaigns, a period of transition was expected and would not have alarmed anyone at the CFA.

Instead, he instantly looked at home. Maybe it was to be expected given his father's connections to the club and the popular photographs of Erling as a child wearing sky blue.

The Community Shield defeat set tongues wagging up and down the land, but Haaland's smile after missing a clear chance in the closing stages suggested he knew what was coming.

That match was a distant memory after just one Premier League game, when his brace earned the three points at West Ham.

With two hat-tricks before the end of August against Crystal Palace and Nottingham Forest, the goalscoring machine was in fine working order.

He made it three hat-tricks in three successive home matches during the unforgettable 6-3 home win in the Manchester derby.

He also claimed the match ball in the January win over Wolves, meaning he hit four Premier League hat-tricks 46 games quicker than anyone has previously achieved.

Haaland also hit three in the FA Cup thrashing of Burnley and an incredible five in the Champions League Round of 16 second leg with RB Leipzig.

Decisive strikes in the closing stages came with a pressure penalty at home against Fulham and an acrobatic finish to win a group-stage tie with Borussia Dortmund.

An example of how Haaland has added a fresh dimension to Guardiola's armoury came in the defeat of Brighton at the Etihad, when a long, direct ball from Ederson saw Haaland brush off the not unsubstantial frame of defender Adam Webster and roll the ball into an empty net.

The goals came more slowly as the end of the season approached and trophies appeared on the horizon, but by that point Haaland was giving

90 www.mancity.com

THE PLAYERS

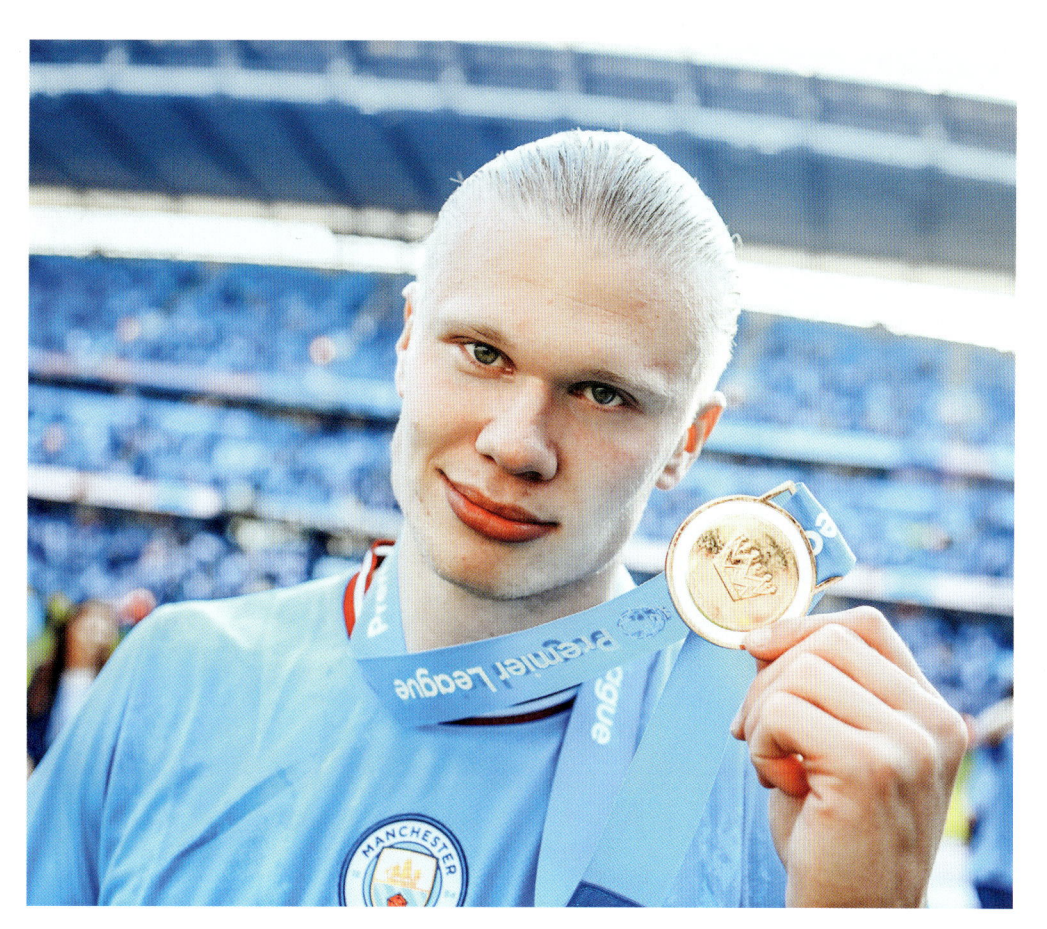

more to the team in possession than he ever had before.

Having had time to work with Guardiola, his job evolved into an essential cog in the winning machine in all aspects of the build-up.

The Catalan has always asked more of his strikers than to just put the ball in the net and Haaland's hard work to create space in the pivotal meetings with title rivals Arsenal and the latter stages of the Champions League demonstrated the complete package he could become.

It seems astounding to say there is more to come from Erling Haaland, but as 2022/23 finished in glory, there was the sense that our No.9 is ravenously hungry for more.

## STATS

| DOB: | Nationality: |
| --- | --- |
| 21 JULY 2000 | NORWEGIAN |
| From: | Joined: |
| LEEDS, ENGLAND | 1 JULY 2022 |

#10

## MIDFIELDER

# JACK GREALISH

**The title of most expensive English signing puts a lot of weight onto one man's shoulders.**

And when Jack Grealish joined City from Aston Villa for a record-breaking fee ahead of the 2021/22 campaign, the spotlight shone brightly on the England international.

The boy from Brum achieved one of his lifelong ambitions – winning the Premier League title – in his debut season with City, but he knew he could do more than that.

For players like Grealish, his performances aren't defined by the number of assists or goals he accumulates but by the persistence, agility and opportunities he brings to the pitch.

And he wanted to do more of that, not just in the Premier League but also on the biggest of stages – the Champions League.

His campaign was off to a flying start with convincing wins over West Ham and Bournemouth before a minor injury ruled him out for the remaining August fixtures.

He marked his return to action with his first goal of the season in our 3-0 win over Wolverhampton Wanderers in September. Grealish went on to win every game he featured in prior to the pause of play for the 2022 World Cup in Qatar.

On his return from international duty in December – where he featured in all of England's games prior to their departure in the quarter-finals – Grealish assisted Erling Haaland twice in our 3-1 win over Leeds United.

Grealish continued to be an imperious figure in Pep Guardiola's team following his return from Qatar as we saw another level to his game.

In our 15-match unbeaten run in the Premier League which helped City secure our third consecutive title, Grealish scored three goals and assisted four.

The most fouled player couldn't be stopped. He had the highest passing accuracy of any winger to attempt at least 200 passes in the Premier League with 87.6%.

And only our own Kevin De Bruyne created more chances in open play in the Premier League than Grealish, the pair creating 69 and 46 respectively.

We returned to the top of the table for a brief moment following our 3-1 win over Arsenal. Grealish's goal gave City the lead and inspiration needed to go on and secure all three vital points against our title rivals.

It became evident that Grealish's game and mindset had come to full fruition under Guardiola in our 4-1 win over Liverpool and embodied City's power and desire to succeed.

Grealish put a stop to a chance for Liverpool in the 26th minute after he dashed half the length of the pitch to deny Mo Salah the opportunity to play a dangerous pass into the City box.

The City winger turned creator moments later when he assisted Julian Alvarez, who levelled the score. The England international went on to score in our thrilling comeback to top off one of his finest games for the club, earning him the man of the match award.

Those 60 seconds of inspiration at both ends of the pitch personified City's ethos. It was another example of how Grealish has played every minute with a smile and become a fan favourite while doing so.

He was racking up more distance, passes, goals, assists and wins this

THE PLAYERS

campaign compared to any other and the past 18 months of hard work were to thank for it.

As the business end of the season approached and three pieces of silverware were in touching distance, Grealish continued to be a key cog in the City system.

A goal and assist in our 4-1 win over Southampton, an assist in our 3-0 FA Cup semi-final win over Sheffield United and featuring for the entirety of our Champions League quarter-final and semi-final clashes with Bayern Munich and Real Madrid respectively saw Grealish's limits tested within a short time period.

And he prevailed.

At 27 years old, he won his second Premier League title and his first FA Cup trophy following our 2-1 win in the all-Manchester final.

And when you thought it couldn't get any better, Grealish became one of 10 English players to win the Treble and to have featured in the Champions League final.

As he celebrated on the Ataturk Olympic Stadium pitch with tears in his eyes, you could tell that winning feeling is something Grealish will continue to chase next season.

## STATS

**DOB:**
10 SEPTEMBER 1995

**Nationality:**
ENGLISH

**From:**
BIRMINGHAM, ENGLAND

**Joined:**
5 AUGUST 2021

#14

THE PLAYERS

DEFENDER

# AYMERIC LAPORTE

**Since Aymeric Laporte joined Manchester City in January 2018, the Spain international has often proved to be the man for the big occasion.**

For those of a sky blue persuasion, among a number of highlights, the commanding centre-back will be fondly remembered for his ability to score goals and produce phenomenal performances in vital moments.

This is perfectly reflected by his winning goal in the 2021 League Cup final victory over Tottenham Hotspur, when he powered home a header from close range with nine minutes remaining at Wembley.

His cup final heroics weren't the first time he delivered in a high-pressure environment, though, as he scored our second goal in a title-sealing win over Brighton on the final day of the 2018/19 season.

With Pep Guardiola's side needing to match or better Liverpool's result against Wolves at Anfield to retain our league crown, we found ourselves a goal down when Glenn Murray headed home for the Seagulls.

Sergio Aguero equalised shortly after, and Laporte then handed us the lead before half-time as we went on to record an impressive 4-1 success on the south coast to lift the title.

With this in mind, perhaps it's no surprise the Catalan would turn to the silky defender when needing to add vital experience and expertise into his side either from the bench or from the off in 2022/23.

His first appearance of the campaign came in our epic 6-3 victory over Manchester United at the Etihad Stadium in October.

As the season progressed, 23 outings for club and country followed (including three matches at the World Cup in Qatar) before he was handed starts in huge back-to-back league fixtures with Leeds and Everton.

Having comprehensively beaten title rivals Arsenal (4-1) two games earlier and recorded a hard-fought win over Fulham in our previous outing (2-1), City viewed the matches with the Whites and Toffees as vital tests if we were to claim a third successive Premier League title.

Thanks to the Spanish defender's performances in fantastic team displays, Guardiola's team passed with flying colours.

Against Sam Allardyce's side in the first of the two assignments, Laporte marshalled the backline expertly as we recorded a 2-1 success thanks to Ilkay Gundogan's first-half brace.

## THE PLAYERS

He then impressively repeated the trick at a raucous Goodison Park as our captain scored two more goals alongside Erling Haaland's strike, which helped secure a 3-0 win on Merseyside.

The three points over Sean Dyche's team proved to be enough to seal the league crown with the Gunners' loss to Nottingham Forest the following weekend confirming our status as champions before our home meeting with Chelsea.

This was, of course, the first part of our historic Treble and Laporte certainly played a key role in our FA Cup success by recording the second most passes in the competition among his team-mates.

Then, in the first-ever all-Manchester final, with the game hanging in the balance at 2-1 in our favour at Wembley, he was introduced in the closing stages to help see out the famous win.

Victory in Istanbul followed a week later as we won a maiden Champions League trophy in our illustrious 129-year history with Laporte featuring four times en route to the showpiece.

As the curtain fell on the 2022/23 campaign in the most wonderful of circumstances, the 29-year-old had managed to secure 12 trophies in sky blue.

## STATS

**DOB:**
27 MAY 1994

**Nationality:**
SPANISH

**From:**
AGEN, FRANCE

**Joined:**
30 JANUARY 2018

#16

## MIDFIELDER

# RODRIGO

**With one sweetly timed and majestic sweep of his right foot on a summer's night in Turkey, Rodrigo ensured his name will forever be etched in Manchester City folklore.**

The Spanish international's 68th minute moment of magic at Istanbul's Ataturk Olympic Stadium not only delivered the ultimate prize of the Champions League as City overcame Inter 1-0 to be crowned European champions.

It also cemented City's elevation to the rarefied plinth only reserved for the game's true all-time immortals, by also securing the Treble of Champions League, Premier League and FA Cup.

Wherever one looked across Pep Guardiola's gilded squad there were heroes aplenty. Both that memorable night in the country where Europe collides with Asia as well as across the course of a season that truly was like no other.

But it felt somehow fitting and only appropriate that, on the biggest stage of them all, it was Rodrigo who delivered when a moment of magic was required to overcome the challenge of a dogged and dangerous Inter, and deliver the trophy the club cherished and yearned for above all others.

Because, by whatever metric one chooses to employ, the Spanish holding midfielder's impact and influence on City was simply immense across a season for the ages.

The all-important holding midfield pivot in Guardiola's wonderfully assembled City side, the 27-year-old was the veritable glue who helped bond all of City's separate elements into a cohesive, potent and beautiful whole.

Four seasons into his stay at the Etihad after his arrival from Atletico Madrid, Rodrigo's standing and importance to Manchester City has never been more apparent or appreciated.

Across the course of a draining, 11-month-long marathon campaign that began in late July at the King Power Stadium in a Community Shield match with Liverpool and ended in a corner of Istanbul that will now be forever Blue, Rodrigo proved a veritable rock of ages, his intelligence, diligence and understanding of his vital role proving utterly fundamental to Guardiola and City.

Of course, few understand the responsibilities of the midfield pivot more that Pep, who helped redefine the way a holding midfielder was both seen and appreciated across the course of his own stellar playing career with Barcelona.

Fast forward to today and few now would argue that Rodrigo has refined and made the role his own at City.

Having learnt, prospered and further matured alongside Fernandinho – the undisputed past master of the holding midfield role – in his first three seasons at the Etihad, the Spaniard's tactical know-how and maturity took centre stage with Ferna having departed in the summer of 2022.

Quite simply, he proved indispensable to all that the club achieved across our glorious Champions League, Premier League and FA Cup campaigns.

It says everything that for many City fans, his was more often than not the first name on their team sheets.

And the fact that no player made more appearances than the Spaniard (56) or started more games (52) spoke volumes as to his importance – and

## THE PLAYERS

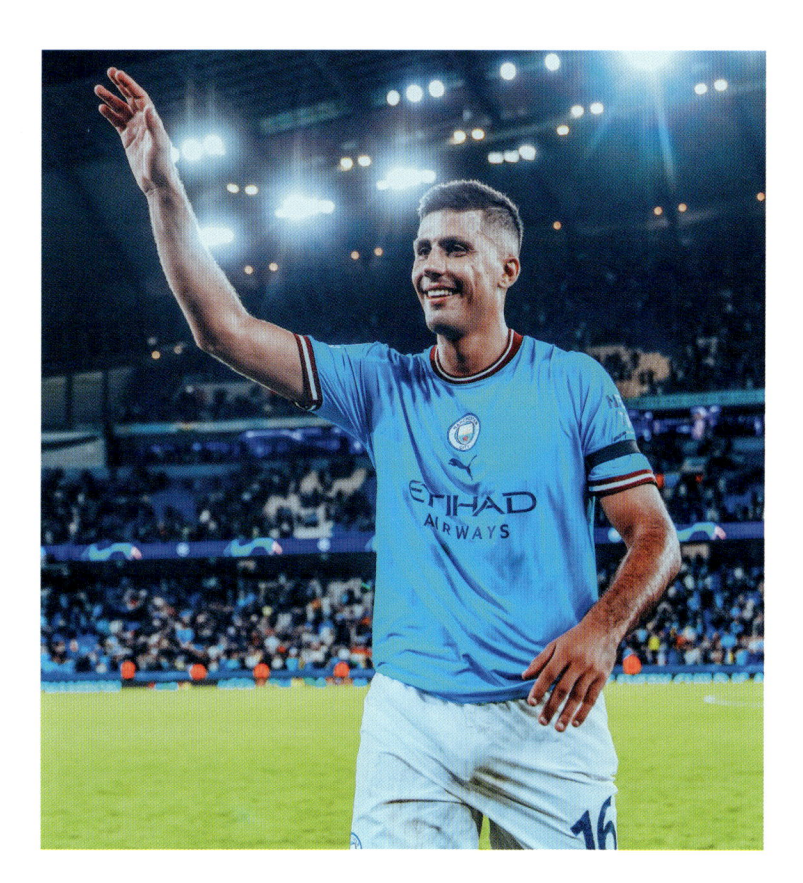

the way Guardiola implicitly valued and trusted his quality and delivery.

The Champions League final aside, there were also other crucial goals – not least a brilliant European strike against Bayern Munich in a pulsating 3-0 quarter-final first leg victory.

Reflecting on his enormous contribution ahead of that final in Istanbul, the City boss was fulsome in his praise and admiration for Rodrigo's contribution.

"[He has been an] incredible signing for us," Pep said.

"Seeing his development as a football player, to read better some situations. He solved it with his incredible mentality. He's so important."

The exciting aspect for City is, that having only turned 27 in the summer, Rodrigo's best years are still ahead of him.

And given the way his career trajectory has panned out so far at the Etihad, it's a fair bet that many more glorious chapters await!

## STATS

**DOB:**
22 JUNE 1996

**Nationality:**
SPANISH

**From:**
MADRID, SPAIN

**Joined:**
4 JULY 2019

www.mancity.com 103

#17

## MIDFIELDER

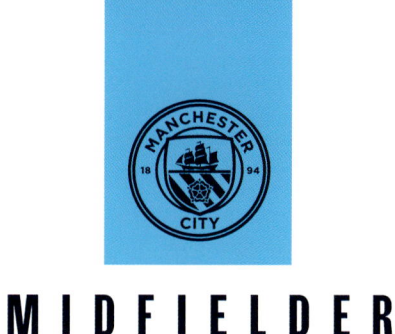

# KEVIN DE BRUYNE

**It was a magnificent season for our brilliant Belgian.**

Kevin De Bruyne has established himself as one of the world's greatest players over the past five or six years, but 2022/23 could be argued as his best yet.

An inspirational footballer, a creative genius and a leader on the pitch in so many ways, KDB's stats during our quest for the Treble beg the question: Is there a better player in world football at this moment?

Including 11 international matches for Belgium, De Bruyne has racked up 60 appearances in the last calendar year with almost no extended rest period.

His 49 games for City saw him push his body to the limit, occasionally to his own cost as he continued to help his team achieve footballing immortality, as witnessed in a second successive heart-breaking Champions League final exit with injury.

If one player deserves to shine during the biggest club match in world football, it is surely our humble, quiet yet inspiring No.17.

As City adjusted to the arrival of Erling Haaland, it was De Bruyne who quickly tuned into the Norwegian's wavelength and by the end of their first season, they had forged one of the most lethal understandings in the modern game.

When De Bruyne picks up the ball, Haaland will invariably start his run or find a pocket of space, knowing that the ball will arrive at the perfect pace, height, or angle.

It is a devastating partnership that blossomed during our greatest ever season.

And one glance at his season stats confirms what every City fan already knows – KDB is one of our greatest players of all time and, at his peak, he is a joy to watch and almost unstoppable.

He registered an astonishing 28 assists in all competitions in 2022/23, eight more than any other player from Europe's top five leagues – the nearest being Lionel Messi with 20 – which speaks volumes of his phenomenal productivity.

It is the fourth time he has topped 20-plus assists as a City player, having achieved the feat in 2016/17 (20), 2017/18 (21) and 2019/20 (22). During that time, only two other Premier League players have reached that milestone in one season (Christian Eriksen in 2016/17 with 23, and Mesut Ozil in 2015/16 with 20).

De Bruyne created an average of 3.4 chances per 90 minutes in all competitions in 2022/23, the best rate of any Premier League player with a minimum 1,000 minutes played – so that pans out at one goalscoring chance made every 25 minutes of every game he played last season.

He also assisted 16 goals in the Premier League in 2022/23, the division's best, and only Cesc Fabregas has managed more than the four occasions KDB has assisted 15 or more goals in a single Premier League campaign.

And the records and milestones continue to fall as his stellar career progresses.

His delightful chip for Haaland's headed goal against Southampton in April was his 100th Premier League assist in only his 237th appearance for City, achieving the landmark 56 games faster than the next best, Fabregas, who took 293 matches.

But the accolades don't end there.

KDB's eight assists for Haaland in the Premier League in 2022/23 is the most one City player has assisted another in a single season in the competition and his six Champions League assists last term was also the most in the competition for 2022/23 – and he tied with Wrexham's Sam Dalby as joint-top assist king in the FA Cup with four, two of which came in the final!

Most of De Bruyne's 10 goals were superb strikes, too – and many were in crucial matches.

His sublime free-kick away to Leicester secured a 1-0 victory, while his magnificent goal against Arsenal at the Emirates put the Blues on the way to a 3-1 win, and he was on target again in the 4-1 triumph over Liverpool.

Perhaps his best performance of the season was in the Etihad return leg against Arsenal, where, in a must-win game, he immediately took the contest by the scruff of the neck and his early goal on seven minutes was followed by an assist for John Stones.

Another strike arrived early in the second period as City swept the Premier League leaders aside 4-1, making it two huge performances against our title rivals that yielded three goals and two assists.

And, of course, when the Blues needed a goal at the Bernabeu, it was the Belgian maestro who delivered with a bullet of a low drive that fizzed past international team-mate Thibaut Courtois to ensure City began the Champions League semi-final return leg against Real Madrid on level terms.

Big-game players step up to the plate when they are needed, and De Bruyne does it time and time again.

It's easy to run out of superlatives for this magnificent footballer who has just had the season of his life and – worryingly for our opponents – he just seems to get better year on year.

An incredible campaign and a wonderful contribution.

## STATS

**DOB:**
28 JUNE 1991

**Nationality:**
BELGIAN

**From:**
DRONGEN, BELGIUM

**Joined:**
30 AUGUST 2015

www.mancity.com 107

#18

THE PLAYERS

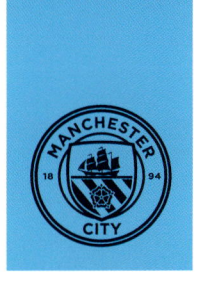

# GOALKEEPER

# STEFAN ORTEGA MORENO

**Goalkeepers are different, so the saying goes.**

But from the moment he joined City last summer, German shot-stopper Stefan Ortega Moreno provided a comforting sense of familiarity and security as he instantly settled into life in Manchester.

The 30-year-old had arrived at the Etihad from Arminia Bielefeld armed both with extensive experience from his time in the Bundesliga and a driven sense of ambition and excitement about the challenge that lay ahead.

Ortega Moreno was both old enough and wise enough to know that Ederson was likely to remain City's number one.

But equally, he would have been aware that given the depth of quality within the squad and Pep Guardiola's insatiable thirst for success on all fronts, opportunities – and the chance to acquire silverware – would arise.

Eleven months and a historic and era-defining Treble later, it's fair to say that the move has paid handsome dividends and then some for both player and club.

From the get-go, it was apparent that Ortega Moreno was the perfect fit working alongside Ederson and fellow experienced keeper Scott Carson.

The trio not only boasted exemplary skills, attitude and professionalism.

Allied to that, the harmony and togetherness they displayed – added to the desire to keep improving under the expert tutelage of renowned goalkeeping coach Xabi Mancisidor – only added an extra layer of quality to the club's already hugely respected goalkeeping department.

From Ortega Moreno's perspective, swapping the rigours of battling at

## TREBLE WINNERS

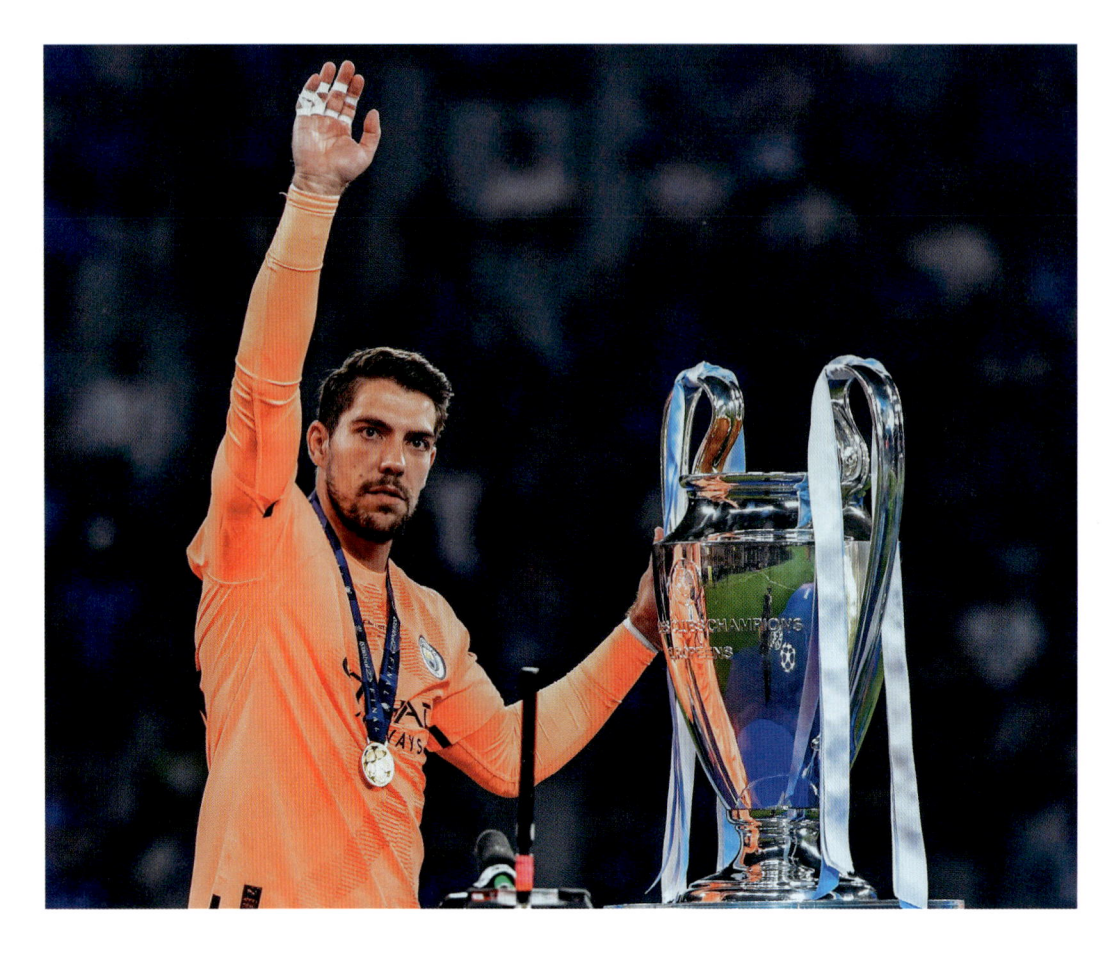

the wrong end of the Bundesliga to joining a squad regularly contesting the game's ultimate prizes was a challenge and opportunity too good to pass up.

"I'm ambitious enough to show my best performances and to try to be the best and I can't wait to work with the goalkeeping team," Stefan had declared on joining the club.

And having featured in our pre-season clash against Club America on the summer tour to the United States, Ortega Moreno's competitive debut saw him return to his home country as he featured in a Champions League group game away at Borussia Dortmund.

Ortega Moreno impressed enormously, keeping a clean sheet to help Guardiola's side record a goalless draw to seal top spot in Group G, and it was an encouraging portent of what was to come from the German.

Even better was to follow in what was only his second appearance at the Etihad.

Having figured in a 3-1 Champions League home success against Sevilla, Ortega Moreno then produced a quite stunning display to help City overcome Chelsea 2-0 in a fiercely fought Carabao Cup fourth round encounter.

The keeper earned widespread praise for his stellar performance having produced a series of outstanding saves, illustrating just why City had been so keen to bring him to Manchester.

But arguably, it was in our triumphant FA Cup campaign where Ortega Moreno's influence and impact was most profound.

The German played in every minute of our march to a seventh FA Cup triumph in total – and was one of the pivotal figures as Guardiola's side overcame Manchester United 2-1 in the final.

Indeed, such was his impact that Bruno Fernandes' somewhat fortuitous first-half penalty in that first-ever all-Manchester Wembley showpiece was the only goal Stefan conceded in City's cup-winning campaign.

All told, Ortega Moreno went on to make 14 appearances across all competitions, keeping nine clean sheets and conceding just seven times.

From City's perspective, by those sheer metrics alone, it's evident his first year proved a resounding success.

And with Premier League, Champions League and FA Cup winners' medals safely secured in his own trophy cabinet, for Ortega Moreno the move to City has been everything he would have hoped for – and so much more besides!

## STATS

**DOB:**
6 NOVEMBER 1992

**Nationality:**
GERMAN

**From:**
HOFGEISMAR, GERMANY

**Joined:**
1 JULY 2022

#19

## FORWARD

# JULIAN ALVAREZ

**Despite tasting success in his native Argentina with River Plate, Julian Alvarez arrived at the Etihad Stadium in the summer of 2022 as a relative unknown.**

That's far from the case 12 months on.

Premier League, Champions League and FA Cup triumphs, plus the small matter of a World Cup winners' medal. Those achievements would be the envy of all but a select few professionals. Julian Alvarez has become the first to achieve all four in a single season.

There were early indications that Pep Guardiola and his scouts had unearthed another gem during the club's pre-season tour to the United States, with his pace and energy catching the eye in victories over Club America and Bayern Munich, and it wasn't long before that translated into goals.

Seven days after that final triumph over the Bavarians, in fact, with Alvarez demonstrating his poacher's instinct on his competitive debut against Liverpool in the Community Shield.

It means the Argentine holds the distinction of being the only player to score in every competition for City in the 2022/23 season.

Indeed, rather than wilt under the sizeable shadow of City's attacking talents – not to mention a certain Norwegian acquisition who arrived on English shores around the same time – his potent blend of style and industry have seen him become a key figure under Guardiola.

Alvarez would mark his first Premier League start in the best possible fashion in late August, grabbing a brace in a 6-0 victory over Nottingham Forest.

The first, caressed under Forest stopper Dean Henderson from a tight angle, was followed by a stinging drive into the roof of the visitors' net, showcasing the array of finishes he has in his repertoire.

It's a quality which has caught the eye of fans and pundits alike, with former City striker Paul Dickov likening his clinical nature to that of Alvarez's fellow Argentine, Sergio Aguero.

Having been on target again in our 5-0 win over FC Copenhagen, the forward would round off the Champions League group stages with another impressive display, finding the net and grabbing two assists in a 3-1 victory against Sevilla.

The headline from our triumph against the Spaniards was undoubtedly a first senior goal for 17-year-old Academy graduate Rico Lewis but it was Alvarez who was the architect, slotting the youngster in behind having won possession back on the edge of the visitors' box.

Indeed, for all of the Argentine's ability on the ball, his tenacity and work rate make him just as much of an asset off it.

That standout display against Sevilla set the tone for a memorable November, which ended with Alvarez being named Etihad Player of the Month, with three goals and two assists ahead of the World Cup break.

He'd proven he could mix it with the best that English football had to offer, but now it was time for El Arana to show what he was capable of on a global stage.

Argentina went into the Qatar World Cup as one of the favourites, and recovered from a shock opening defeat to Saudi Arabia to win the competition for the first time since 1986.

Alvarez, despite only having 13 senior caps for La Albiceleste before the tournament, was at the centre of that historic success, featuring in every match and grabbing four goals in the process.

He returned to the City Football Academy a world champion, but the Argentine's attentions were immediately turned back to gaining further accolades at club level.

## THE PLAYERS

Another goal, this time from the penalty spot, helped Guardiola's men begin our path to FA Cup glory with a 4-0 win over Chelsea, with the forward continuing to make an impression as the final furlongs of an historic campaign came galloping into view.

A new contract in recognition of a stellar first season at the Etihad Stadium would follow in March, but Alvarez's campaign was far from over.

One month later, he would once again demonstrate his finishing repertoire in devastating fashion, whipping an unstoppable effort into the top corner from distance against Fulham.

It was a stunning strike, and one which helped Guardiola's men regain top spot for the first time in two months at a crucial point in our battle with Arsenal for the Premier League crown.

That title was secured following the Gunners' defeat to Nottingham Forest in late May, and it was Alvarez who would star in the first match since that triumph, as City beat Chelsea 1-0 at the Etihad Stadium.

Clever movement, a quick touch out of the feet, bottom corner finish, Alvarez wheeling away to celebrate.

By this point in the season, that sequence of events had become commonplace for the latest Argentine to make waves in Manchester.

## STATS

**DOB:**
31 JANUARY 2000

**Nationality:**
ARGENTINIAN

**From:**
CALCHIN, ARGENTINA

**Joined:**
31 JANUARY 2022

#20

## MIDFIELDER

# BERNARDO SILVA

**At the beating heart of this Manchester City team across 2022/23 was Bernardo Silva.**

The Portuguese star is almost unique in modern football with his mix of sublime skills and technique coupled with a work ethic that sets him apart from other playmakers.

It seems there is no role within the City team that he cannot adapt to and make his own and he has been one of the Blues' most influential players for so long and it is no coincidence that only Rodrigo (56) played more than his 55 appearances in our Treble-winning campaign – the most games he's played in a single season for the club.

Throughout his previous six years at the Etihad Stadium, the versatile bundle of invention, energy and tricks had amassed 11 major honours and delivered key goals and assists in Manchester derbies, Premier League showdowns and seismic Champions League clashes.

He continued this phenomenal habit throughout the 2022/23 campaign, which many believe was his best yet in a City shirt.

Having not started our opening two matches of the season, the 28-year-old would have been champing at the bit to ignite his seventh term in sky blue.

And he did just that when playing the entirety of our exciting 3-3 draw with Newcastle at St James' Park in what was our third Premier League assignment of the season.

He grabbed an excellent goal and an assist as City battled back from two goals down against Eddie Howe's Champions League-bound side.

This set the tone for a sparkling season both personally and as part of the group.

A driving force within the team, Bernardo has often been the catalyst in games where City needed a fillip, leading by example with his never-say-die attitude and will to win.

Whether on the wing, as a false nine, a No.10 or even a deep-lying attacking midfielder – the best way to describe his habit of collecting the ball from the back and driving forward – Bernardo has a bit of everything in his locker.

And he is a matchwinner, too, as illustrated in the epic 4-0 Champions League semi-final second leg victory over Real Madrid, which secured our passage to the European showpiece.

In what was an electric first-half display by City, Bernardo scored twice as he produced a stellar performance which earned him the Player of the Match award – leading Pep Guardiola to sound the salute for his midfield maestro.

"[He is] one of the best players I have ever seen in my life" – high praise from a manager who has had quite a few good players in his time!

A statistical dive into his 2022/23 season certainly shows why the Catalan holds Bernardo in such high regard.

Firstly, his immense versatility was highlighted as he played 23 times as a central midfielder, 14 times on the right side of midfield and on occasion at left-back – most impressively in our vital 3-1 win away to Arsenal in February.

Perhaps this is unsurprising when looking at his average distance travelled in the Premier League, which stands at 11.8 kilometres per 90 minutes – the most of any City player last year.

In fact, Bernardo accounted for each of the top three highest distances covered in a single league game by a sky blue player in 2022/23.

Hard work on and off the ball is a key principle to the way Guardiola's side operates and the Portugal international is massively productive when in possession.

## THE PLAYERS

Among the players who played the majority of their matches in central midfield, he led all of the engine room operators in the division for total ball carry distance per 90 minutes in the league (229 metres).

These immense stats translate into the Champions League, too.

Across every player who competed in the 2022/23 competition, the 28-year-old regained possession of the ball in the final third 25 times in the Champions League last season – seven more times than any other player.

Guardiola's midfield dynamo en route to the Treble, Bernardo proved to be City's standard bearer and led by example, and it was no surprise that he was heavily involved in the winning goal that secured a 1-0 win over Inter in the Champions League final.

And as for his popularity with the City fans, he is off the charts, with the diminutive Portugal star adored by the supporters.

A wonderful campaign by a wonderful footballer.

## STATS

**DOB:**
10 AUGUST 1994

**Nationality:**
PORTUGUESE

**From:**
LISBON, PORTUGAL

**Joined:**
1 JULY 2017

# 21

## DEFENDER

# SERGIO GOMEZ

**The 2022/23 season represented Sergio Gomez's debut campaign in sky blue and he will have gained a lot from it, especially the chance to work with Pep Guardiola.**

He was delighted to join City when he arrived in August 2022 and uppermost in his mind when he put pen to paper was the opportunity to learn from the boss.

In his first interview, he waxed lyrical about the Catalan, telling us: "In Pep Guardiola I have a chance to learn and develop under the most outstanding manager in world football.

"To be able to be part of this club is a dream come true for me and something any young player would aspire to.

"The number of trophies City have won over the past few years has been incredible and the style of football the team plays under Pep is the most exciting in Europe.

"Playing for and being guided by Pep and his coaches is going to be very special."

You got the feeling as the season concluded in June 2023 that the three gold medals he picked up for being involved in our Premier League, FA Cup and Champions League successes will have been trumped by the level of development he'll have gone through under the former Barcelona and Bayern manager.

On the eve of his move to City, he's sure to have been advised on the drive and dedication of his new manager Guardiola as his previous boss at Anderlecht was none other than Vincent Kompany.

Kompany, as club captain for eight seasons, including his final three campaigns in sky blue under the City boss, will have seen first-hand the level of detail that Guardiola goes into – and the improvement Gomez was bound to see in his own game.

He certainly left the Belgian club with plenty of self-confidence, having made 49 appearances across the 2021/22 campaign as well as being voted their Player of the Year.

He began his sky blue career with two substitute appearances, coming on for comfortable home victories over Crystal Palace and Nottingham Forest in August before starting the following month's away Champions League 4-0 victory at Sevilla.

He came off the bench as a late sub in the 4-0 away win at Wolves before playing a more active role in the 6-3 Manchester derby victory over United.

With Kyle Walker struggling with a groin injury early on at the Etihad, Gomez replaced him on 41 minutes, with the Spanish international contributing to the thumping win in front of a delighted home crowd.

He was in from the start three days later, again excelling in the 5-0 home win over Copenhagen in the Champions League before coming off the bench the following weekend in the 4-0 home top-flight victory over Southampton.

Then came the nadir of his season, receiving a 30th-minute red card in the return game away at Copenhagen, the match eventually finishing 0-0.

Cup matches continued to be the avenue Guardiola took to give Gomez game-time from the start, the attacking left-back playing in the 3-1 home Champions League win over Sevilla as well as League Cup and FA Cup home wins over Chelsea.

His involvement in the former competition came to a surprising end at the quarter-final stage, as City went down 2-0 to Southampton, who were relegated from the Premier League at the end of the season.

Gomez continued to be involved from the bench across January, February, March and April, contributing across the Premier League, FA Cup and

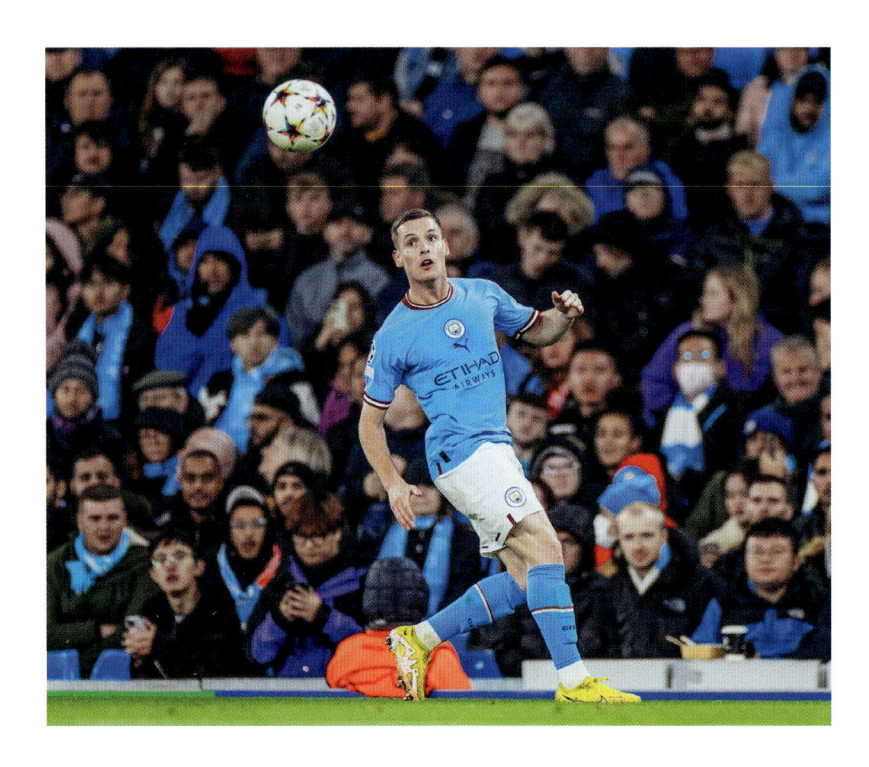

Champions League, three competitions City, of course, went on to win.

His next involvement from the start came on the big stage – at Wembley as City took on Sheffield United in the FA Cup semi-final.

Gomez excelled in the inverted full-back role at the national stadium, playing 90 minutes and impressing greatly in the 3-0 victory.

In fact, Guardiola name-checked him after the game, telling the media in his post-match press conference that Gomez was a player he could rely on after seeing him excel against the Blades, a huge fillip for the starlet defender.

After briefly dropping back to bench duties in the 3-0 victory at Everton, a vital result in the title-race, he was in from the start in the 1-0 home win over Chelsea, a day of much joy and merriment as City celebrated a third straight Premier League title victory.

With Guardiola aiming to keep everyone fresh for finals to come against United and Inter in the FA Cup and Champions League, Gomez continued in the starting line-up for away games against Brighton and Brentford before watching on as City achieved the Treble.

He may not have played in those final duo of games but he can have felt proud of the contributions he'd made along the way.

## STATS

**DOB:**
4 SEPTEMBER 2000

**Nationality:**
SPANISH

**From:**
BADALONA, SPAIN

**Joined:**
16 AUGUST 2022

#25

## THE PLAYERS

# DEFENDER

# MANUEL AKANJI

**Some signings take months of meticulous planning, some are just sudden opportunities that are too good to turn down.**

Manuel Akanji's move to City on deadline day last summer fell into the second category.

Pep Guardiola had assessed his squad in the early weeks of the season and decided he needed defensive reinforcements.

When it became clear the Swiss international was available, the club wasted no time in securing the Borussia Dortmund man. It was a whirlwind few days for him, with the arrival of a new child coinciding with switching clubs.

Since that moment, no defender has played more than Akanji, with the No.25 appearing in 48 of the 55 games we have played.

Initially, those outside the club assumed Akanji would be in the supporting cast – only filling in when players were absent through injury or suspension.

Far from it, he was one of Guardiola's go-to men.

Over the course of the campaign, he played in the middle, on the left and on the right, even stepping up into the hybrid midfield role that eventually became John Stones' own on occasion.

Fans were immediately impressed with his passing during his debut display against Sevilla and he continued to be a reliable member of the side.

However, as with many in the squad, his game went to a new level after the winter World Cup.

Guardiola settled on his favoured personnel and his preferred shape, and suddenly City's defence was almost impossible to breach.

**TREBLE WINNERS**

The Blues went on a 25-game unbeaten run that secured a third straight Premier League title, a second FA Cup under Guardiola and last but certainly not least, our maiden Champions League success.

Akanji was there every step of the way.

Alongside Stones, Ruben Dias, Nathan Ake and Kyle Walker, he was part of the meanest defence at home and against the giants of the continent.

An injury to Ake meant Akanji had to go to the left for a crucial top-of-the-table clash with Arsenal, where he would come directly up against one of the Premier League's in-form men in Bukayo Saka.

Not only did Akanji shackle the England winger, he attacked with a vigour that pushed our title challengers deep into their own half.

He remained there for the thumping second leg victory over Real Madrid in the semi-final of the Champions League, as well as the all-Manchester FA Cup final.

However, he was back on the right just a week later for the date with Champions League destiny in Istanbul.

The defender's athleticism may be the first thing that catches the eye when he's monitoring strikers – only Erling Haaland and Walker clock quicker top speeds in matches than him – but it's his composure on the ball that has made his transition to this City side so seamless.

Progressing the ball forward in a tidy, efficient manner is a key element of what defenders are asked to do by Guardiola.

Across the whole of the 2022/23 Champions League, only Toni Kroos and our own Rodrigo – masters of their craft in midfield – played more line-breaking passes than Akanji.

Those are passes that take opposition players out of the game and find a team-mate in a more advanced position.

However, given he's a defender and so spends most of his time far from goal, only one of those passes went into the 18-yard box.

That just so happened to be for Bernardo Silva in the final. When the little Portuguese winger saw his cross deflected, Rodrigo stepped up and the rest is history.

That move would not have been possible without the timing of Akanji's burst forward and the weight of his pass.

So much more than just a utility player, Akanji is Guardiola's man for all seasons.

## STATS

**DOB:**
19 JULY 1995

**Nationality:**
SWISS

**From:**
WIESENDANGEN, SWITZERLAND

**Joined:**
1 SEPTEMBER 2022

#26

## FORWARD

# RIYAD MAHREZ

**The most creative African player in the history of the Premier League.**

This towering achievement for Riyad Mahrez crowned his own impact on City's Treble-winning season.

By the end of the history-defining campaign, Mahrez had accumulated 61 assists across his 10 seasons in the English top flight.

The Algerian international surpassed Didier Drogba, who previously held the record of 55 assists. And that's not the only mark in history Mahrez made this season, but we'll get to that.

Since joining City ahead of the 2018/19 campaign, Mahrez has continued to be one of the most direct, threatening and agile right wingers in the Premier League.

And let's not forget how jaw-droppingly good his first touch is.

Before the 2022/23 fixtures, Mahrez had 128 goal involvements in 254 games – and was looking to be just as influential once the action got under way. He more than delivered.

The 32-year-old featured in 30 Premier League games while also being a key figure in Pep Guardiola's cup line-ups throughout the course of the season.

Just prior to the international break, Mahrez was an instrumental figure in our Champions League campaign, taking to the pitch in all six of our Group G games against Sevilla, Borussia Dortmund and FC Copenhagen. With two goals and one assist, the Algerian was proving his worth.

Over the course of his City career, Mahrez developed a knack for scoring in City's biggest games. And on the return to Premier League action after the World Cup, he scored the crucial goal in our 1-0 win over Chelsea in January.

## TREBLE WINNERS

He was rampant on the right wing, scoring a brace and assisting Erling Haaland in our 4-2 win over Tottenham Hotspur despite the visitors taking a two-goal lead.

During our illustrious 15-league game unbeaten run, which helped us overcome an eight-point deficit and claim a third consecutive Premier League title, Mahrez was a reliable figure.

From setting up Kevin De Bruyne, who gave City the lead in our 4-1 win over Liverpool, to assisting both goals in our 2-1 win over Leeds, the Algerian was a key cog in Guardiola's title-winning squad.

It came as no surprise that by the end of the campaign he led all wingers in the Premier League for successful passes per 90 minutes with 44.9.

The 32-year-old was also a regular name in City's starting XI in our FA Cup matches throughout the course of 2023, and bagged himself an impressive brace in our 4-0 win over Chelsea in the third round.

But it was his performance in the semi-final which really stood out in England's most prestigious cup competition.

Mahrez's 66-minute hat-trick – which included a spectacular solo goal in which he ran from City's half before finding the back of the Sheffield United net – broke records.

Not only did he score the first FA Cup semi-final hat-trick at Wembley Stadium, he was also the first City player to score a treble at England's home.

He was a regular name in the lead-up to our win over Manchester United in the FA Cup final in a month of silverware and celebrations.

THE PLAYERS

And while he didn't feature in the Wembley showpiece, where City beat Erik ten Hag's side 2-1 to lift the trophy, our team wouldn't have got there had it not been for Mahrez's magic.

And just as the celebrations of winning the Double settled, the Treble came along.

Given his enormous contribution over the past five years, it was fitting that Mahrez was present in Istanbul as City sealed the greatest season in the club's history by lifting the Champions League.

That took his extraordinary success at the Etihad to 11 major trophies. No surprise given his talent, technique and desire to win.

## STATS

**DOB:**
21 FEBRUARY 1991

**Nationality:**
ALGERIAN

**From:**
SARCELLES, FRANCE

**Joined:**
10 JULY 2018

www.mancity.com 131

#31

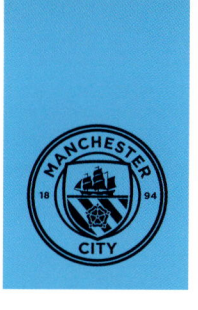

## GOALKEEPER

# EDERSON

**After more than 10-and-a-half months and 5,500 minutes of football, it was Ederson who had the final crucial touch of our remarkable season.**

Seconds away from a historic Treble, City just had to survive one last corner and one final opportunity for Italian side Inter to take the Champions League final into extra time.

Ederson had already made several major contributions in the final, including an astonishing save to deny Romelu Lukaku from close range, shifting his feet to instinctively keep out his header.

And collecting a cross on the edge of his box deep into the game to take the pressure off the defence prompted celebrations from the City fans inside Istanbul's Ataturk Stadium.

Supporters watched through their fingers as Inter's Robin Gosens flicked a near-post header goalwards but Ederson flew to turn it away, and seconds later he was hugged by Nathan Ake before dropping to the floor as the referee blew the final whistle.

It capped yet another brilliant season from the Brazilian when he was once again a reliable and pivotal part of City's success.

Ederson has now won the Premier League title in five of six seasons at the Etihad Stadium, proving to be the perfect keeper for Pep Guardiola's system – brilliant on the ball, alert to danger and capable of making crucial saves.

The 29-year-old made 35 league appearances, reaching that tally in each of his seasons with the club, keeping 11 clean sheets.

While he didn't claim the Golden Glove for most clean sheets for what would have been a fourth successive year, it was still an impressive campaign and one that saw him become the 17th goalkeeper to keep 100 shutouts in Premier League history.

He reached the landmark in a crucial 2-0 win over Newcastle in March, becoming the third quickest to the milestone.

In all competitions, Ederson kept 18 clean sheets – a number he has reached in each of his six seasons in Manchester – with seven of them coming from 11 matches in the Champions League. He also remained unbeaten in his only 45 minutes of domestic cup football as a second-half substitute against Bristol City in the FA Cup.

Summer signing Stefan Ortega Moreno was predominantly used in the FA Cup and Carabao Cup and along with Scott Carson, the keepers have built a close-knit unit working with coaches Xabi Mancisidor and Richard Wright.

In the Champions League, Ederson excelled as City remained unbeaten throughout our successful campaign.

The No. 31 was beaten only once at the Etihad Stadium in five games, in the 2-1 Group G victory over Borussia Dortmund, keeping crucial clean sheets against Bayern Munich and Real Madrid in the quarter-finals and semi-finals.

City didn't concede more than one goal in any European game, with Ederson in the side that drew 1-1 away to RB Leipzig, Bayern and Real in the knockout stages.

He saved 28 of the 31 on-target shots that he faced in the Champions League, for a save percentage of 87.1% – the highest of the 30 goalkeepers to face 20 or more such shots.

But it's not just his saving ability that makes him the ideal keeper, with his ball-playing skills making him an attacking threat.

Ederson was one of four goalkeepers to claim an assist in the Premier League – with his brilliant drilled pass against Brighton in October picking out Erling Haaland, and the City striker finished the opportunity in style.

He is always looking to get his team attacking and City created chances with an expected goals value of 8.43 from the open-play sequences Ederson was involved in, the most of any goalkeeper in the Premier League

THE PLAYERS

last season with his involvement leading to 54 shots, more than any of his rivals.

Against high-pressing teams, he is able to take the ball under pressure and he received more open-play passes in his own penalty area than anyone else, with 679 in total.

His vision and ability to pick out the right pass is why he is such an influential member of the team that thrives on possession and movement.

Players who received a pass in open-play from Ederson in the Premier League had 3.7 passing options available to them on average after receiving the ball – the highest figure for any goalkeeper to complete at least 150 passes.

But it wasn't just in the Premier League where his quality on the ball was important, with Ederson keeping the same calmness on the ball at the Santiago Bernabeu, Allianz Arena and Ataturk among other stadiums on our European adventure.

And in the final seconds of the season, Ederson made sure that he and this fantastic City team secured their place in the history books.

## STATS

**DOB:**
17 AUGUST 1993

**Nationality:**
BRAZILIAN

**From:**
OSASCO, BRAZIL

**Joined:**
1 JULY 2017

www.mancity.com 135

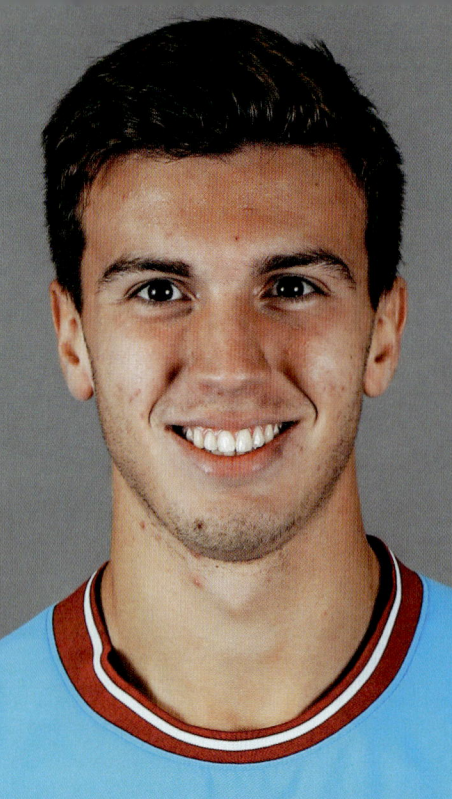

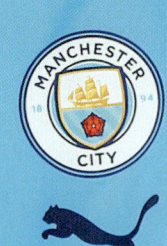

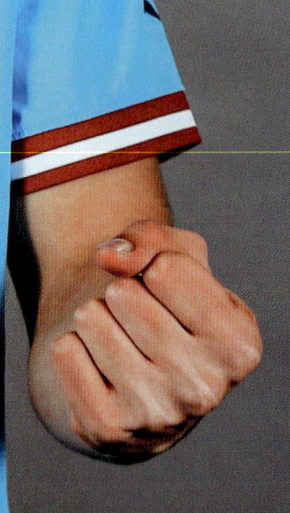

#32

## MIDFIELDER

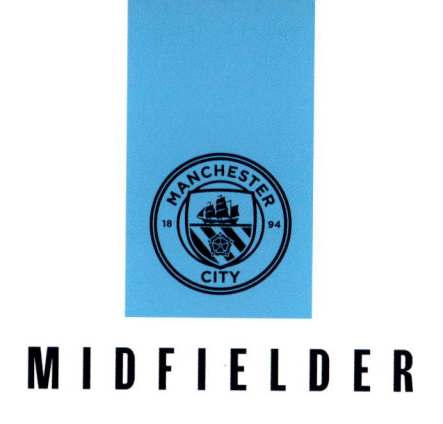

# MAXIMO PERRONE

**City have a long and rich association with exciting Argentinian players, stretching back to 2008.**

Those who have proudly worn the sky blue of the club and the blue and white of La Albiceleste have provided a swathe of memorable and iconic moments at the Etihad Stadium.

These undeniably include Carlos Tevez captaining us to FA Cup glory in 2011, Willy Caballero's penalty heroics in a 2016 Carabao Cup final success and Sergio Aguero's spine-tingling goal against QPR in 2012, to name a few.

Since the arrival of Pablo Zabaleta 15 years ago, a total of 10 players who originate from Argentina have represented City, winning a combined 36 major honours.

The latest of these is midfield starlet Maximo Perrone – who is looking to follow in the footsteps of his countrymen who have enjoyed immense success in Manchester.

In a January transfer window where Pep Guardiola himself admitted City were unlikely to make substantial additions to his squad in the winter of 2023 – the 20-year-old was the only new face to arrive at the City Football Academy.

A move to the reigning Premier League champions and a side who were relentlessly chasing a historic Treble may have seemed a somewhat daunting task for a player who had only played for Velez Sarsfield in his homeland.

But Perrone settled into his new surroundings quickly and was named among the substitutes for our trip to Tottenham Hotspur in January.

The opportunity to train and rub shoulders with some of world football's elite players was one he was relishing, saying in early February: "I keep myself calm. I know I'm here to grow and that's my goal.

"(Everyone has welcomed me) very well. I met a very good group of people, above all.

"I have to train. My goal is to train, give my best in every training session, and then things will come whenever they come.

"There's no better place than this right now."

The versatile midfielder didn't have to wait long to make his debut, either, producing a composed performance in our 4-1 win over Bournemouth on the south coast after coming on from the bench with 18 minutes remaining.

This would be the first of two outings he's made for the club since arriving at the Etihad, as he featured in City's 3-0 FA Cup fifth round win over Bristol City days after we picked off the Cherries.

Although these occasions were the only times the sky blue faithful saw him operate for the club, in the pair of cameo appearances he showcased his sparkling potential to those in attendance and watching around the globe.

Perrone was also a permanent feature in first-team training since his South American switch, and was among the substitutes for all of our UEFA Champions League knockout matches apart from the first-leg trip to RB Leipzig and our semi-final double header with Real Madrid.

As Rodrigo's piledriver secured our maiden Champions League title, he once again witnessed the historic moment from the bench as the roof came off an electric Ataturk Olympic Stadium in Istanbul.

THE PLAYERS

These experiences at football's top table will no doubt prove valuable for the 20-year-old who has lived and breathed what it takes to win the Treble – and is one of a select few players who have done so.

And, as the curtain fell on the 2022/23 campaign in the most wonderful of ways, the immense talent City have on our hands was shown once again as Perrone was named in the 100-player list for the 2023 Golden Boy award.

## STATS

**DOB:**
7 JANUARY 2003

**Nationality:**
ARGENTINIAN

**From:**
BUENOS AIRES, ARGENTINA

**Joined:**
23 JANUARY 2023

www.mancity.com 139

#33

## GOALKEEPER

# SCOTT CARSON

**As Pep Guardiola has consistently explained, City's strength lies in the collective. Regardless of the amount of minutes a player gets, every member of the squad has a hugely important role to play off the pitch.**

The fact that Guardiola has made multiple references to Scott Carson throughout the 2022/23 season may seem odd to those outside the dressing room, but to those inside the club, it comes as no surprise how appreciated the goalkeeper is.

"He is a guy when he talks everybody listens," said Guardiola when asked about Carson's character and the role he plays within the team.

"He helps take quality training sessions, especially after a game. We have him in the locker room and with the staff you cannot believe the impact [he has], we are very pleased to have him."

The 37-year-old has had an illustrious career and, with that, he brings a wealth of experience most players only dream of having.

After spending two seasons on loan with City, Carson joined Guardiola's squad permanently in 2021. And his influence and impact has been profound.

He's worked alongside fellow keepers Ederson and Stefan Ortega Moreno, and has brought the competitive best out of both. And through this, he has made City's goalkeeping unit the envy of their peers.

And while Carson did not take to the pitch during our 2022/23 campaign,

## TREBLE WINNERS

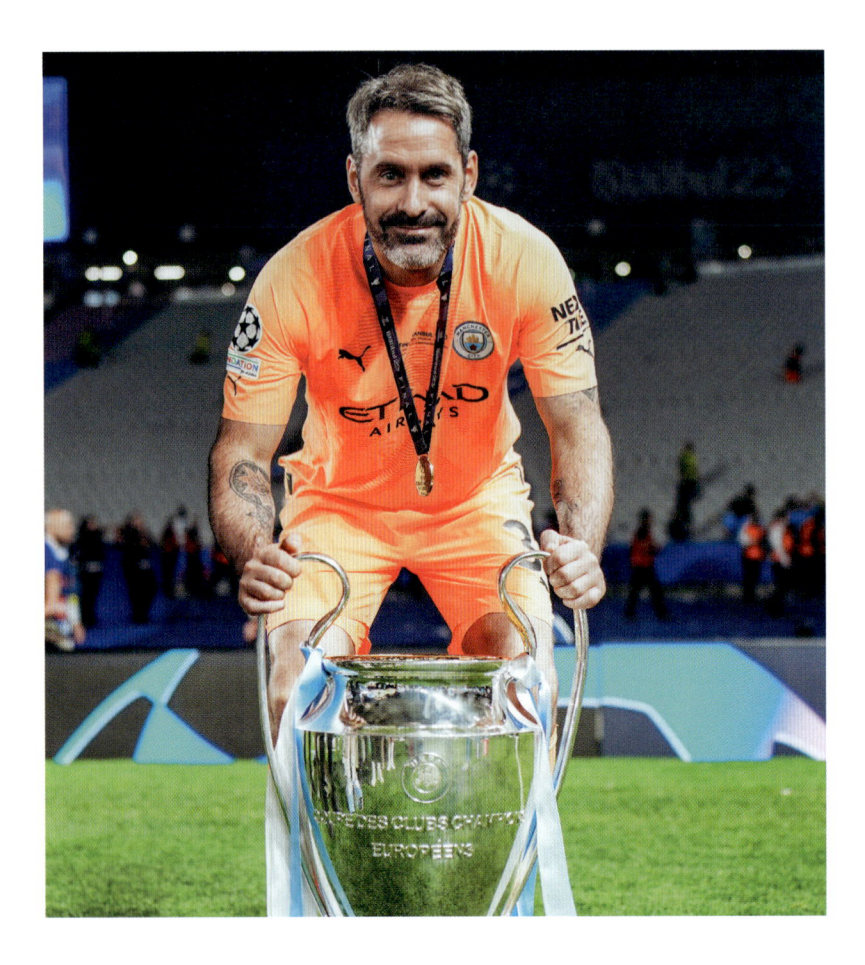

the esteem in which Guardiola and City hold him in was echoed when he signed a contract extension in May.

"I just love getting out there and diving around. I've always felt I've given 100% at every club I've been at and even now I still think I've probably improved in the last couple of years I've been here," said Carson on the Official Man City Podcast.

"I feel I've done a lot more behind the scenes [rather than playing]. I've not just come here and done the minimum I could. I've set standards, even at my age, I've got a work ethic that I hope people have looked at and if they want to play for as long as I have they see what I do day in, day out.

"I love working with Pep, Xabi Mancisidor and our incredible players every day. Hopefully I can help all of our goalkeepers be at their best."

Across his two decades in the game, he's honed his craft overseas at Turkish side Bursaspor, as well as in spells around England, including at Liverpool.

A unique aspect of Carson's experience is that he had previously been part of a Champions League-winning team, unlike any other player in City's 2022/23 squad list.

And it came in handy.

There was a neat symmetry of success in Istanbul as he was part of the Liverpool team to lift the trophy in the same stadium in 2005, mirrored by City's triumph in the final 18 years later.

And in doing so he added his name to an exclusive list of players, equalling former AC Milan duo Paolo Maldini and Alessandro Costacurta's record for the longest gap between securing Champions League/European Cup medals for a player.

As City ramp up for another exciting season, Carson's experience and leadership skills will continue to be invaluable as the team prepare for the 2023/24 campaign.

In Carson's own words: "Not playing isn't going to stop me from every single day working hard, coming in with a smile on my face and if the manager needs me, I'm going to be ready."

## STATS

| | |
|---|---|
| **DOB:** 3 SEPTEMBER 1985 | **Nationality:** ENGLISH |
| **From:** WHITEHAVEN, ENGLAND | **Joined:** 8 AUGUST 2019 |

#47

## MIDFIELDER

# PHIL FODEN

**Just seven days before his 23rd birthday, incredibly Phil Foden collected his fifth Premier League winners' medal with his boyhood club Manchester City.**

A mere few weeks later, the Stockport-born midfielder had won every trophy he could in a City shirt after a Manchester derby FA Cup final at Wembley and that incredible Champions League night in Istanbul.

For Foden, born in May 2000, it was the first Treble by an English club in his lifetime and the culmination of watching our incredible rise as a fan and then as a crucial member of Pep Guardiola's squad.

As a youngster he was a City ballboy and mascot as well as an Academy player before making his debut just a few months after turning 17.

From there his impact has continued to grow and in the 2022/23 season, he was once again crucial to City's success.

In a campaign that was disrupted by an ankle injury, surgery following appendicitis and the mid-season break for the World Cup, he still made 48 appearances for the Blues in all competitions.

That was three more than the previous season and helped him to a tally of 15 goals, the third successive season he has been in double figures, and at his best-ever strike rate with a goal every 177 minutes.

Among the most memorable of those was a brilliant hat-trick in an astonishing 6-3 victory over Manchester United at the Etihad Stadium.

Erling Haaland also scored three that day to become the first player in 28 years to score a treble in a Manchester derby. However, it would only be another nine minutes before Foden claimed his own hat-trick!

Those strikes took his career total for City to 50, making him the youngest player to reach a half-century of goals under Guardiola (22 years, 127 days), even surpassing the great Lionel Messi (22 years, 16 days).

More important contributions were to come, including a brilliant individual goal in a vital victory over Champions League-chasing Newcastle United at the Etihad in March.

Eddie Howe's side were one of the surprise packages of the season and it was a potentially tricky clash as we chased down Arsenal at the top of the table, but Foden made the breakthrough after a wonderful weaving run.

He also had a big effect on maintaining the challenge on three fronts, notably in a tough FA Cup tie at exciting Championship side Bristol City where a sold-out Ashton Gate crowd were hoping for a major upset.

But Foden extinguished any potential shocks with an early goal and a late second in 3-0 victory.

The title was wrapped up before our final home game of the season, the 1-0 win over Chelsea, which was Foden's 100th Premier League win in his 127th outing, making him the fastest player to reach a century of victories in the competition's history.

With a hectic schedule in the final weeks of the campaign, Guardiola would often rotate his starting line-ups to keep his players fit, fresh and firing as we closed in on a magnificent end to the season. Although Foden found himself among the substitutes on occasions, his importance to the team didn't diminish.

THE PLAYERS

And when Kevin De Bruyne was forced off through injury in the 1-0 Champions League final victory over Inter, the City boss instinctively turned to the Englishman, who delivered an assured and quality display in Istanbul.

He came close to creating a less nervy finish with a brilliant chance created for himself following an exquisite turn, but he was denied by a smart save from Andre Onana.

But City saw out the win and Foden celebrated as one of the City fans – it just so happened that he's good enough to be on the pitch.

Signing a new contract in October 2022 that extends his stay at the Etihad Stadium until 2027, it's going to be fascinating to see how many more medals he can add to a collection that has 14 winners' gongs already.

## STATS

**DOB:**
28 MAY 2000

**Nationality:**
ENGLISH

**From:**
STOCKPORT, MANCHESTER, ENGLAND

**Joined:**
1 JULY 2016

www.mancity.com 147

# #80

## MIDFIELDER

# COLE PALMER

**It's been a season of steady progress for Cole Palmer.**

A foot injury had disrupted what was rapidly developing into an exciting finale to his 2021/22 campaign, with the winger providing a handful of eye-catching performances around the turn of the year, particularly in the FA Cup against Swindon Town.

It can be difficult for young players to build on what could be considered a 'breakthrough' campaign but, having more than doubled his appearance tally during our Treble-winning season, Palmer's stock has continued to rise under the watchful eye of Pep Guardiola.

Despite featuring in seven of our first 11 Premier League matches, the 21-year-old's playing opportunities mainly came in the form of our cup competitions. He certainly didn't disappoint.

After impressing in Carabao Cup triumphs over Chelsea and Liverpool before the turn of the year, Palmer would become a mainstay in our march to the FA Cup, featuring in all but one knockout round and the final.

Another eye-catching performance against Chelsea would follow, repaying the faith that Guardiola had placed in the youngster when facing some of English football's heavyweights.

And he would even get his name on the scoresheet in a 6-0 victory against Burnley in the quarter-finals, reacting quickest to a loose ball to volley home from close-range at the Etihad Stadium.

There was an added maturity to the youngster's game, with his elegant dribbling style, deceptive turn of pace and excellent close control. He looked at home on the grandest stage, and his tactical intelligence and technical brilliance saw Guardiola deploy him in a variety of positions, including a central role on several occasions.

## TREBLE WINNERS

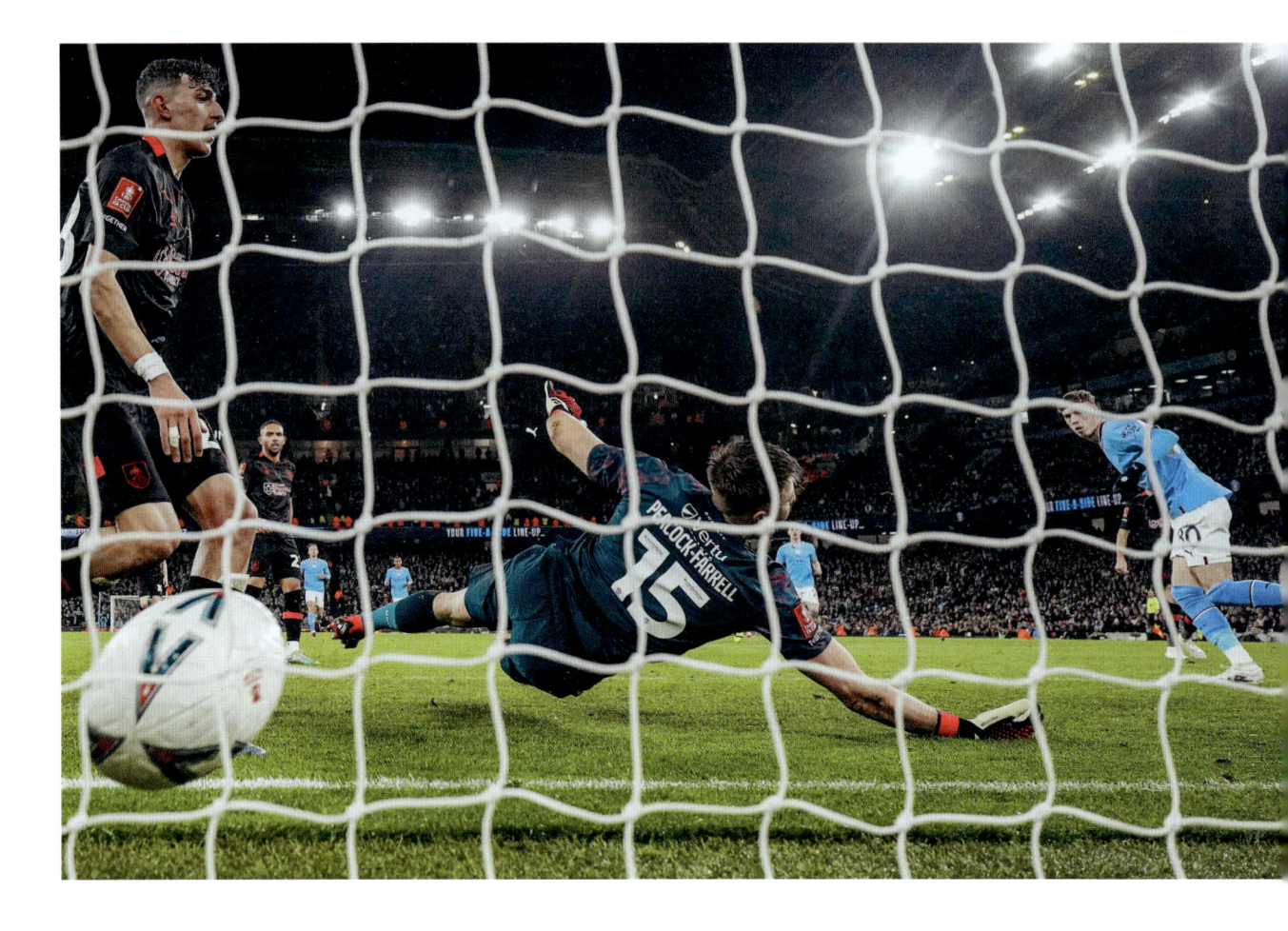

He even went close to marking one of those appearances, in a 5-0 Champions League win over FC Copenhagen, with a spectacular goal from distance, forcing a fine save from opposition goalkeeper Kamil Grabara.

Further game time would come towards the end of the campaign, as the demands of City's busy fixture schedule placed a greater emphasis on squad rotation.

It was an opportunity that Palmer wasn't about to pass up, playing a starring role in our 1-0 triumph over Chelsea at the Etihad Stadium, our first match since being crowned Premier League champions for the third successive season.

It was the winger's incisive ball into Julian Alvarez which sparked the only goal of the game, but there was so much more for City fans to be enthused by beyond the assist itself.

Instead, it was the manner of the 21-year-old's performance, undeterred by coming up against one of the Premier League's best-ever right-backs in Cesar Azpilicueta, which really caught the eye.

Palmer was a constant threat out wide, regularly dragging the Chelsea captain into uncomfortable positions and looking to exploit space in behind the visiting defence.

At 33 and operating in an out-of-sorts Chelsea side, Azpilicueta's best years were, perhaps, a little behind him, but he's remained one of the Londoners' most consistent performers over the past few years. Cole's performance against someone of that calibre demonstrated the heights that he hit on that sunny afternoon at the Etihad.

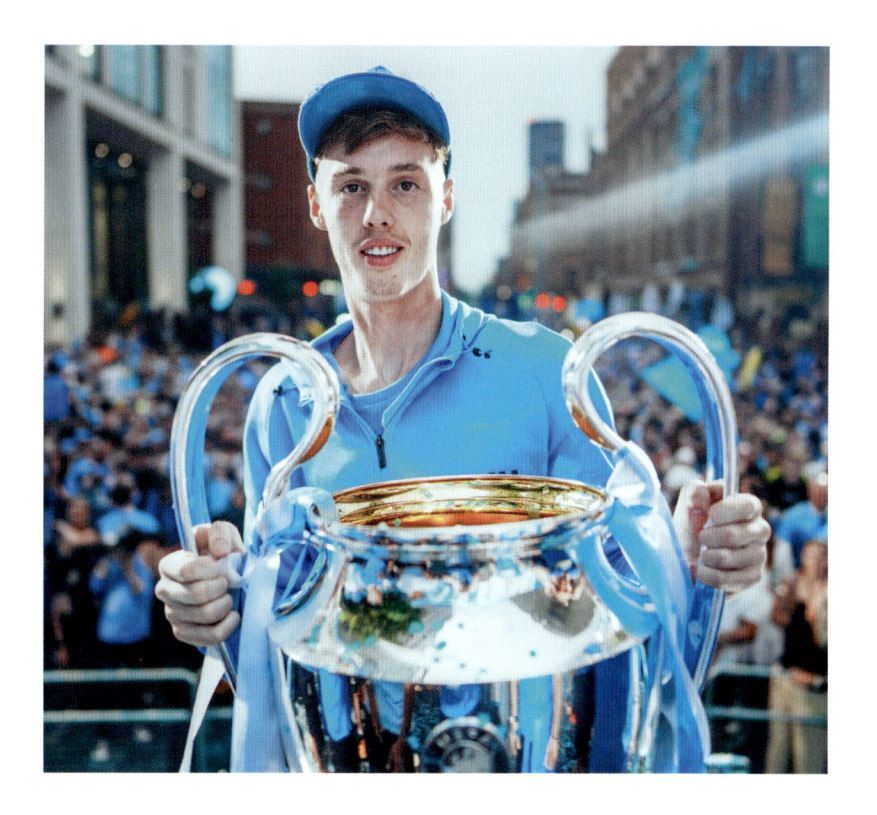

Palmer impressed once again just three days later after coming off the bench away to Brighton. The winger was unfortunate not to add another assist to his tally on the south coast, patiently working the opening out wide after combining with Ilkay Gundogan before clipping an inch-perfect cross into Erling Haaland.

The goal was ultimately disallowed for a foul in the build-up, but it was yet another indication that Guardiola, among the array of attacking talents he has at his disposal, has another patiently waiting in the wings.

## STATS

**DOB:**
6 MAY 2002

**Nationality:**
ENGLISH

**From:**
MANCHESTER, ENGLAND

**Joined:**
24 APRIL 2018

# 82

THE PLAYERS

## DEFENDER

# RICO LEWIS

**When Rico Lewis lifted the Under-18 Premier League title at the end of 2021/22 season, he will have set his sights high.**

Even in his wildest dreams, the Bury-born defender could hardly have accounted for how the next 12 months of his life would go.

It started with an invite to the pre-season tour. Every year, youngsters join the core of Pep Guardiola's squad for a brief foray to another corner of the globe to put the plans in place for the season to come.

Spending every waking hour together, it's an opportunity for those on the periphery to impress.

In Houston, Texas and Green Bay, Wisconsin, Lewis clearly did just that. Still 17 at the time, he came on for the closing stages of a friendly with German giants Bayern Munich in front of almost 80,000 people and immediately looked at home.

A return to Manchester and the start of the Premier League season brought fresh hopes and, for Lewis, renewed inspiration when it became apparent he was a valued part of Guardiola's plans.

A late substitute appearance in a convincing win over AFC Bournemouth at the Etihad Stadium got the home debut out of the way in the most comfortable fashion possible at this level.

However, it wasn't long before the teenager became one of Guardiola's thought leaders on the pitch.

He was the youngest player ever to score on their first Champions League start when he fired into the roof of the net at home against Sevilla while playing a more conventional full-back role.

City fans love an Academy graduate, especially one that's been a blue all their life.

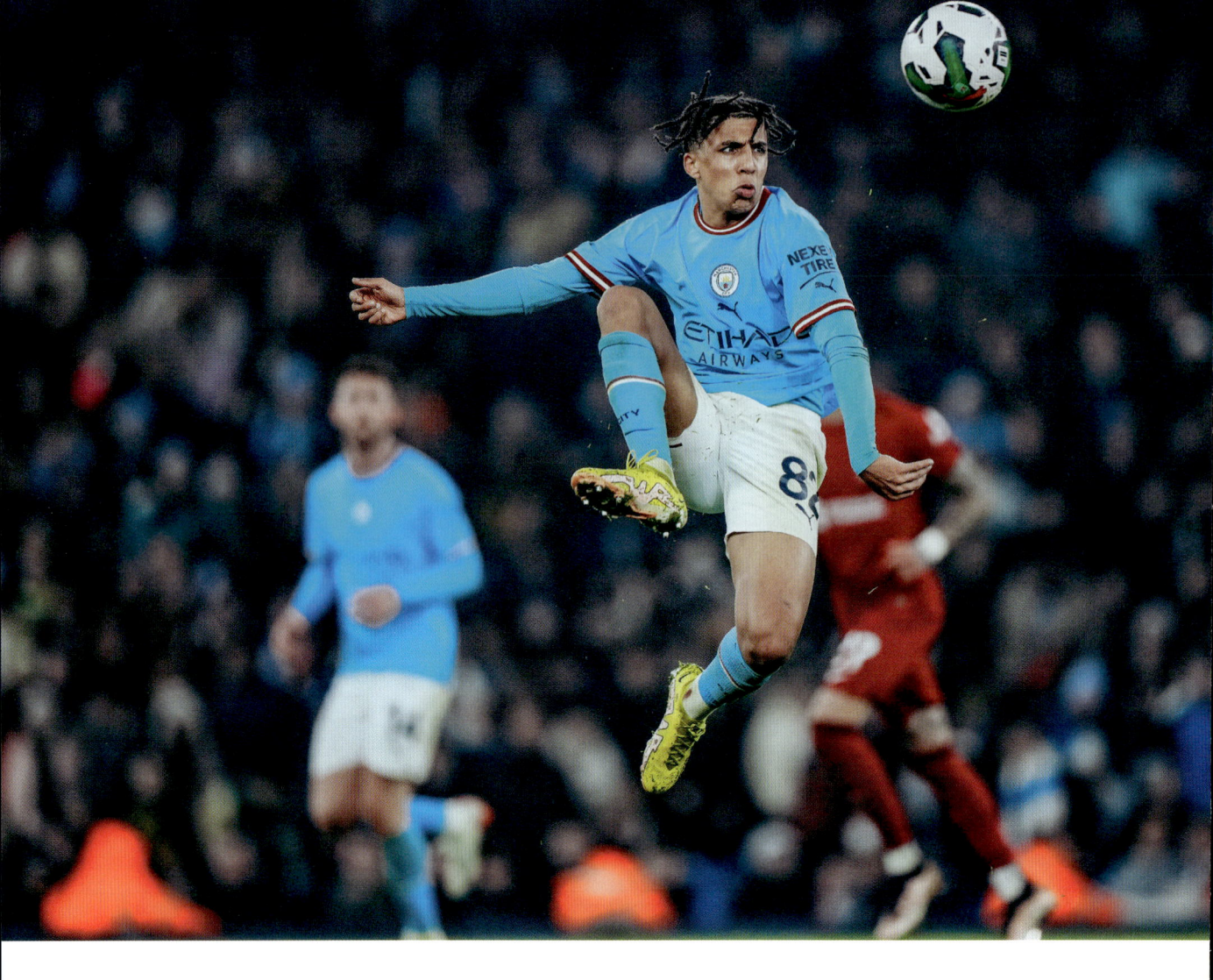

Lewis' talent was immediately evident to all in the Etihad Stadium and this performance against the side that would go on to lift the Europa League cemented his status as a member of the team.

He was visibly moved by the standing ovation after his late substitution. After all, he is a boy living the dream.

Following the World Cup, he was tasked with marshalling the likes of Luis Diaz, Raheem Sterling and Heung-min Son – some of the Premier League's best attacking talents.

Guardiola was at no stage reticent to throw him into the fiery cauldron of football matches at the highest level.

The son of a boxing trainer in Radcliffe, Lewis' on-pitch persona is that of a fighter. While only slight in stature, there has been no opponent too daunting for him in his first campaign in senior football.

As the end of the season approached, Guardiola reverted back to the experienced names that have seen and done plenty before in their career.

However, he continued to praise Lewis' enthusiasm for all of the challenges that were thrown at City and the impact that had on a squad brimming with players with full medal drawers already.

You only had to watch his in-play reactions on the touchline at the Ataturk

THE PLAYERS

Olympic Stadium during the closing stages of the Champions League final to understand what this means to him.

Sent out of the dugout to warm up, the youngster instead spent the last 20 minutes on his haunches as Ederson held firm to seal the trophy.

It won't be long before the 18-year-old's attention turns to doing it all again.

With the backing of Guardiola, there's no telling the heights Lewis can reach.

## STATS

| DOB: | Nationality: |
|---|---|
| 21 NOVEMBER 2004 | ENGLISH |
| From: | Joined: |
| MANCHESTER, ENGLAND | 1 JANUARY 2001 |

www.mancity.com 155

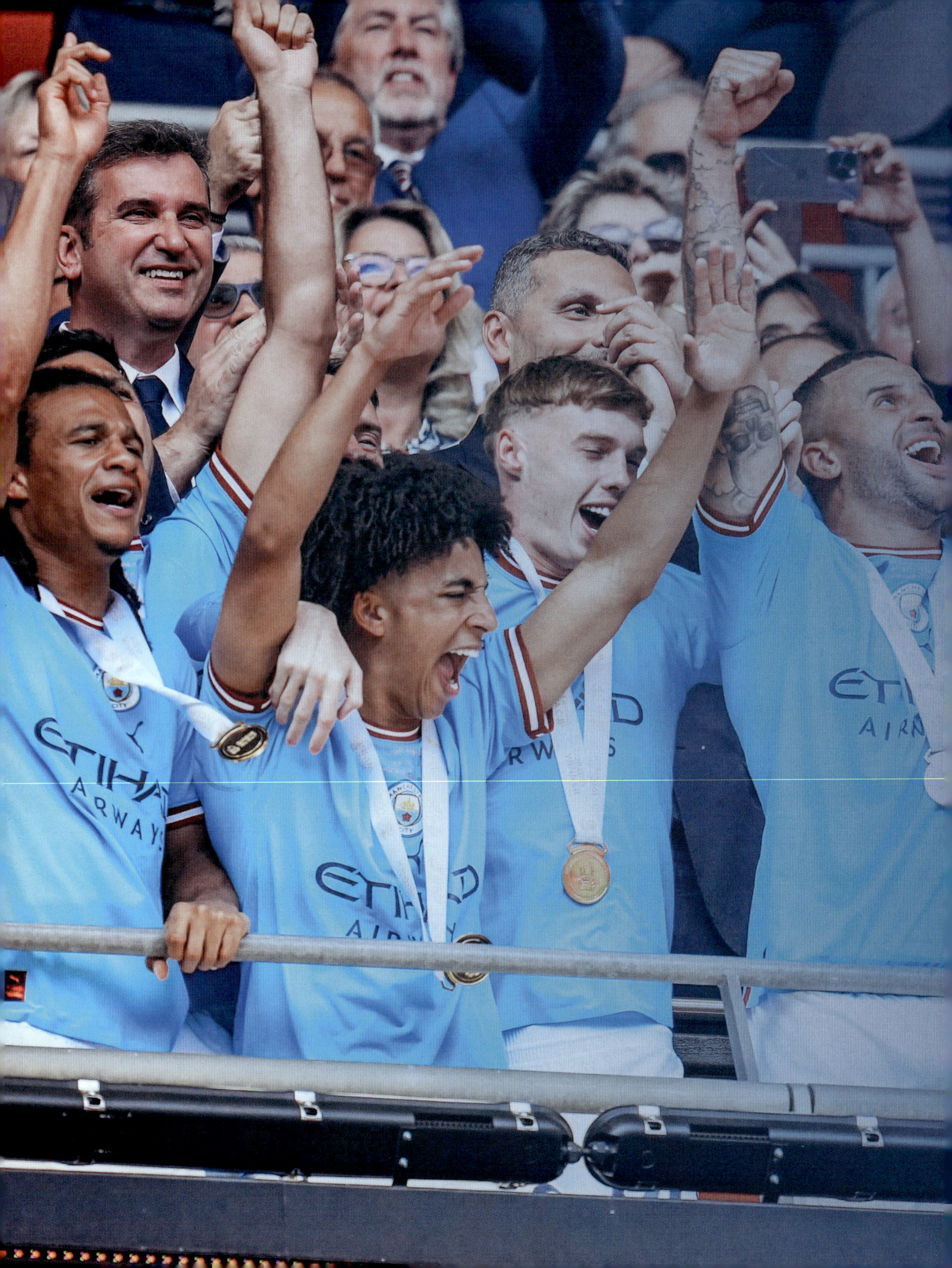

# 3

THE STORY OF
THE FA CUP

# WEMBLEY WONDERS
# DELIVER
# THE DOUBLE

## TREBLE WINNERS

**The FA Cup has been probably the trickiest of the domestic silverware for Pep Guardiola to win during his seven years of remarkable success at the Etihad Stadium.**

He guided Manchester City to the trophy in 2019 as his side became the first English club to win every domestic honour available in one season.

A record-equalling 6-0 victory over Watford at Wembley added the trophy to the Carabao Cup and Premier League title as well – not to mention the Community Shield collected in the campaign's curtain-raiser.

Before this season, it was the only time that Guardiola had got his hands on the famous trophy, but it doesn't tell the full story of why more success has come elsewhere.

The FA Cup has always been a special competition for English football fans and holds special memories for generations of City supporters.

City have won the trophy on seven occasions in total, with the first in 1904, meaning the Blues boast the longest time span of any team between winning their first major honour and most recent.

We won it again in 1934, after Bert Trautmann's brave heroics in 1956, with Joe Mercer's famous side in 1969 and again in 2011 after an agonising 44-year wait for silverware.

Guardiola, who won the Copa Del Rey in 2009 and

THE STORY OF THE FA CUP

www.mancity.com 159

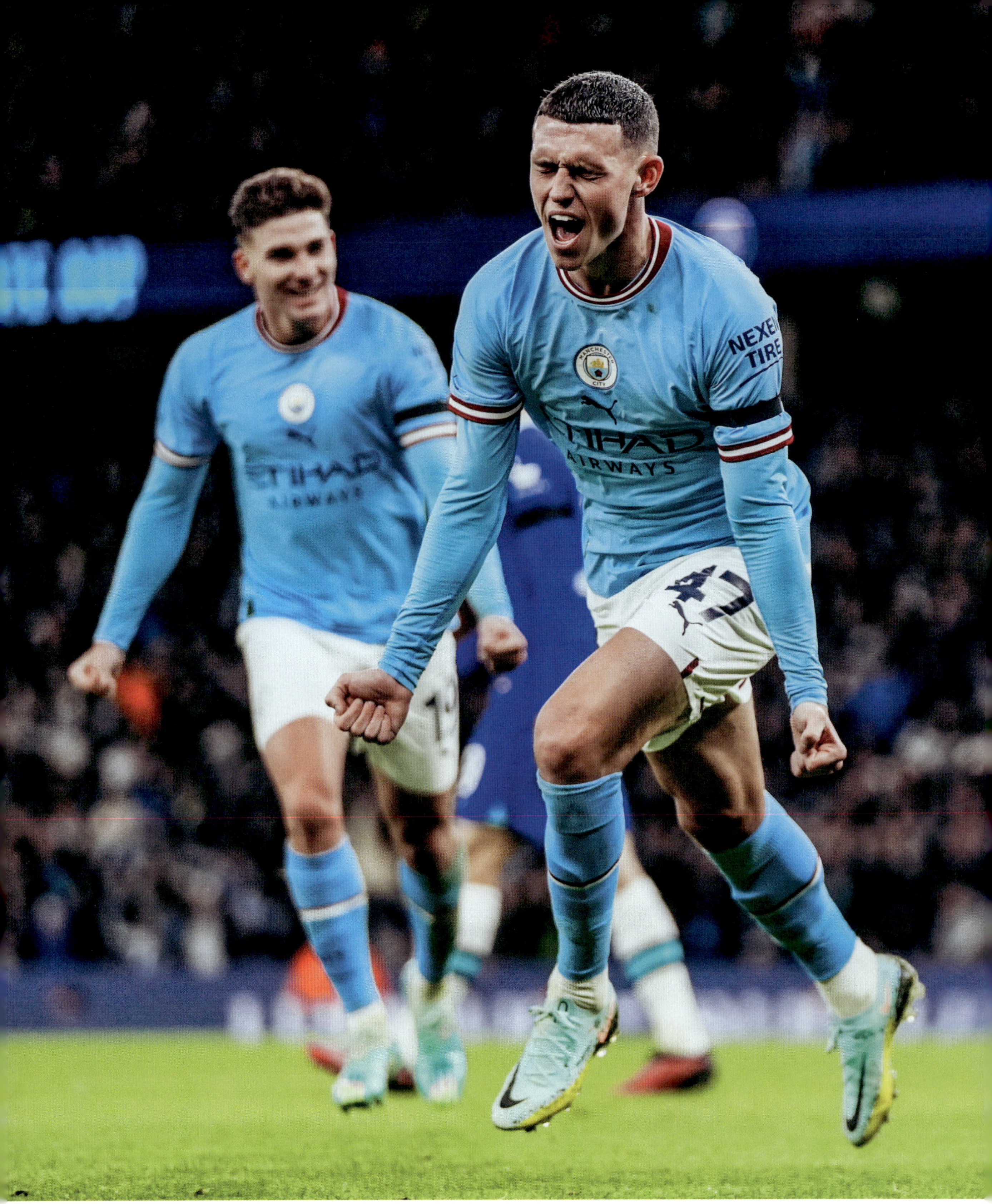
NEXEN
TIRE
AIRWAYS

> "What a season. The skills are there but it is the special mentality. When you have these players who play the game like a friendly game, they handle the pressure like, OK, let's have fun, you are becoming a good, good team. Otherwise, you cannot do it"

2012 with Barcelona and the DFB-Pokal in each of his three seasons at Bayern Munich, has spoken about his love of the traditions of the oldest football competition in the world, which dates back to 1871.

"When I read about the impact of the oldest cup in the world, that starts with over 700 teams from the beginning, it's really special," he has said.

"I love England for that reason, they maintain the traditions. They have a mix of traditions and being open to new things and that is quite interesting."

But City have often been the victims of our own success, with the business end of the season seeing the need to attack a Premier League title race and the latter stages of the Champions League as well as the FA Cup.

In four of the previous six seasons, City have been defeated in Wembley semi-finals, and were knocked out in the fifth round on another occasion.

That shows how much the prize is coveted with strong line-ups pushing for every trophy available in a squad with a determined winning mentality.

Going the distance in the league and Europe has often seen City playing semi-finals during a packed schedule of must-win matches and facing sides with the FA Cup as their major priority.

The luck of the draw can often be important. In the 2022/23 third round draw, non-league clubs Wrexham, Boreham Wood and Chesterfield were in the hat along with a host of lower-league sides hoping for the opportunity of facing the champions of England.

But the romantic cup draws were elsewhere as City were handed a tough pairing at home to Premier League rivals Chelsea – the finalists in five of the previous six years.

City had already knocked the London side out of the Carabao Cup with a 2-0 victory in November thanks to goals from Riyad Mahrez and Julian Alvarez.

And the two sides met again at Stamford Bridge in the Premier League on 5 January, three days before the FA Cup clash, with substitute Mahrez once again on target to secure a crucial 1-0 victory.

Guardiola made seven changes for the rematch at the Etihad, with Stefan Ortega Moreno taking his place as the cup keeper and Mahrez in the starting line-up.

## TREBLE WINNERS

It was the Algerian winger who was deadly again, making the key breakthrough as well as scoring the final goal of an impressive 4-0 victory.

Ahead of the game, not everything was going well for new Chelsea manager Graham Potter, who had taken over in September, and visiting fans were chanting the name of his predecessor Thomas Tuchel as City showed no mercy.

Mahrez opened the scoring midway through the first half with a sublime free-kick from 25 yards after being fouled himself, curling a sumptuous strike into the top right corner.

Seven minutes later, Julian Alvarez, fresh from his heroics at the 2022 World Cup for winners Argentina, doubled City's advantage.

Referee Robert Jones awarded a penalty after the VAR spotted a handball by Chelsea striker Kai Havertz and, despite keeper Kepa Arrizabalaga trying to put him off, Alvarez made no mistake from the spot.

And the game was virtually over before half-time with a wonderful team goal that saw Phil Foden finish confidently after brilliant passing and movement from Rodrigo, Mahrez and Kyle Walker.

Foden was bundled over late in the second half in the penalty area by Kalidou Koulibaly – and Mahrez converted from the spot to wrap up a comfortable victory.

"To have played the way we played and to score four goals and keep a clean sheet, it was a good day for us," Mahrez said after his two goals.

"It was a good [free-kick] to be fair. I think someone touched it a little bit so it made it faster. It was good to start with. After that we played very good.

"I was going to take the first [penalty], but Julian asked me, so of course I said yes.

"He's a striker, he needs goals, it's good for him. The second one I wanted to take. Everyone was involved today so it's good."

With one of the early favourites knocked out, fans

www.mancity.com 163

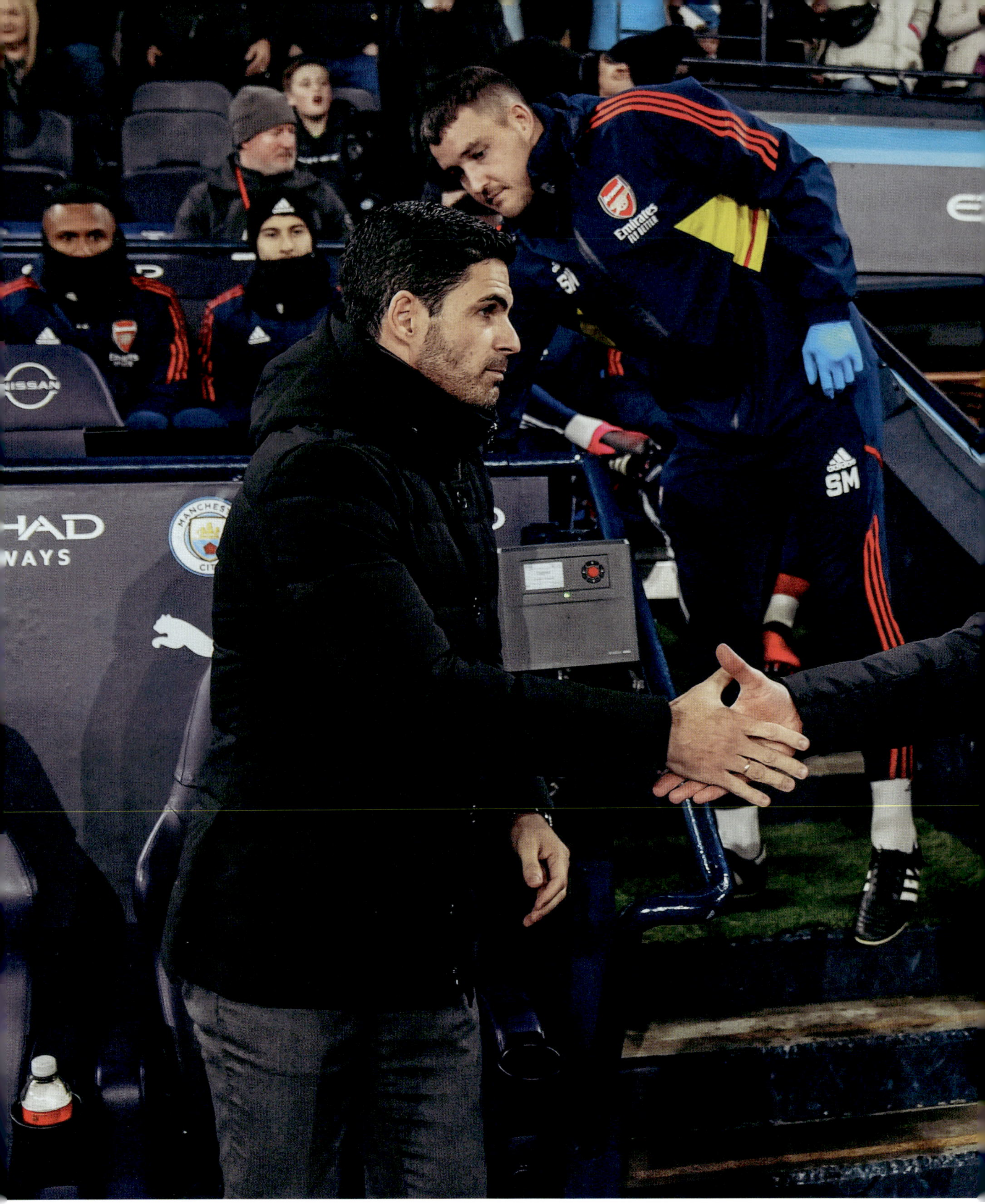
HAD
WAYS
Emirates
FLY BETTER
SM
SM
NISSAN

THE STORY OF THE FA CUP

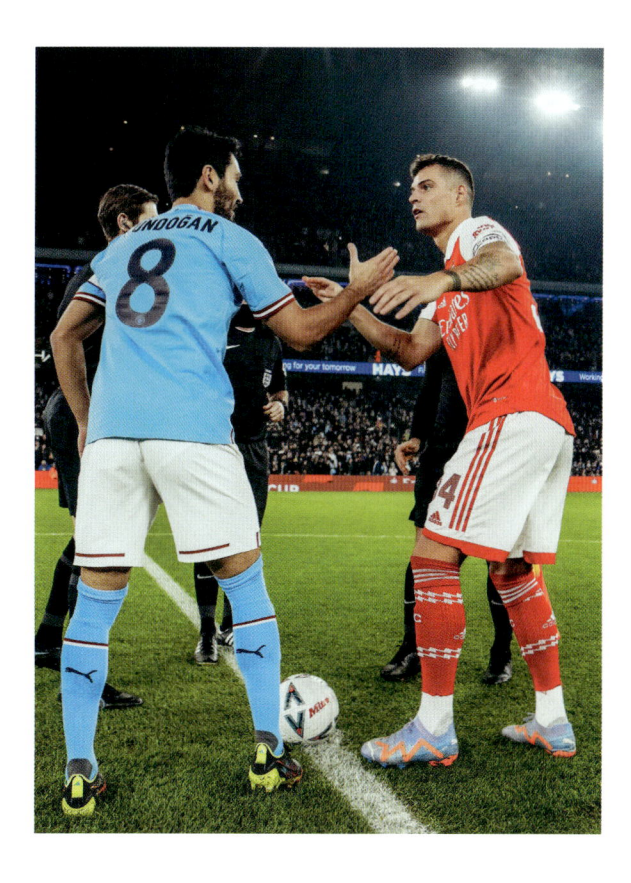

might have been hoping for a kinder draw in the fourth round but this time they were drawn against the country's in-form side in Premier League leaders Arsenal.

Arsenal were playing thrilling football under Guardiola's former City assistant Mikel Arteta and were eight points clear at the top of the table when the two sides met on 27 January.

Guardiola spoke highly of the Gunners, who had blazed a trail in the first half of the season, helped by their summer recruits Gabriel Jesus and Oleksandr Zinchenko, two key figures in City's recent success.

The two sides had not yet met in the Premier League, and victory in the FA Cup for either side could potentially deliver a psychological blow ahead of their two clashes as well as taking another step in the competition, although Guardiola didn't see it that way.

www.mancity.com 165

## TREBLE WINNERS

"It will be different at the Emirates and different [at home in the league]," the boss said. "Of course we play and see what they do and see what we do.

"I'm pretty sure that for the second one we will change something, either players or the way we play. Maybe they will do something we don't expect or we do something they don't expect."

But City did go into the game with a slight edge, with six wins from the seven fixtures against Arsenal since Arteta left City for North London, although the only defeat came in the FA Cup – at the semi-final stage in 2020.

The visitors were full of confidence and Ortega Moreno had to be at his best to keep out early strikes from Takehiro Tomiyasu and Leandro Trossard, making his full debut, while Eddie Nketiah was also off-target with another opportunity.

City, too, carried plenty of threat with Erling Haaland close to the opener, once with an audacious overhead kick from 30 yards after beating Gunners keeper Matt Turner to a through ball.

However, the only goal of the game came from perhaps an unlikely source in Nathan Ake's right foot, with the Dutch defender expertly steering in a low shot after good work from Alvarez and Jack Grealish.

It capped a superb night for the left-back, who came out on top in a personal duel with the dynamic in-form England winger Bukayo Saka in another outstanding

www.mancity.com 167

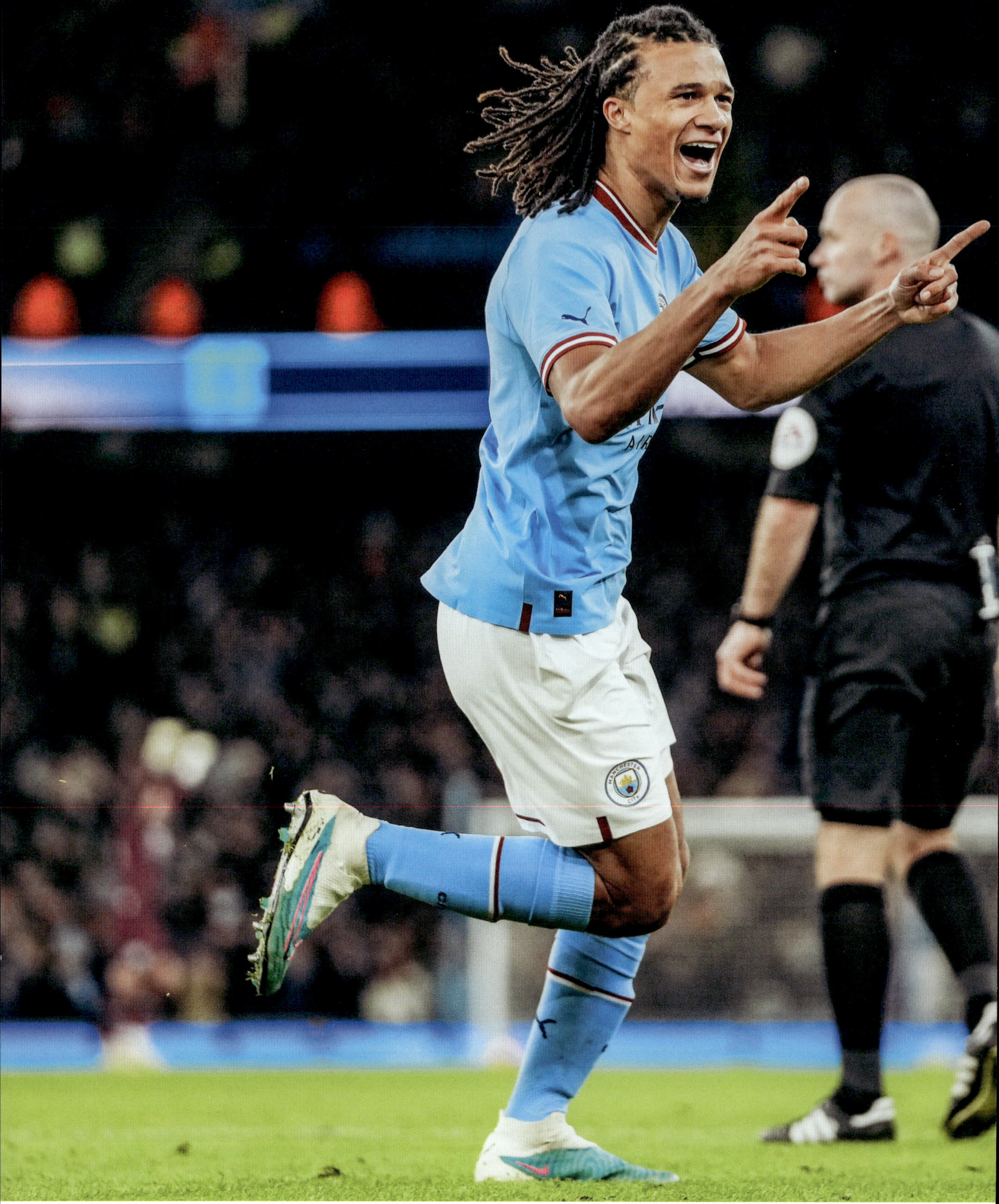

THE STORY OF THE FA CUP

performance, in a season when he was such a key figure in Guardiola's backline.

"What an incredible right foot, I didn't expect it!" Ortega Moreno said of his team-mate. "I was really happy for him because in the last few weeks he's played so good. He helped us a lot in this situation, and he deserves it."

It was the first part of an epic treble of matches against the Gunners, with City travelling to the Emirates two weeks later and securing a 3-1 victory with goals from Kevin De Bruyne, Jack Grealish and Haaland that brought the title race to the boil.

And in the final weeks of the season, we would win 4-1 again at the Etihad to take a big advantage into ultimately becoming Premier League champions for the third season in a row.

Meanwhile, the FA Cup adventure continued with a fifth-round trip to Championship side Bristol City, with a sold-out Ashton Gate hoping to see a major upset.

It was the first time we had ever faced the Robins in the FA Cup and a vibrant young side went into the game unbeaten in their previous 12 matches and full of confidence.

www.mancity.com 169

## TREBLE WINNERS

Kalvin Phillips was recalled to the starting line-up and almost made an instant impact with a 20-yard strike that thundered off the crossbar in the third minute.

But the 4,000 visiting fans didn't have to wait long for the opener with Foden turning in Mahrez's wonderful low cross in the seventh minute.

Ruben Dias and De Bruyne went close to doubling the lead before half-time while Ortega Moreno picked up a hand injury that saw him replaced by Ederson at the break.

The Brazilian continued the defensive record of remaining unbeaten, although the game wasn't killed off until the final 15 minutes.

Foden added his and City's second to round off a quick flowing move before De Bruyne wrapped up a 3-0 victory with a wonderful 25-yard strike in the dying minutes.

It was the former Academy player who caught the eye of Guardiola, with the coach happy to see him playing with his trademark swagger and style after injury and going to Qatar 2022 with the England squad.

"Phil scored one in the last [Premier League] game, now two, his dynamic and rhythm and work ethic [is back to his best]," the Catalan said.

"Footballers have ups and downs. Phil's has been up and up and up, but with the World Cup and his ankle, he has had a bit of a down.

"Phil has always had a high level. His impact since he

"When I read about the impact of the oldest cup in the world, that starts with over 700 teams from the beginning, it's really special. I love England for that reason"

arrived with us has been amazing. When you work like he works, football always pays off for you."

The sixth-round draw saw us paired with another Championship team with leaders Burnley coming to the Etihad for what would be an emotional reunion with City legend Vincent Kompany.

It would be the first return in a professional capacity for the former captain, who was such an integral part of City's success over the previous decade.

The Belgian spent 11 unforgettable years in Manchester, winning four Premier League titles, two FA Cups and four League Cups.

Defending and leadership were his two main attributes but along the way he left a list of magical moments

www.mancity.com 171

## TREBLE WINNERS

such as a crucial winner against title rivals Manchester United in the 2011/12 Premier League success and his magnificent long-range strike to secure a vital 1-0 victory over Leicester City on his final appearance at the Etihad in 2019.

With a statue outside the stadium, Kompany's fabled status is secured but in the build-up to the tie, Guardiola predicted that he will one day become the City boss, particularly after guiding Burnley to promotion as champions with a phenomenal season.

It was in that spectacular form that he brought his side to the Etihad on 18 March but, after a warm reception from the crowd as well as embraces from Guardiola and another club legend Mike Summerbee in the week he received his OBE, it was to be a chastening afternoon.

There was no sentiment shown as City ruthlessly took apart the Clarets 6-0 with Haaland claiming his sixth hat-trick of his record-breaking season.

It was a week to remember for the brilliant Norwegian,

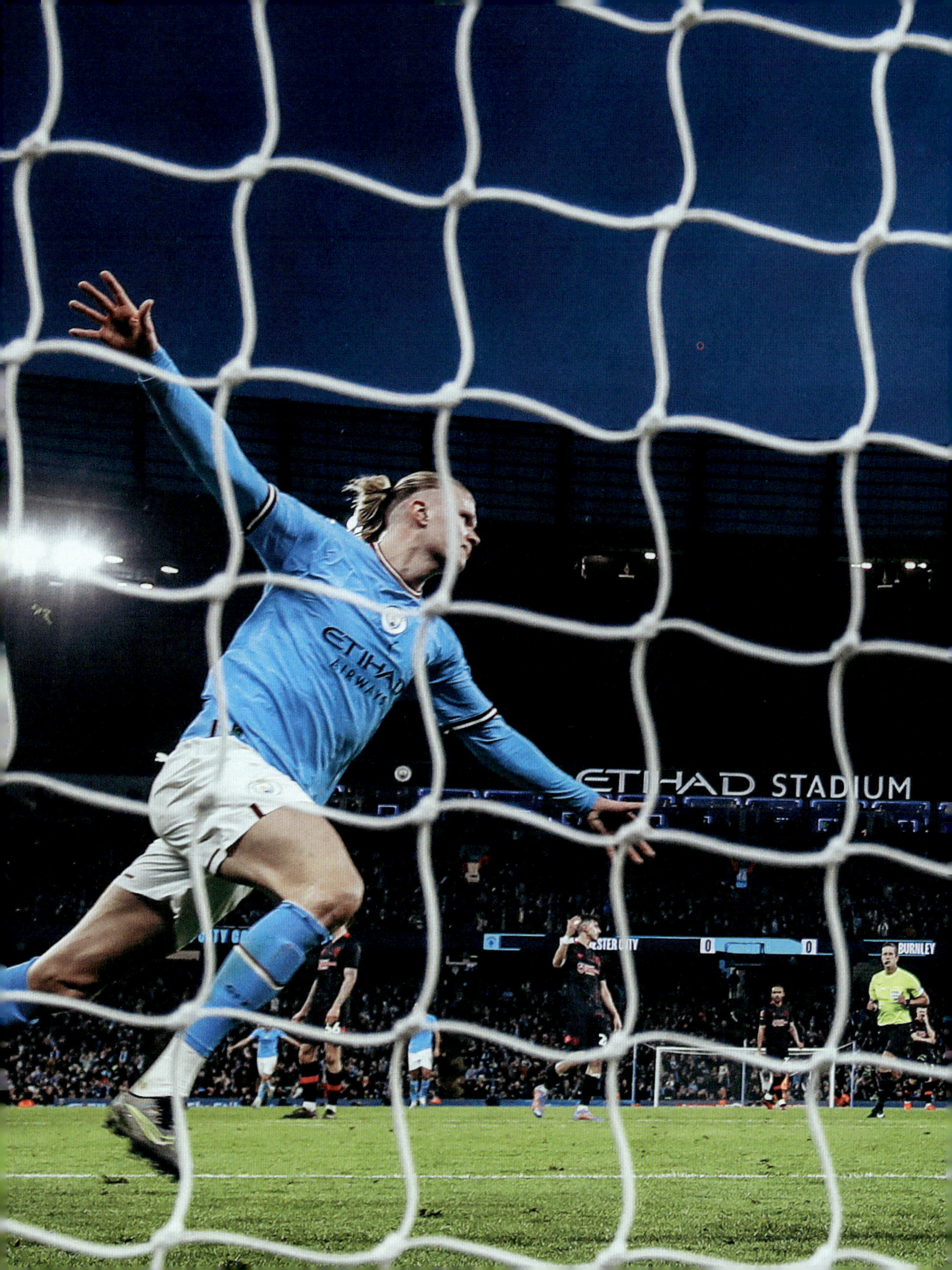
ETIHAD STADIUM
ETIHAD AIRWAYS
BURNLEY
0
0

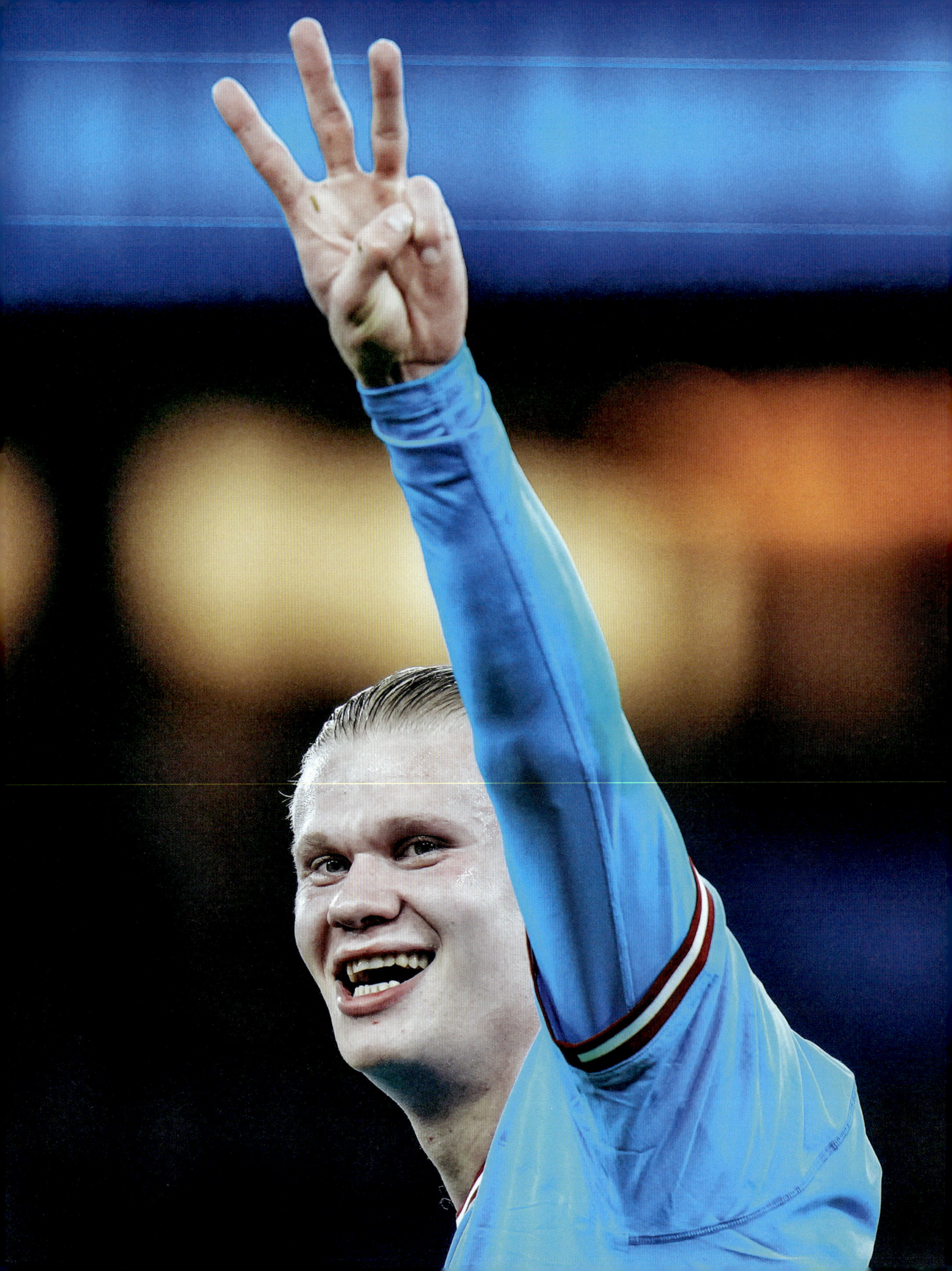

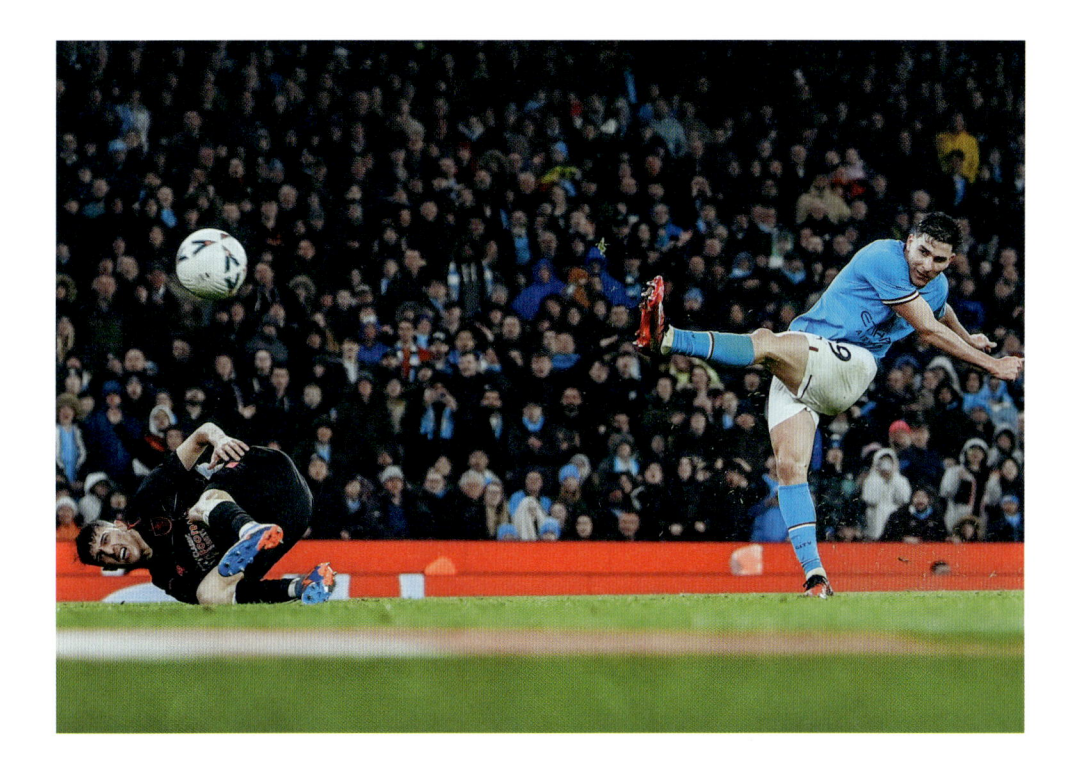

which started with the only goal in a crucial 1-0 victory over Crystal Palace and was followed by five goals in a 7-0 Champions League demolition of German side RB Leipzig.

After a bright start from the visitors, Haaland ran onto Alvarez's threaded pass to poke the Blues ahead.

It quickly became two when the striker neatly finished Foden's low cross after the winger was cleverly released by De Bruyne.

Just before the hour, Foden's low shot struck the bottom of the post and inevitably it was Haaland who was in the right place to finish for yet another treble, and he was soon replaced by Cole Palmer when Alvarez added a fourth moments later.

Palmer took barely two minutes to get in on the goals before Alvarez rounded off the scoring with the pick of the bunch.

The Argentinian had made a stunning impact since joining up with his new team-mates in the summer, as well as starring at the World Cup.

It earned him a new contract extension in the days before the game and he celebrated with a wonderful strike, racing onto De Bruyne's through ball before cutting inside and unleashing an unstoppable shot.

"I was, I've got to be honest, honoured to receive the reception from my former club Man City," Kompany said.

"It felt like a very friendly atmosphere towards me but, in the end, on the pitch it felt hostile.

"So, we're still here to compete and my goal next time is to see if we can do something better, if this game can be different."

City went into the semi-final draw alongside a rejuvenated Manchester United and a brilliant Brighton side that had excited the Premier League with a brash and bold style of football but avoided both, instead drawing Championship promotion hopefuls Sheffield United.

Coming between a Champions League quarter-final second leg at German giants Bayern Munich and a crucial Premier League clash with Arsenal, it was perhaps a kinder draw.

The Blades' main focus was a return to the top flight and they would be further weakened by the fact that loanees James McAtee and Tommy Doyle would not be permitted to play against their parent club.

## TREBLE WINNERS

Both had been in brilliant form at Bramall Lane, leading the charge in a campaign which would eventually lead to promotion and Doyle, the grandson of former City players Mike Doyle and Glyn Pardoe, who won the FA Cup in 1969, scored a spectacular 90th-minute winner in the previous round.

Guardiola would have preferred them to play and gain experience from the Wembley occasion so it was a frustrating conclusion.

Still, the Yorkshire side proved a tough test but the match would be remembered for magic from Mahrez, as he became the first City player to score a hat-trick at the national stadium as we ran out 3-0 winners.

Sheffield United created a great opportunity in the opening moments from a corner, when the ball dropped to Iliman Ndiaye, but his effort was smothered by the alert Ortega Moreno.

It was to be their best opportunity as the game quickly settled into a pattern of City pushing to find a way through the Blades' structured backline.

176 www.mancity.com

www.mancity.com 177

## TREBLE WINNERS

The breakthrough finally came three minutes before the half-time whistle when Bernardo Silva was caught by Daniel Jebbison's swiping challenge inside the box and Mahrez cooly slotted home the penalty.

A second arrived on the hour as Mahrez scythed through the Sheffield United defence before calmly side-footing past the onrushing keeper.

And five minutes later, he had his treble after turning in Jack Grealish's low cross.

"The most important thing is that two or three seasons in a row we've come here in the semi-finals and lost," the hat-trick hero said.

"We wanted to make sure we got to the final. I think I had a good game. It's a good team achievement and we took the game seriously.

"It means a lot to be in the final. We really want to work hard in every competition going. We're in the final of the FA Cup, which is amazing."

City found out their final opponents the following day, with Manchester United making it through after a penalty shootout victory over the Seagulls.

It would be the first-ever all-Manchester final, although the two sides memorably met at Wembley for a 2011 semi-final when Yaya Toure was the matchwinner.

City had thrashed our neighbours in October, with Haaland and Foden claiming hat-tricks in a 6-3 victory, but United had won at Old Trafford 2-1 in a game remembered for a controversial offside call over Bruno Fernandes' equaliser.

In a rivalry that goes back to the 1890s, the 190th derby was always going to be a special occasion.

But there was even more spice added with City going into the final with the chance of securing a Treble after winning the Premier League title with games to spare and securing a place in the Champions League final following victories over Bayern and Real Madrid.

United were the only English side to have achieved the Treble when they did it 1999 and were desperate to hang on to that status.

Under new manager Erik ten Hag, the Reds had claimed a top-four spot and also won the Carabao Cup – their first trophy in six years.

Many pundits suggested that the FA Cup final would be tougher than the European final against Inter in Istanbul, while United travelled to the capital on 3 June full of belief.

But so too did the City fans, although they could hardly have dreamed of the unbelievable start that Guardiola's side would make.

Just 12 seconds into the game, City captain Ilkay Gundogan volleyed in a spectacular opener for the fastest goal in FA Cup final history.

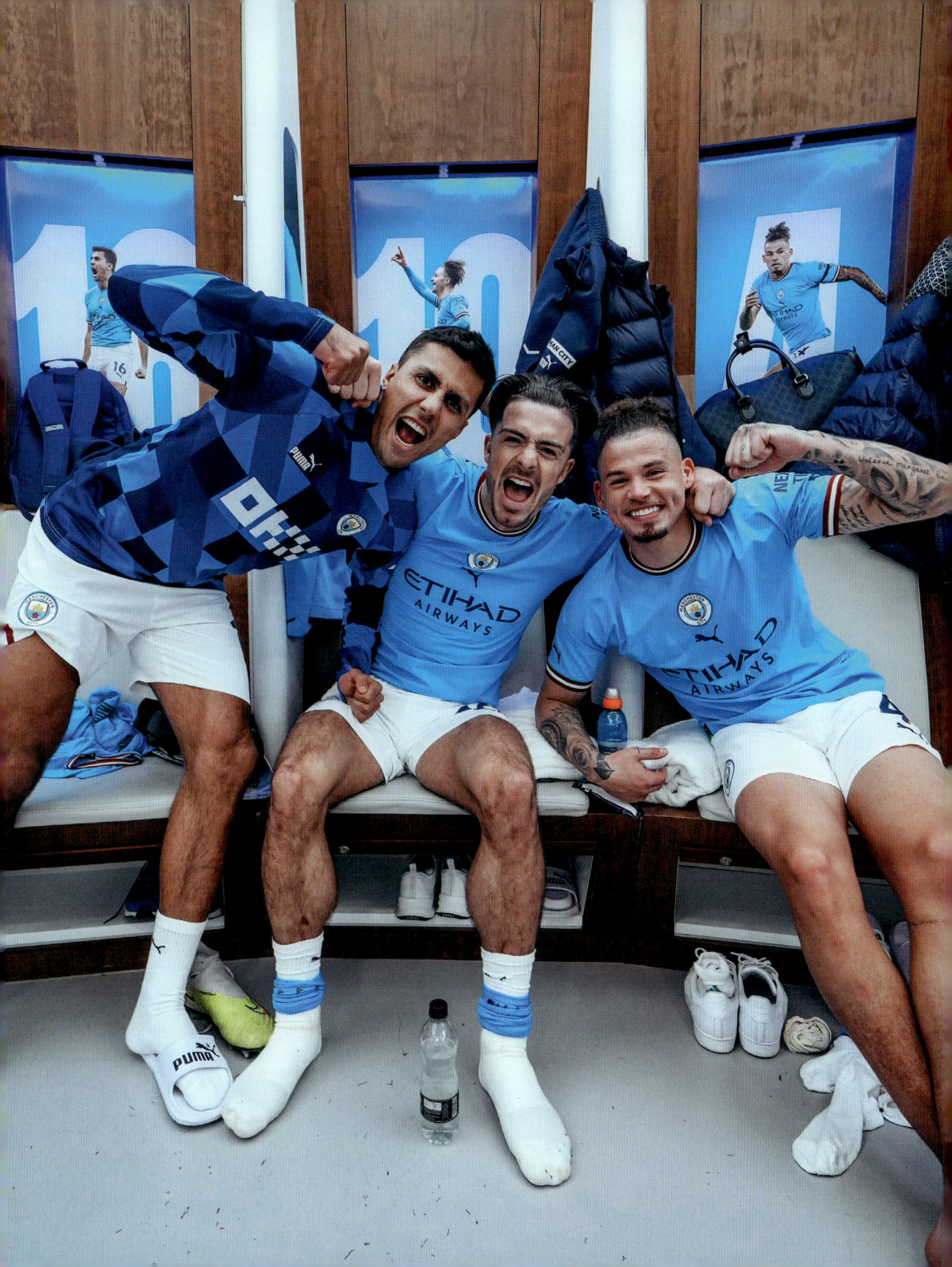
PUMA
ETIHAD
AIRWAYS
PUMA

180 www.mancity.com

## THE STORY OF THE FA CUP

City fans went wild and the team were well on top until United were handed a lifeline when an innocuous cross flicked Grealish's fingers and a penalty was awarded after VAR intervention.

Fernandes converted the spot-kick with United's only shot on target in 90 minutes and the only goal that Ortega Moreno or City would concede in the entire cup run.

It could have altered the initiative but City were able to regain control and Gundogan once again showed his ability to deliver big moments at key stages.

The midfielder, who scored twice on the final day of the 2021/22 season to deliver a dramatic title success in a 3-2 win over Aston Villa, struck another volley in front of the delirious Blues supporters.

With seconds ticking down, United went close to an equaliser in stoppage time with Ortega Moreno denying Raphael Varane and Scott McTominay hitting the top of the crossbar.

But there was sheer delight at full-time as the players sprinted to celebrate with the fans after completing the second league and cup Double in the club's history and the second leg of a historic Treble.

Guardiola wiped away tears after the final whistle and praised his players for another incredible achievement.

"What a season," he exclaimed after the 2-1 win. "The skills are there but it is the special mentality.

"When you have these players who play the game like a friendly game, they handle the pressure like, OK, let's have fun, you are becoming a good, good team. Otherwise, you cannot do it."

For matchwinner Gundogan it would be a second

www.mancity.com 181

## TREBLE WINNERS

trophy lift in his first season as the club captain and another proud moment.

Defender Dias hailed his influence, saying: "A magician, a special player.

"This is my third season with him, so I know him quite well and what he's capable of – even though he's always able to surprise me and everyone.

"He's just an amazing player and an even better person."

Gundogan, meanwhile, said it was a special moment to share with the dressing room and the fans.

"I feel appreciated from the fans, my team-mates, it's an absolute joy to be part of this team, to work with Pep and his staff," he said.

"I have learned a lot throughout the years. I had many ups and a few downs, we have won a lot together and every single trophy feels special. So far it has been amazing."

The squad flew back to Manchester the same night, meeting Elton John at the airport after his performance in the city centre, and the pop legend congratulated them on their achievements.

City celebrated but there was still one more week of hard work and a massive match to come.

But for many supporters, the party went on well into the night.

Beating city rivals United in an FA Cup final was incredibly special, that it came as part of a Treble-winning season was simply remarkable.

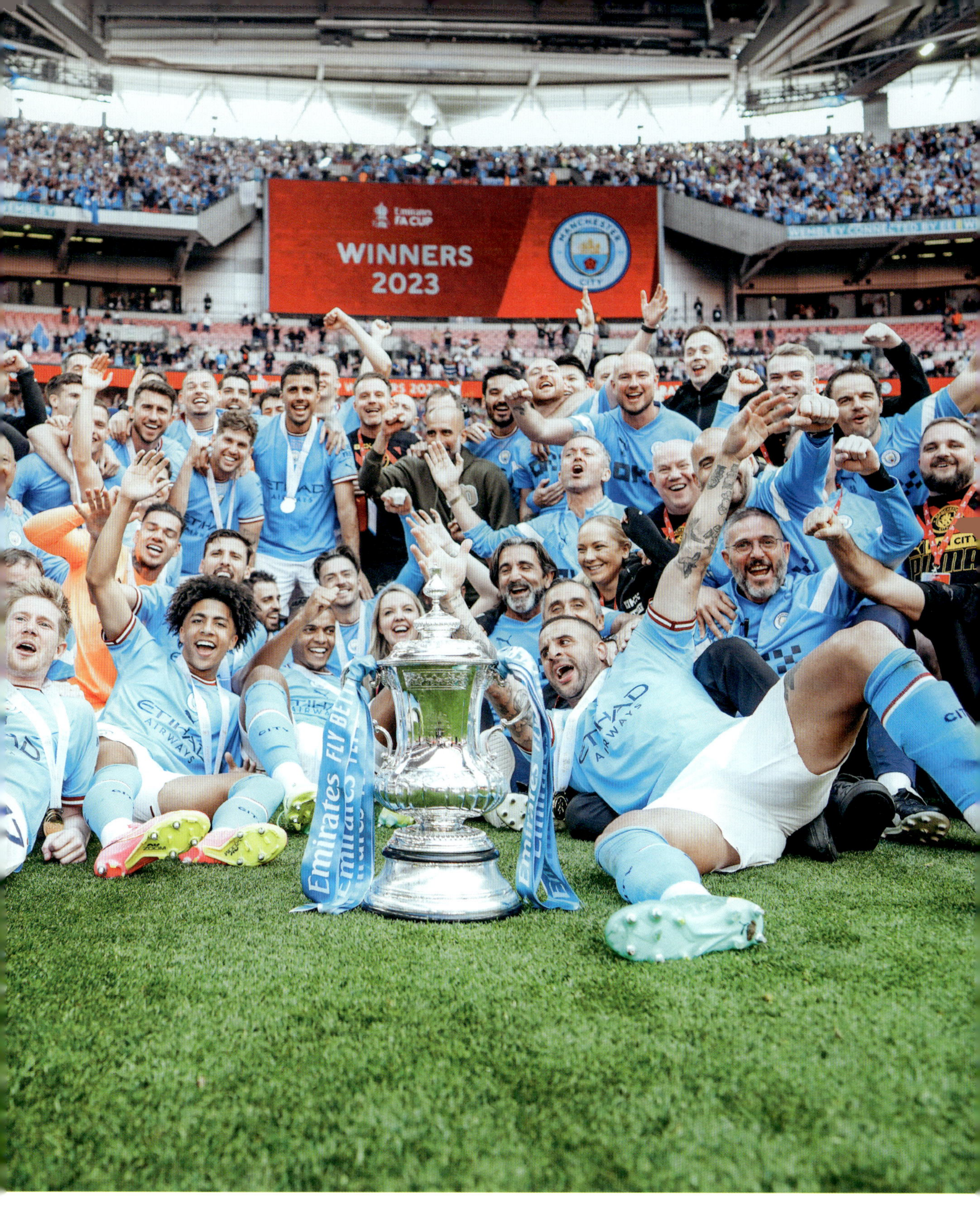
Emirates FA CUP
WINNERS
2023
MANCHESTER CITY

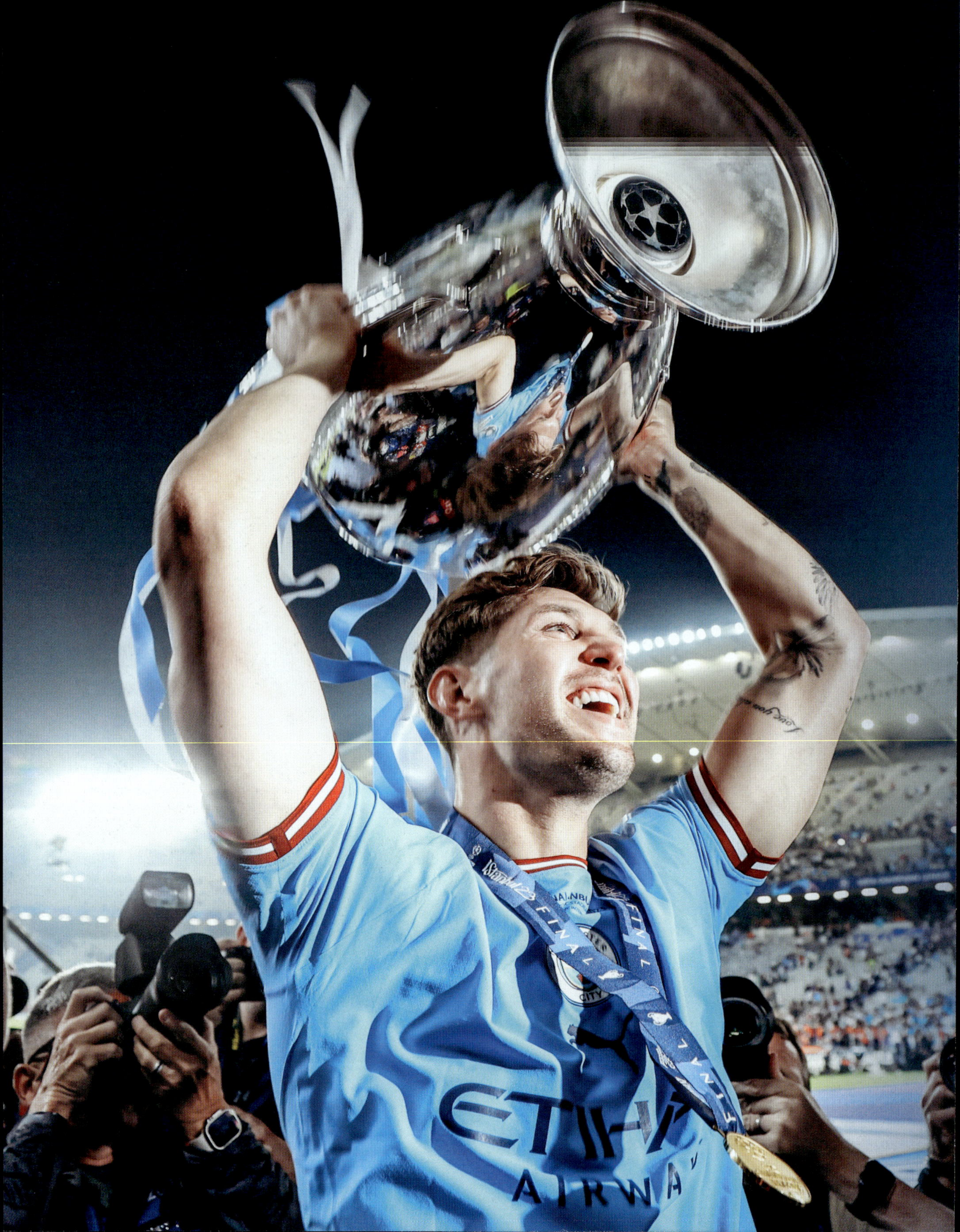
FINAL

# 4

THE STORY OF THE
CHAMPIONS LEAGUE

# TREBLE DREAMS
## COME TRUE IN ISTANBUL

## TREBLE WINNERS

**"It looks like this final was written in the stars."**

That was the emotional verdict of a happy but exhausted Pep Guardiola immediately after the greatest season in Manchester City's illustrious 129-year history was crowned on an unforgettable night in Istanbul.

It may have been more than a century in its inception but City's glorious, seismic and history-making maiden Champions League triumph ultimately all came down to one delicious stroke of Rodrigo's right foot that lit up a corner of west Istanbul and sparked scenes of joy and delirium across Manchester and beyond.

A 1-0 final win over Inter not only secured a revered and long sought-after first-ever Champions League crown for the club, it also delivered the Holy Grail of the Treble and ensured both City and Guardiola's name would forever be stamped amongst the game's true immortals.

At the very edge of Europe, where East collides with West, amidst a melting pot of ancient and modern civilisations, it was the night that saw the Blue Moon rise over Istanbul's Blue Mosque as City finally and gloriously claimed Europe's very own Blue Ribbon prize.

Fittingly, a maiden European success had to be earned the hard way.

But no-one could deny that City hadn't paid their dues in this most unforgiving of tournaments.

Since qualifying for the Champions League for the first time in 2011, the road to Istanbul had seen trials and tribulations aplenty.

First came two chastening group-stage exits under Roberto Mancini.

Then there was a timid, deflating semi-final defeat to Real Madrid in 2016 that meant Manuel Pellegrini's final weeks in charge would end with a whimper.

The arrival of Guardiola in the summer of 2016 ushered in an era of quite brilliant domestic dominance – but success on the European stage remained tantalisingly out of reach.

There was the dramatic and heartbreaking quarter-final loss at the hands of Tottenham in 2019, which ended in VAR controversy.

That was followed by defeat in our first final in 2021

*"A 1-0 final win over Inter Milan not only secured a first-ever Champions League crown for the club, it also delivered the Holy Grail of the Treble and ensured both City and Guardiola's name would forever be stamped amongst the game's true immortals"*

against a Chelsea side many felt we were superior to.

And, perhaps most crushing of all, came last season's semi-final defeat to Real Madrid that saw us uncharacteristically concede late goals before losing on aggregate.

It led some to wonder whether City were afflicted by some kind of curse when it came to chasing the trophy affectionately known as Old Big Ears.

Others, meanwhile, spoke of an obsession.

But Pep and his players ignored all the outside noise.

The management staff and a squad packed to the ginnels with quality of the very highest order – and reinforced by the incredible impact of Erling Haaland – knew that the time had come for City to take that final giant leap and turn dreams into reality and so ensure fantasy became fact.

And in a football-mad city like no other in Europe, full of beautiful, breath-taking vistas with minarets piercing the sky and where the mighty Bosphorus separates Europe from Asia, deliverance was finally at hand.

This is the story of how history was made…

www.mancity.com 187

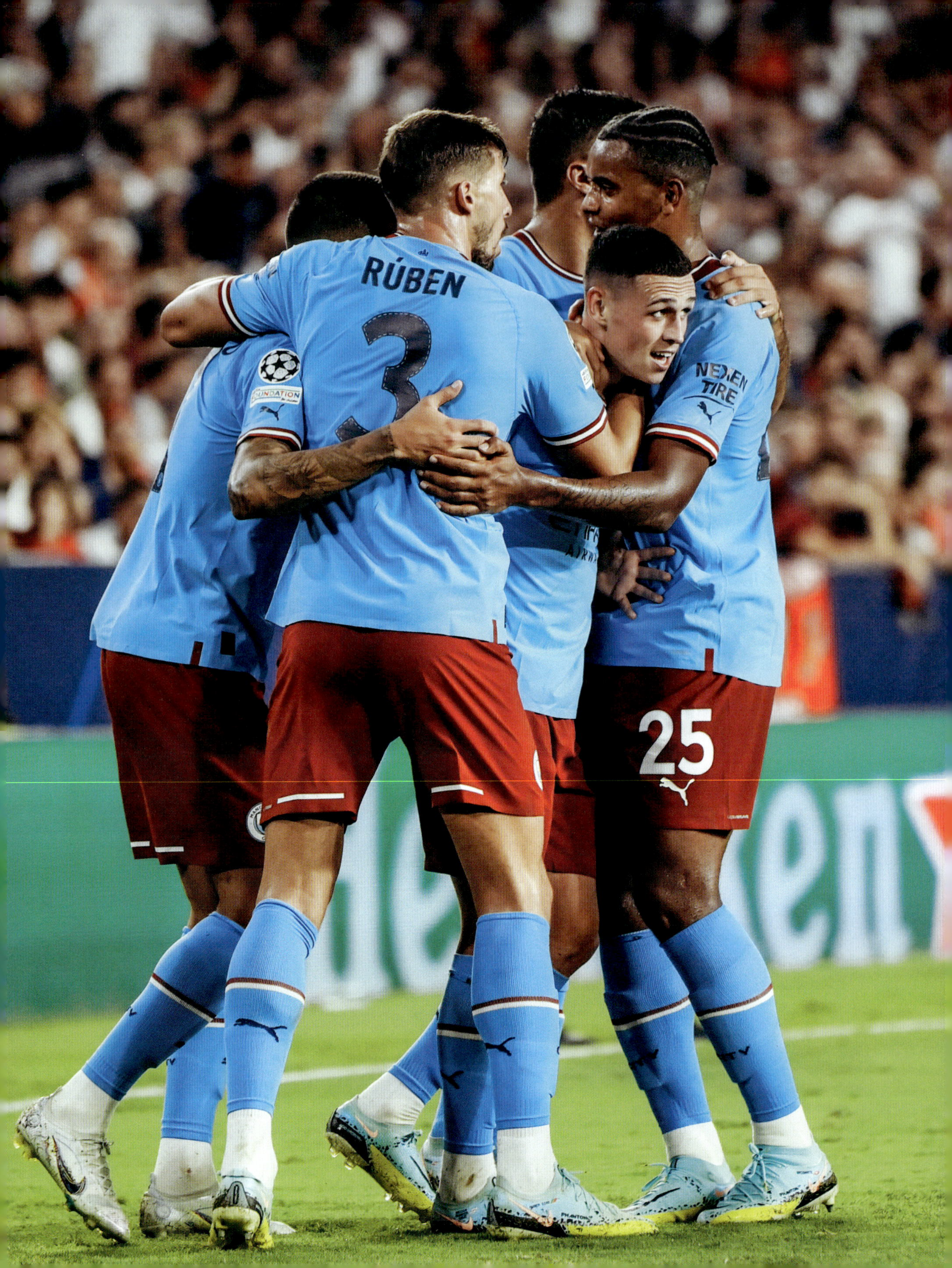
RÚBEN
3
NEXEN TIRE
25

# GROUP STAGES

Matchday One
September 6, 2022

## SEVILLA 0
## CITY 4
(Haaland 20, 67, Foden 58, Dias 90+2)

As opening statements of intent go, a dominant 4-0 win away at Sevilla more than set the tone for what was to come.

The Spanish side had established a formidable record in European competition, having already won the UEFA Cup/Europa League a record six times when we met on a sultry September evening in Andalucía. They had no answer, however, to a City display which married artistry and athleticism to quite devastating effect.

Summer signing Erling Haaland continued his dazzling start to life at the club as he claimed another brilliant brace of goals sandwiched by a fine Phil Foden strike, to take his tally for the season to 12 in just seven games.

And an injury time effort from Ruben Dias set the seal on a magnificent night's work by Pep Guardiola's men.

With new signing Manuel Akanji producing an assured, classy display at the back alongside Dias just five days after signing from Borussia Dortmund, and fellow summer arrival Sergio Gomez impressing too on his first full start, it was a night loaded with positives aplenty.

"Manuel trained one day and a half with us, but he showed what experience he has at Dortmund and what a good central defender Manchester City brought to us," a satisfied Guardiola declared afterwards.

"He has quality similar like Aymer (Laporte) – he can break the lines with the pass.

"City brought me and the club a fantastic player.

"We weren't good in the first half, but when they were playing better, we scored the second thanks to a brilliant goal from Phil (Foden).

"We made more passes in the first half rather than looking for Erling, but I still prefer to have him!

"His numbers (Haaland's) are quite similar at other clubs. He just has an incredible sense for goal."

**CITY:** Ederson, Cancelo, Dias, Akanji, Gomez, Rodrigo (Phillips 78), De Bruyne (c) (Mahrez 78), Bernardo, Foden (Palmer 70), Haaland (Alvarez 70), Grealish (Gundogan 62)
**Subs not used:** Ortega, Carson, Ake, Lewis, Wilson-Esbrand

## TREBLE WINNERS

### Matchday Two
### September 14, 2022

# CITY 2
(Stones 80, Haaland 84)

## BORUSSIA DORTMUND 1
(Bellingham 56)

If that Sevilla game had demonstrated the poise and panache that underpin Pep's Blues, a battling, come-from-behind triumph against Borussia Dortmund in our second group assignment served as a reminder that City also possessed character and grit by the bucket-load, too.

A Dortmund side packed with quality looked set to claim the Etihad spoils after Jude Bellingham's close-range header early in the second half had fired them ahead.

City, however, once more illustrated our priceless capacity to fight to the end and always find a way to win.

A spectacular, long-range John Stones drive unleashed 10 minutes from time had already almost lifted the roof off the Etihad, not to mention the Dortmund netting, to draw City level.

But then, just four minutes later, there were yet more Haaland heroics as Erling struck in incredible fashion to deny his former team-mates.

The Norwegian produced a quite astonishing 84th-minute acrobatic finish at the far post, executing a balletic leap to somehow meet Joao Cancelo's stunning long-range assist and send City three points clear at the top of Group G.

A 21st match without defeat at the Etihad also saw City equal the longest unbeaten run in UEFA Champions League history.

And for the boss, the manner of Haaland's spectacular strike carried extra special echoes of the past.

"Maybe the people who know me know the influence of Johan Cruyff in my life as a person, a mentor, a manager," Pep Guardiola reflected afterwards.

"Years ago, he scored in Camp Nou an incredible goal versus Atletico Madrid, it was quite similar today with Haaland and the moment he scored it I thought, 'Johan Cruyff', it was quite similar.

"They were two really nice goals!"

**CITY:** Ederson, Stones, Akanji, Ake, Cancelo, Rodrigo, Gundogan (c) (Bernardo 58), De Bruyne, Grealish (Foden 58), Haaland (Phillips 90+2), Mahrez (Alvarez 58)
**Subs not used:** Ortega Moreno, Carson, Dias, Gomez, Palmer, Lewis, Wilson-Esbrand

THE STORY OF THE CHAMPIONS LEAGUE

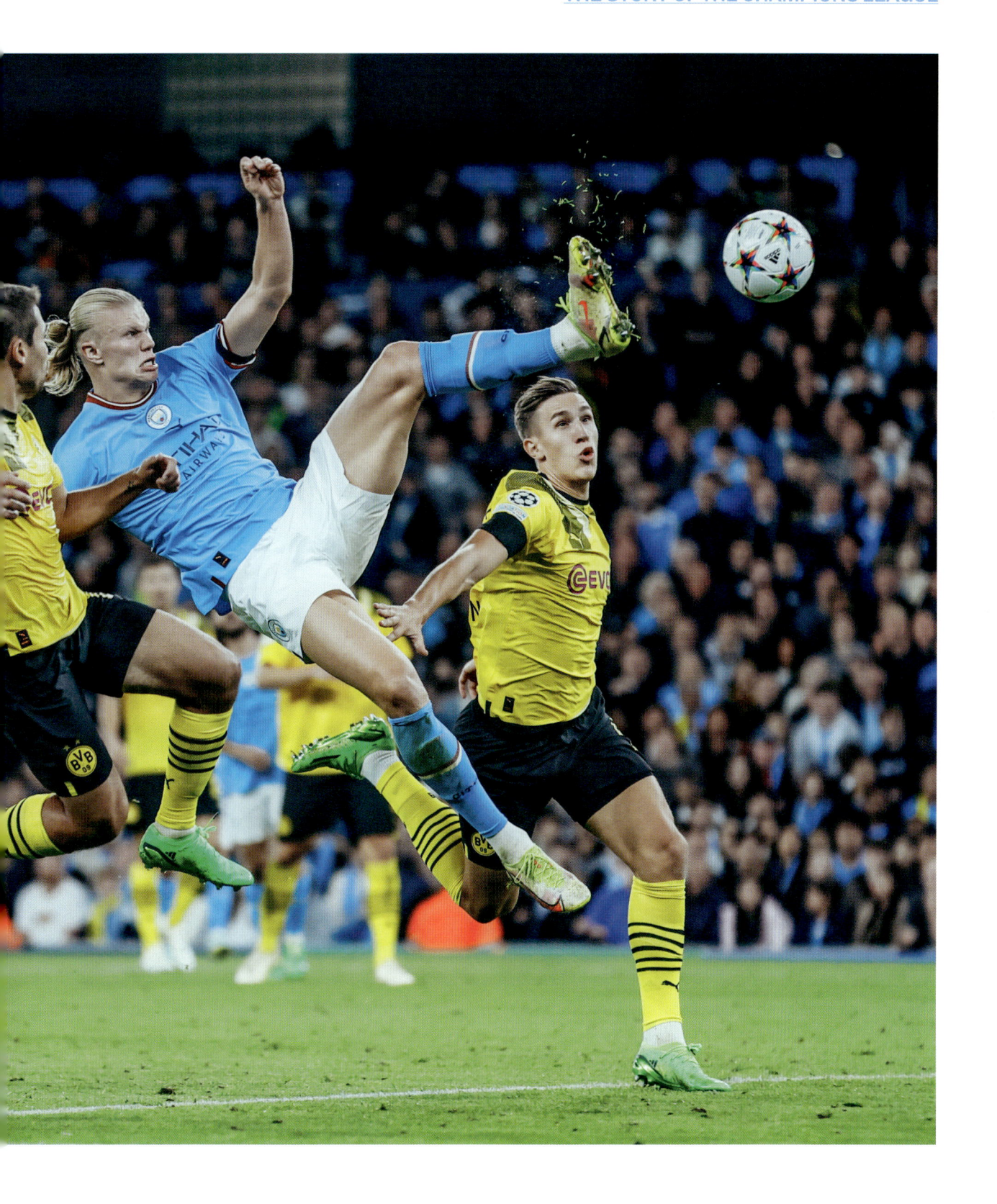

www.mancity.com 191

TREBLE WINNERS

**Matchday Three**
**October 5, 2022**

# CITY 5
(Haaland 7, 32, Khocholava 39 og, Mahrez 55, Alvarez 76)

# FC COPENHAGEN 0

An emphatic five-star rout of Danish champions FC Copenhagen left City sitting pretty at the halfway point of the group stages as our European campaign continued to march on from strength to strength.

There's nothing ever routine about City of course but this was as impressive and comfortable a victory as one could wish for as Pep Guardiola's players made it nine points from nine in Group G.

A brilliant first-half brace from Erling Haaland had got City motoring before a Davit Khocholava own goal all but sealed the deal before the break.

Riyad Mahrez then marked his 200th appearance for City by converting a second-half penalty before substitute Julian Alvarez rounded off another excellent Etihad night's work.

A third straight group-stage triumph left City requiring just one more point to secure our passage into the knockout stages and Guardiola full of admiration for his side's remarkable and relentless work ethic.

"Today we see the reasons why the last years have been successful for this club. After playing Manchester United on Sunday, we were able to be humble enough to respect the opponent," the City boss declared.

"This is the secret of this game. It was the work ethic. Yesterday we trained for 20 minutes, and everyone was focused and paid attention.

"This is the reason why this season and seasons before with different players for every three days we are there; this is the biggest title we can get.

"Beyond the Premier League, Champions League… everything. This is the best."

**CITY:** Ederson, Cancelo (Lewis 57), Dias, Laporte, Gomez, Gundogan (c), Bernardo (Wilson-Esbrand 66), Grealish, Mahrez, Alvarez, Haaland (Palmer 45)
**Subs not used:** Ortega Moreno, Carson, Ake, Rodrigo, De Bruyne, Akanji, Foden

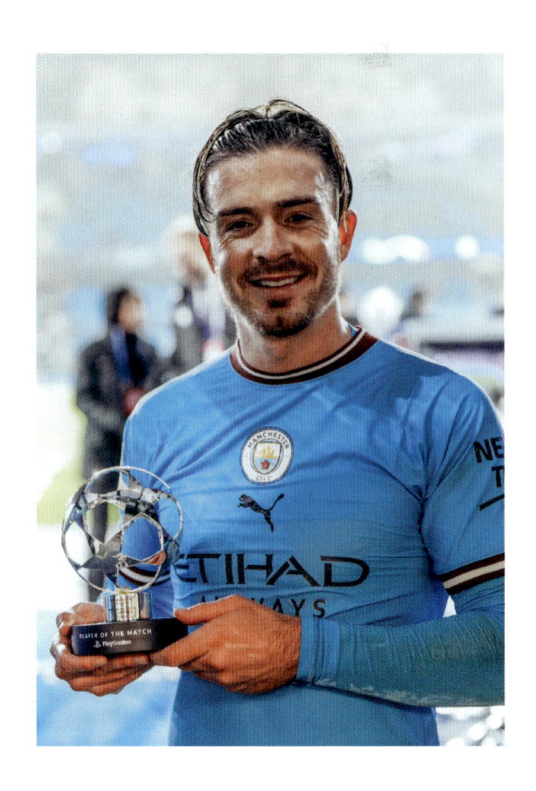

THE STORY OF THE CHAMPIONS LEAGUE

www.mancity.com 193

TREBLE WINNERS

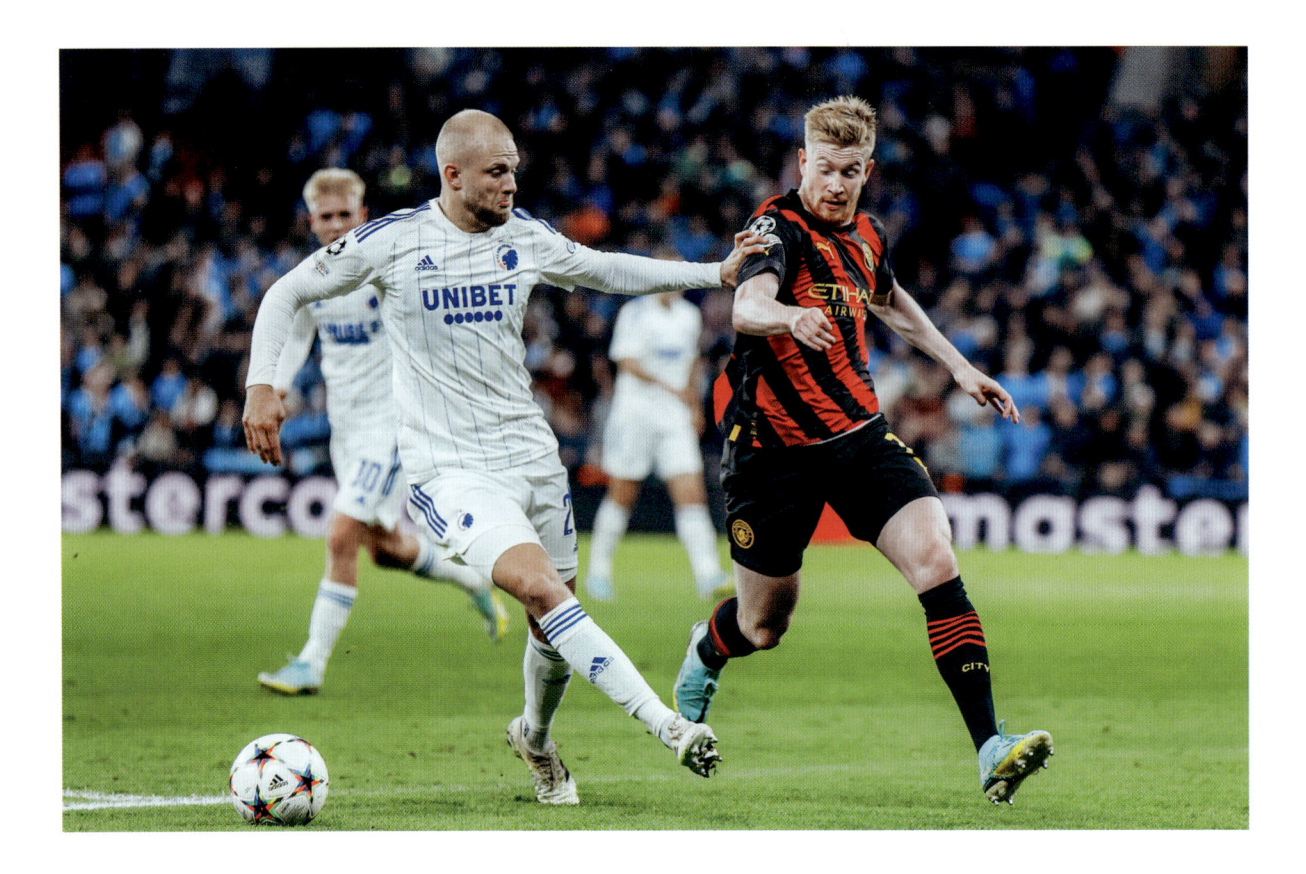

Matchday Four
October 11, 2022

# FC COPENHAGEN 0
# CITY 0

**Ten-man City's winning streak may have been blunted on what proved a frustrating evening in the Danish capital.**

But it was still a case of job done at the Parken Stadium as a point – combined with Sevilla's later 1-1 draw at Borussia Dortmund – confirmed City's passage through to the knockout stages.

VAR emerged as the main talking point from the night.

A spectacular early strike from Rodrigo was then subsequently overturned following a VAR check for a Riyad Mahrez handball.

Another VAR call by referee Artur Dias then saw City awarded a 24th-minute penalty – only for Mahrez's subsequent spot-kick to be saved.

And the TV monitor again took centre stage on the half-hour when Sergio Gomez was shown a straight red card for a late challenge on Copenhagen's Hákon Haraldsson after referee Dias was again advised to take another look.

However, despite that numerical disadvantage City still carried the bigger threat, but ultimately a point proved more than sufficient.

"Really satisfied, with the team that gives everything, 10 v 11 in Europe, the physicality of them, we concede few (chances), we started really well, then many things happened," Pep Guardiola reflected afterwards.

"Now we are going to recover, prepare for the next games, go to Dortmund and try to get results, and Sevilla, to finish first in the group stage."

**CITY:** Ederson, Cancelo, Akanji, Laporte (Ake 88), Gomez, Rodrigo, Gundogan (c), De Bruyne (Bernardo 77), Mahrez (Dias 32), Grealish (Foden 77), Alvarez
**Subs not used:** Ortega Moreno, Carson, Haaland, Palmer, Lewis, Wilson-Esbrand

THE STORY OF THE CHAMPIONS LEAGUE

## Matchday Five
### October 25, 2022

# BORUSSIA DORTMUND 0
# CITY 0

**For the second successive group game, City were again forced to settle for a goalless draw on our travels – with Riyad Mahrez once more denied from the penalty spot.**

But a battling display at a packed and partisan Westfalenstadion was still enough to ensure Pep Guardiola's side would top Group G – and with a game to spare.

It was also a memorable evening for goalkeeper Stefan Ortega Moreno, who made his competitive debut for the club following his summer move to the Etihad from Arminia Bielefeld.

Back playing in his home country, the German produced a fine maiden display capped by a number of key saves which helped keep Dortmund at bay.

The only frustration for City was seeing Dortmund keeper Gregor Kobel guess correctly to dive and keep out Mahrez's 60th-minute spot-kick after the Algerian had been brought down by Emre Can.

That quibble aside for central defender John Stones, the achievement of winning the group with a game to spare spoke volumes as to City's iron-clad mindset.

"I think topping the group is always our goal from the start of the season. There were a lot of tough teams in the group as well," the England international pointed out.

"To keep recreating that and topping the group, getting through to the next stage, is massive for us as a club and a team. It's really a happy dressing room after the game.

"It's not easy to do. It's something I'm extremely proud of and the lads are as well. To do it with one game to go is something special."

**CITY:** Ortega Moreno, Stones, Dias, Ake, Cancelo (Akanji 45), Rodrigo, Gundogan (c), Foden (Grealish 81), Mahrez (Palmer 88), Alvarez, Haaland (Bernardo 45)
**Subs not used:** Ederson, Carson, Laporte, De Bruyne, Lewis, Wilson-Esbrand

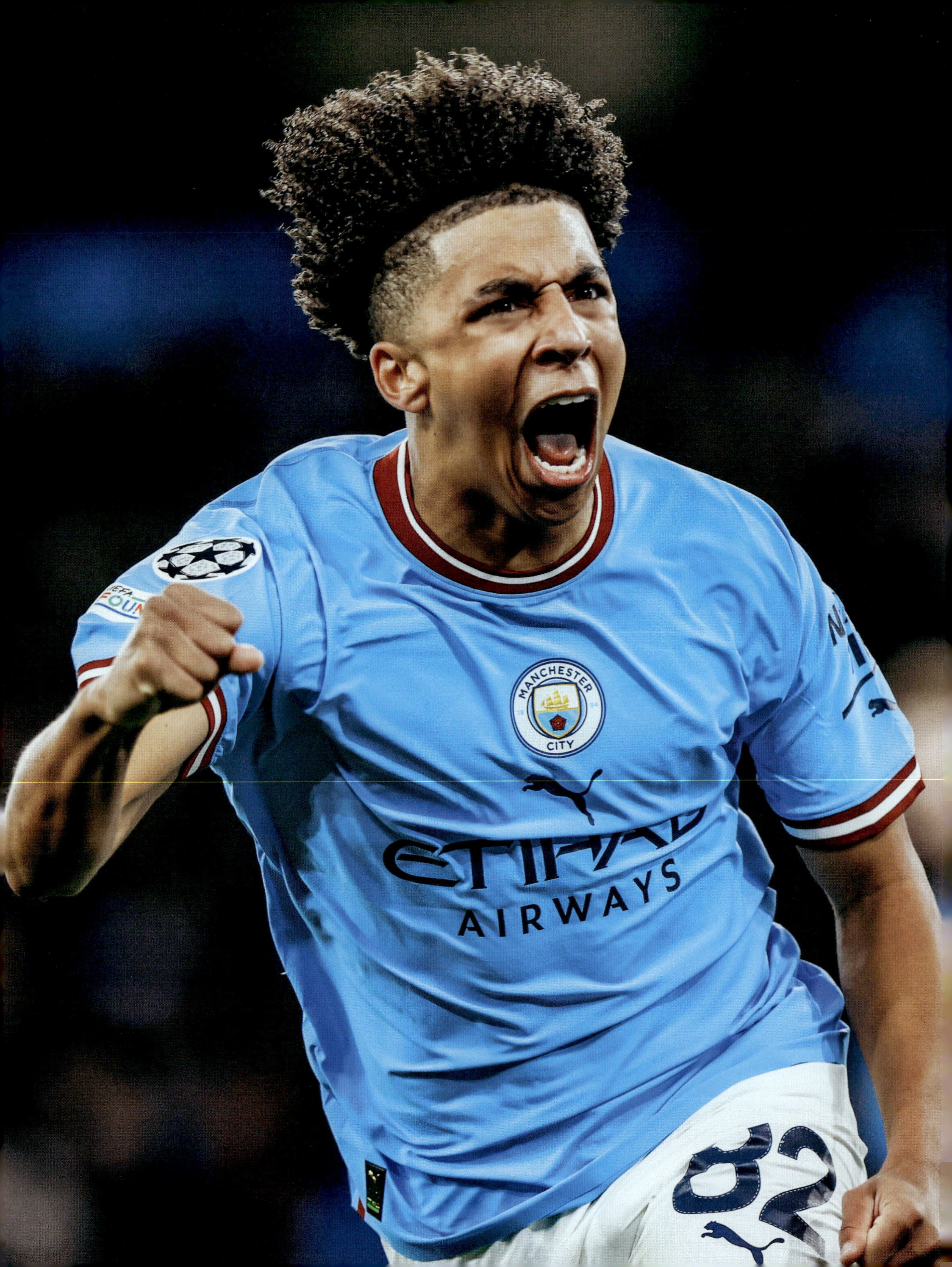
MANCHESTER CITY
ETIHAD AIRWAYS
82

THE STORY OF THE CHAMPIONS LEAGUE

Matchday Six
November 2, 2022

## CITY 3
(Lewis 52, Alvarez 73, Mahrez 83)

## SEVILLA 1
(Mir 31)

**City rounded off a memorable Champions League group campaign in style on what proved an Etihad night to remember for teenage history maker Rico Lewis.**

Having found ourselves trailing to the Spanish visitors after a 31st-minute Rafa Mir goal, City were in need of second-half inspiration, and it was provided by our then 17-year-old defender seven minutes after the restart.

The Bury-born Academy graduate rifled home a quite brilliant leveller on his full debut and, in the process, became the youngest player in Champions League history to score on his first start.

The subsequent introduction of Kevin De Bruyne from the bench then helped City ensure we converted our territorial dominance into tangible reward.

An exquisite 73rd-minute KDB through-ball provided the platform for Julian Alvarez to power through and round the Sevilla keeper before converting from a narrow angle.

Six minutes from time, Alvarez then turned provider, setting up Riyad Mahrez to round off a hugely impressive group campaign.

And for Pep Guardiola the impact of Lewis only added to the sense of satisfaction and accomplishment.

"Rico's so smart. He made a standing ovation all the way down, he played really well," the City boss declared.

"He is so clever, so intelligent. If you say something, he doesn't need to practise more because he knows what happened during the game.

"We see him every day. We don't give presents here. Not just because he is a City fan from the Academy is he going to play. You have to earn it.

"In the training sessions we always thought this guy has something special.

"It's good to qualify but we finished well. The money for the club is important. The prestige. It was a good night for the club."

**CITY:** Ortega Moreno, Lewis (Cancelo 85), Dias, Laporte, Gomez (Wilson-Esbrand 70), Gundogan (c) (Bernardo 57), Palmer (De Bruyne 70), Foden, Mahrez, Grealish (Rodrigo 45), Alvarez
**Subs not used:** Ederson, Carson, Stones, Ake

www.mancity.com 197

TREBLE WINNERS

# KNOCKOUT STAGES

### Round of 16, first leg
### February 22, 2023
## RB LEIPZIG 1
(Gvardiol 70)

## CITY 1
(Mahrez 27)

In the midst of a tough and demanding schedule that saw the side play five consecutive games on the road, City secured a more than satisfactory draw in eastern Germany as the Champions League knockout stages got underway.

City had dominated the early stages of what proved an absorbing encounter at the Red Bull Arena and deservedly powered in front thanks to Riyad Mahrez's clinical 27th-minute shot.

But Leipzig responded in kind after the break and drew level 20 minutes from time when Croatian defender Josko Gvardiol headed home from a corner.

Though Ilkay Gundogan came agonisingly close to restoring City's advantage almost immediately afterwards, it was a result that set things up perfectly for the deciding return leg.

And the City boss expressed his satisfaction as he looked ahead to the Etihad decider.

"We had good chances in both halves and we are going to decide it in Manchester," was Pep Guardiola's verdict.

"I am happy for all of the game, not just the first half.

"It's a competition where in the group stages, many important teams are out. And it's difficult. We knew it. It was our fourth game away in 10 days, with all the travel.

"We are a good team. We do many, many good things and we continue to do this."

**CITY:** Ederson, Walker, Akanji, Dias, Ake, Rodrigo, Gundogan (c), Bernardo, Mahrez, Grealish, Haaland
**Subs not used:** Ortega Moreno, Carson, Phillips, Alvarez, Gomez, Perrone, Foden, Charles, Palmer, Lewis, Robertson

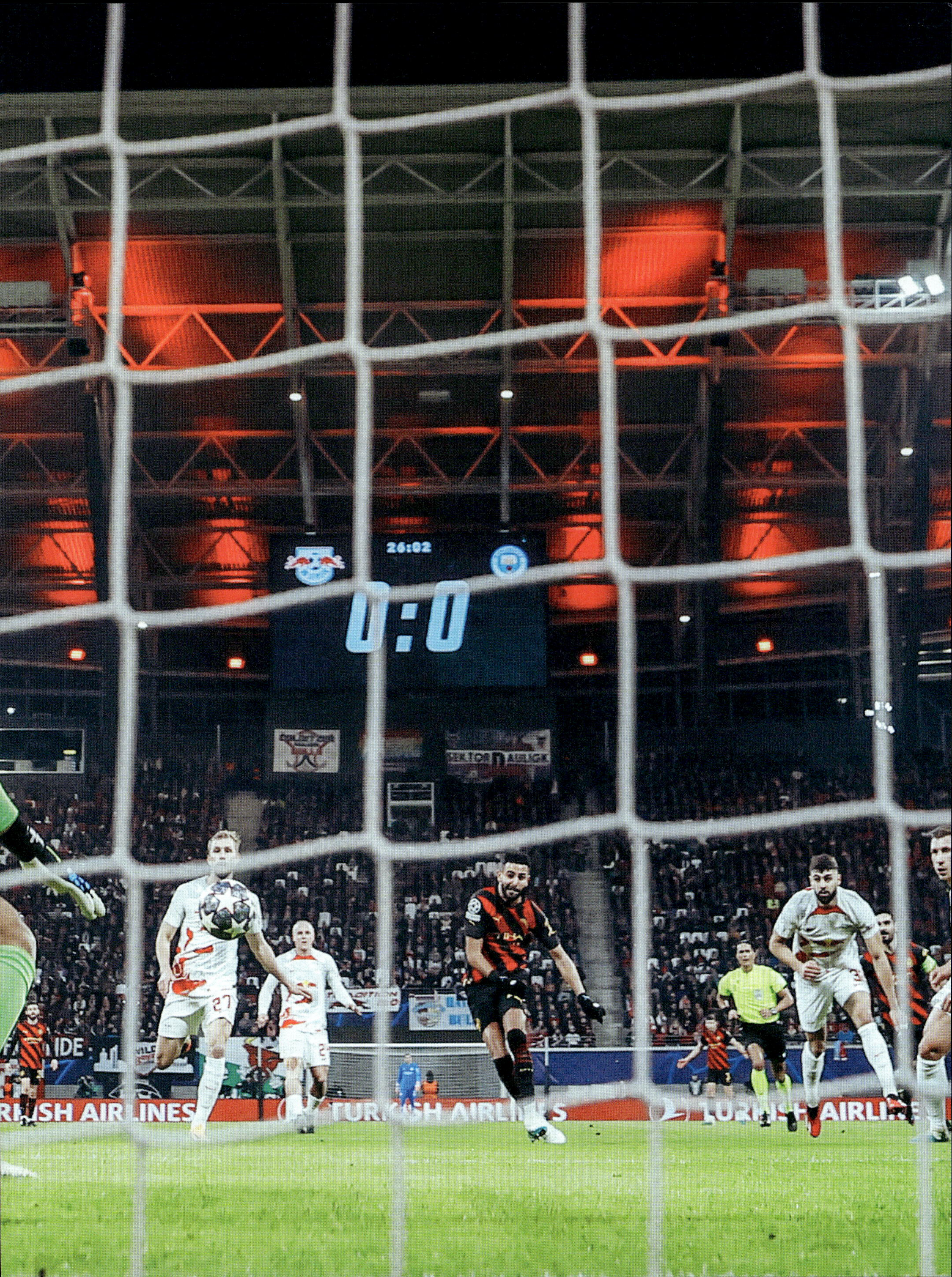
26:02
0:0

Round of 16, second leg
March 14, 2023

# CITY 7
(Haaland 22, 24, 45+2, 53, 57, Gundogan 49, De Bruyne 90+2)

# RB LEIPZIG 0

**A record-breaking, unforgettable night at the Etihad saw City power through into the Champions League quarter-finals and fire a warning shot that ricocheted around the rest of Europe.**

Once again in his extraordinary debut season, Erling Haaland hogged the individual headlines, the City striker claiming a five-goal haul as Pep Guardiola's side reached the Champions League last-eight for the sixth season in a row.

In the process, Haaland became only the third player to net five in a single Champions League game after Luiz Adriano and Lionel Messi, and the feat meant he became the youngest and quickest player to hit 30 goals overall in the competition.

If that wasn't enough, the 22-year-old's mind-boggling

"Once again in his extraordinary debut season, Erling Haaland hogged the individual headlines, the City striker claiming a five-goal haul as Pep Guardiola's side reached the Champions League last-eight for the sixth season in a row"

exploits also saw him reach 39 goals for the campaign, thus breaking Tommy Johnson's club record of 38 goals in a single season – a tally that had stood since 1928/29.

With Ilkay Gundogan and Kevin De Bruyne also on target, it was a performance that saw City at their devastating, incisive best.

And it ensured that the English champions were the side everybody else were understandably keen to try and avoid in the quarter-final draw that was to follow later that week.

As for Haaland, who Guardiola described as "a gift to all of us" – to deliver in such a way in the competition that most inspires him was cause for huge professional and personal satisfaction.

"It was a big night," Erling reflected.

"First of all, to play in the Champions League, I'm proud to play in it – I love this competition as everyone knows.

"To score five goals and to win 7-0 at home, I'm so happy.

"For a lot of goals today I did not think, I was just doing it. The same with every goal, I didn't think.

"A lot of it is being quick in the mind and putting it where the keeper is not."

**CITY:** Ederson, Stones (Gomez 64), Akanji, Dias, Ake, Rodrigo (Phillips 64), De Bruyne, Gundogan (c) (Mahrez 55), Bernardo, Grealish (Foden 55), Haaland (Alvarez 63)

**Subs not used:** Ortega Moreno, Carson, Walker, Laporte, Perrone, Palmer, Lewis

## TREBLE WINNERS

**Quarter-final, first leg**
**April 11, 2023**

# CITY 3
(Rodrigo 27, Bernardo 70, Haaland 76)

# BAYERN MUNICH 0

The business end of the season truly kicked in on a wet and wild April night at the Etihad as City took a huge step towards reaching the semi-finals by overpowering German giants Bayern Munich.

City's route to a potential final was the toughest one possible. The draw pitting us against Bayern in the last eight and then, if successful, facing a return semi-final showdown against Real Madrid.

Any nerves or apprehension, however, were instantly dismissed by a focused, full-blooded display that epitomised the quality and appetite of City's big-game hunters.

Bayern, under the tutelage of new boss Thomas Tuchel, more than played their part in a special match – and carved out a number of fine chances themselves.

City, though, possessed the greater cutting edge, generating a crucial advantage with which to take to Bavaria for the following week's deciding leg.

Rodri, enjoying his best season yet in a City shirt, broke the deadlock in spectacular fashion with a brilliant curling left-foot drive into the top corner after 27 minutes.

City then crucially extended our advantage with 20 minutes left, Erling Haaland turning provider by supplying an inviting cross for Bernardo Silva to head home after Jack Grealish had stolen possession from Dayot Upamecano.

Haaland, inevitably, also got in on the scoring act, claiming City's third six minutes later, as he latched onto the end of John Stones' headed knockdown to sweep a composed finish past Bayern keeper Yann Sommer for his 45th goal of the campaign.

The result extended City's unbeaten run to 25 Champions League home games, the longest by an English team in the competition's history.

It was another special – if draining – night at the Etihad and the manner of both the result and performance particularly resonated with Guardiola given his intricate knowledge of three-times European champions Bayern.

"Emotionally, I'm destroyed," the City boss admitted afterwards. "I have aged 10 more years. It was so demanding a game. It was not comfortable.

"It was an incredible result, but I know a little bit what can happen in Munich," added Guardiola, who managed Bayern from 2013 until 2016, winning three league titles and two domestic doubles.

"If you don't perform really well, they are able to score one, two, three. I know that and the players know that.

"It's an incredible result, but we have to do our game with huge, huge personality. If we don't do our game anything can happen.

"To knock out these teams you have to have two good games, not just one."

**CITY:** Ederson, Stones, Akanji, Dias, Ake, Rodrigo, De Bruyne (Alvarez 68), Gundogan (c), Bernardo, Grealish, Haaland
**Subs not used:** Ortega Moreno, Carson, Walker, Phillips, Laporte, Gomez, Mahrez, Perrone, Palmer, Lewis

www.mancity.com 203

## TREBLE WINNERS

### Quarter-final, second leg
### April 19, 2023
## BAYERN MUNICH 1
(Kimmich 83)

## CITY 1
(Haaland 57)

City's Champions League credentials were further enhanced as a thoroughly deserved draw at the Allianz Arena confirmed a 4-1 aggregate triumph and so booked our passage into the semi-finals for a third season in a row.

Though stepping out at the home of the Bundesliga champions armed with the safety blanket of a 3-0 first-leg victory, there was still serious work to do on a chilly, rainy night in Germany.

Buoyed on by a boisterous, capacity 75,000 crowd, Bayern threw everything plus the kitchen sink at the City backline as they sought to overturn the deficit.

It was a feisty – and at times fractious – encounter, with two genuine heavyweights of European football slugging it out toe to toe.

The evening also threw up a rarity as Erling Haaland saw a first-half penalty miss the target after a Dayot Upamecano handball.

The Bayern defender was fortunate enough to be still on the pitch having seen an earlier red card for a professional foul on Haaland rescinded following a VAR check which showed the City striker was fractionally offside.

Haaland, however, was not to be denied. And 18 minutes into the second half, he demonstrated his class once more by slamming home a superb shot after latching onto Kevin De Bruyne's sumptuous assist.

To their credit, Bayern kept pushing for an equaliser, with substitute Mathys Tel having a goal disallowed for offside.

And the home side were handed a penalty in the 83rd

minute when the ball struck Manuel Akanji's arm, with Joshua Kimmich scoring from the spot, but it was little more than an exercise in pride.

To City went the spoils – and a mouth-watering re-match of last season's semi-final with holders and 14-times champions Real Madrid.

For De Bruyne it was a case of City again applying ourselves in the perfect way when the stakes were high.

"I think going into the semis is what we wanted to do," the Belgian pointed out.

"I've played here before and, in the beginning, you know they're going to come aggressive, and they're going to try and put you under pressure.

"But I think we dealt well with the pressure. We defended when there was a tough moment and at certain times, we created what we needed to create.

"In the difficult moments I think it was a very smart game from us.

"What happened last year (against Real Madrid), happened. I think we played really well in the two games and in the last five minutes [they] changed the course of not qualifying.

"You have to take it on the chin and move on. It happened and it doesn't mean we didn't play well for the majority of the two games.

"However, football is about the details. It happens, and you move on."

**CITY:** Ederson, Stones, Akanji, Dias, Ake (Laporte 66), Rodrigo, De Bruyne (Walker 88), Gundogan (c), Bernardo, Grealish, Haaland (Alvarez 84)
**Subs not used:** Ortega Moreno, Carson, Phillips, Gomez, Mahrez, Perrone, Foden, Palmer, Lewis

## TREBLE WINNERS

**Semi-final, first leg**
**May 9, 2023**

# REAL MADRID 1
(Vinicius Jnr 36)

# CITY 1
(De Bruyne 67)

An enthralling, absorbing encounter between the Spanish and English champions ended with honours even and City going a long way towards exorcising the memory of last season's heartbreaking last-four exit in Madrid.

Back in May 2022, two dramatic injury-time goals and a subsequent penalty in extra time saw Real somehow deny Pep Guardiola's side a place in the final.

Twelve months on, however, City demonstrated there was no emotional baggage attached to our quickfire return to the Spanish capital.

And once again, Kevin De Bruyne demonstrated his sheer class and quality when thrust onto the biggest and most pressurised of stages.

The City midfielder slammed home a stunning second-half leveller after Vinicius Junior's fine first-half strike had given Real the initial advantage.

A high-quality, high-octane encounter saw both sides come close to securing a first-leg advantage.

City were grateful to keeper Ederson for producing two fine late blocks to deny both Karim Benzema and Aurelien Tchouameni.

Earlier, Real counterpart Thibaut Courtois had demonstrated all of his acumen and vast experience in blocking efforts from De Bruyne, Rodrigo and Erling Haaland.

The result extended City's unbeaten run to 21 games across all competitions, a sequence which included 17 wins.

And it set up the mouth-watering stage for an Etihad decider in six days' time.

For Guardiola, the result was merely half-time with all still to play for in that Etihad decider.

However, the City boss was more than satisfied with the application and attitude of his players as he looked ahead to a 'play-off final'.

"It was a really tight game. Congratulations to the team because in this competition and this scenario the teams are always so difficult for their history but especially their quality," Pep declared afterwards.

"We started really well and when we were better, they made an incredible transition from Camavinga and an incredible finish from Vinicius.

"And when they were better than us in the second half, we scored a goal.

"It was a tight game. It's open to Manchester, it will be a final playing at home with our people and we look forward to it.

"The effort was incredible. It's like a play-off now."

**CITY:** Ederson, Walker, Stones, Dias, Akanji, Rodrigo, Gundogan (c), De Bruyne, Bernardo, Grealish, Haaland
**Subs not used:** Ortega Moreno, Carson, Phillips, Laporte, Alvarez, Gomez, Mahrez, Foden, Palmer, Lewis

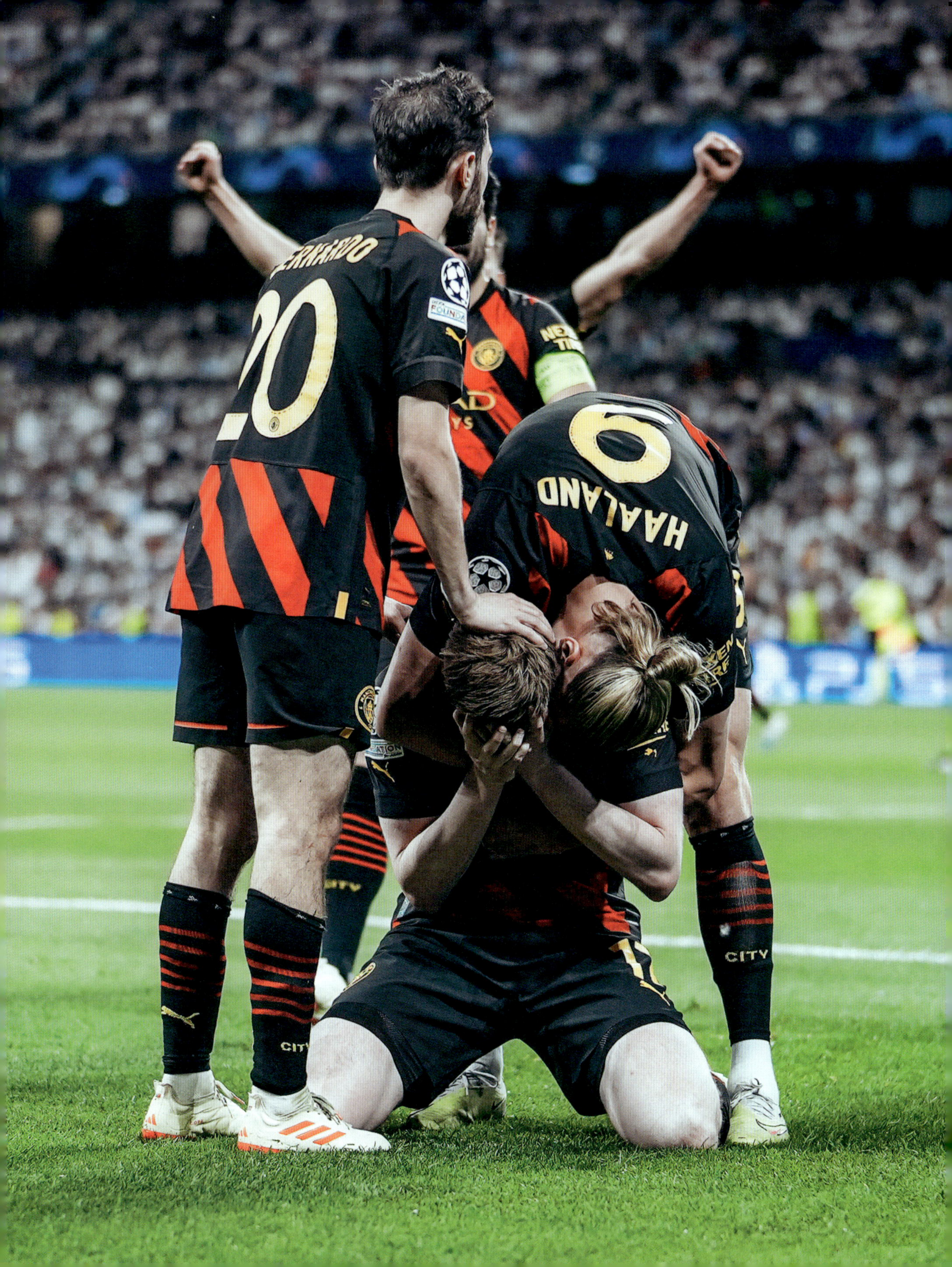
20
CITY

TREBLE WINNERS

Semi-final, second leg
May 17, 2023

# CITY 4
(Bernardo 23, 37, Akanji 76, Alvarez 90+1)

## REAL MADRID 0

As Pep Guardiola had been at pains to stress earlier in the season, "perfection in football doesn't exist".
However, on a glorious, technicolour May evening in Manchester, City served up a treat for the eyes and sustenance for the soul that was as close to the perfect display as it's possible to get.

Real, the 14-times winners and reigning European champions, were simply blown away by a glorious, compelling exhibition of football that served as the template for everything that is good about City.

Guardiola's players proved simply unstoppable – especially in a majestic first 45 minutes that for many observers served as arguably the finest exhibition of football ever seen on these shores.

Roared on by a passionate, exuberant full house and with hundreds of millions more watching spellbound around the globe, City not only banished the spectre of last season's semi-final loss, they also demonstrated they now possessed all the requisite qualities needed to go on and be crowned kings of Europe.

It was high-quality, high-octane stuff that will surely live long in the memory of all those lucky enough to witness the game as Real – the recognised kings of Europe – were outthought, outfought and outclassed.

Real keeper Thibaut Courtois had already performed heroics to block two Erling Haaland headers early in the first half before a Bernardo Silva brace deservedly converted City's superiority into concrete reward.

A superb, sweeping 23rd-minute move ended with Bernardo applying a brilliant close-range finish to open the scoring and raise the roof off the Etihad.

Then, 14 minutes before the break, the Portugal midfielder doubled his and City's tally after despatching a fine looping header as Guardiola's side asserted even more control.

Ederson was called into action after the break to keep out efforts from David Alaba and Karim Benzema, but a

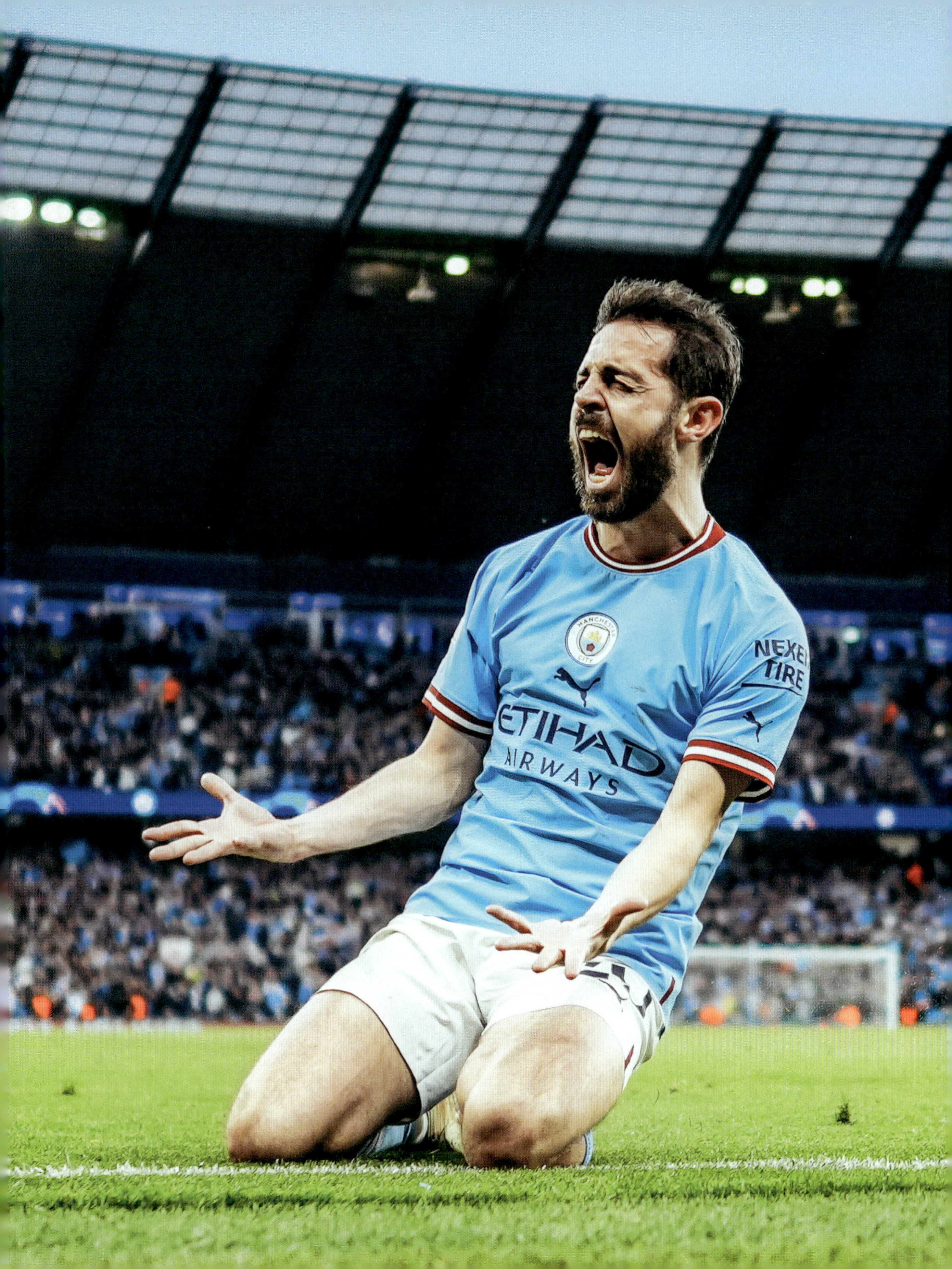
ETIHAD
AIRWAYS
NEXEN
TIRE

TREBLE WINNERS

THE STORY OF THE CHAMPIONS LEAGUE

*"It felt like the night City finally came of age as a truly great European side and at the same time kept Guardiola's squad firmly on course for a potential historic Treble as a remarkable and historic season approached its zenith"*

hungry, ravenous City were not to be denied. And when Manuel Akanji's header deflected in off Eder Militao 14 minutes from time, it lit the Blue touch paper at a joyous Etihad.

Substitute Julian Alvarez then wrapped up a dominant win for the ages with a crisp injury-time strike after latching onto an exquisite Phil Foden pass.

The victory sealed City's passage into our second Champions League final in three years, setting up the prospect of an intriguing final against Italian giants Inter in Istanbul.

It also felt like the night City finally came of age as a truly great European side and at the same time kept Guardiola's squad firmly on course for a potential historic Treble as a remarkable and historic season approached its zenith.

For Guardiola, the pain and frustration of that cruel loss 12 months earlier had served as fuel for the fire that City unleashed on an unsuspecting Real and was nothing less than his players merited.

"These guys have done it for many years and today they got the reward they deserve. A final against an Italian team," Pep declared.

"When the draw was Real Madrid, I said, 'Yeah, I want it'. Today it was there. I'm very pleased for the organisation, the chairman, owner and players. I had the feeling these last days that we had a mix of calm and tension to play these types of games.

"After 10 or 15 minutes I had the feeling that all the pain that we had during one year from what happened last season was there today. It was so tough and hard here last season – we played quite similarly to the way we played today.

"I remember that in an interview Toni Kroos said Madrid was special because they could have been beaten 10-2 at the Etihad. Kroos is one of the best players I have ever seen and trained and when he says that it means we were there and it was really tough losing the way we lose.

"You have to swallow poison and swallow everything, be kind and football and sport always gives you another chance. We accept defeat and today we were there.

"Football and life always gives you an opportunity and the important thing is to never give up and try again."

**CITY:** Ederson, Walker, Stones, Dias, Akanji, Rodrigo, Gundogan (c) (Mahrez 79), De Bruyne (Foden 84), Bernardo, Grealish, Haaland (Alvarez 89)
**Subs not used:** Ortega Moreno, Carson, Phillips, Laporte, Gomez, Palmer, Lewis

TREBLE WINNERS

**Champions League final**
**June 10, 2023**

# CITY 1
(Rodrigo 68)

# INTER 0

With the Premier League already secured and the FA Cup subsequently bagged seven days earlier thanks to a historic 2-1 Wembley win over Manchester United, City stood on the brink of footballing immortality as they stepped out in Istanbul to contest for the biggest prize of them all.

The overwhelming majority of pundits and sages had already made their mind up, acclaiming City as winners before a ball had even been kicked in anger.

For them, the semi-final against Real Madrid had represented the final in all but name.

Pep Guardiola, however, knew far, far better.

He recognised that an Inter side which had conceded in just one game in the knockout stages en route to reaching the Istanbul showpiece represented the toughest of nuts to crack.

The boss also recognised the unique demands and phenomenal pressures associated with the biggest club match in world football.

And at the end of a marathon season like no other, which had kicked off 11 months earlier, Pep also understood that the physical and mental demands thrown up by the never ending campaign would also need carefully navigating too.

Of course, nothing in life, not least the greatest prize of all, comes easy.

So it proved on a hot and tense night at the Ataturk Olympic Stadium.

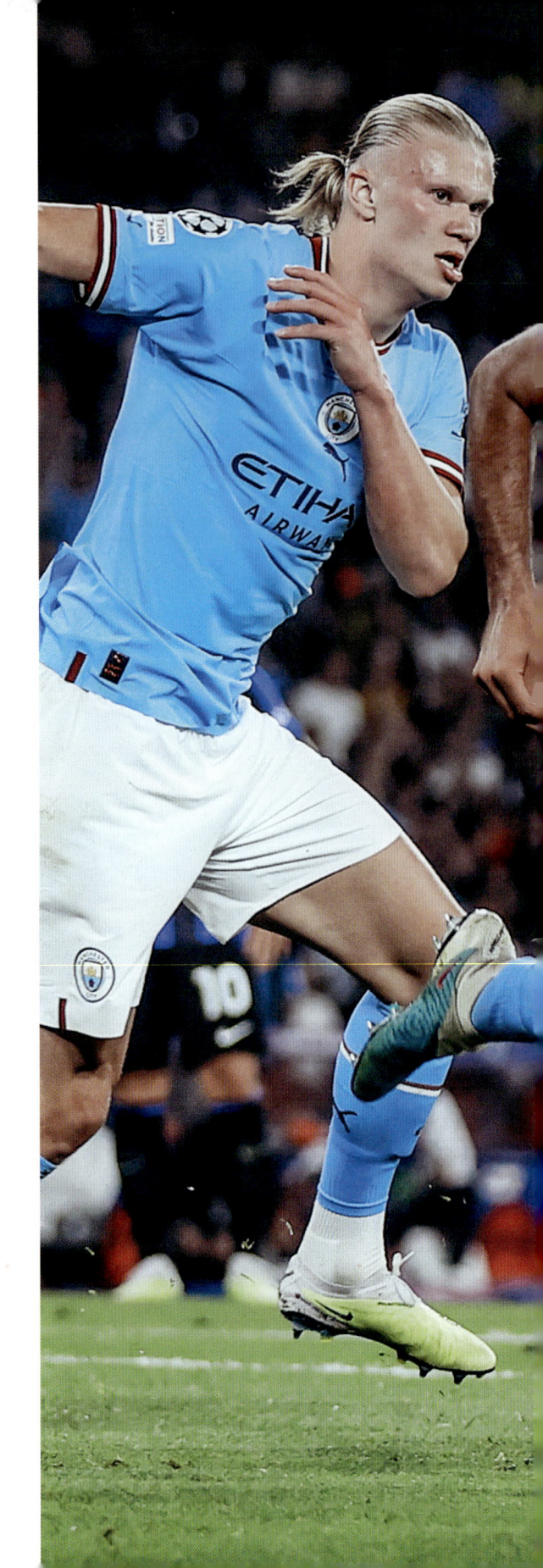

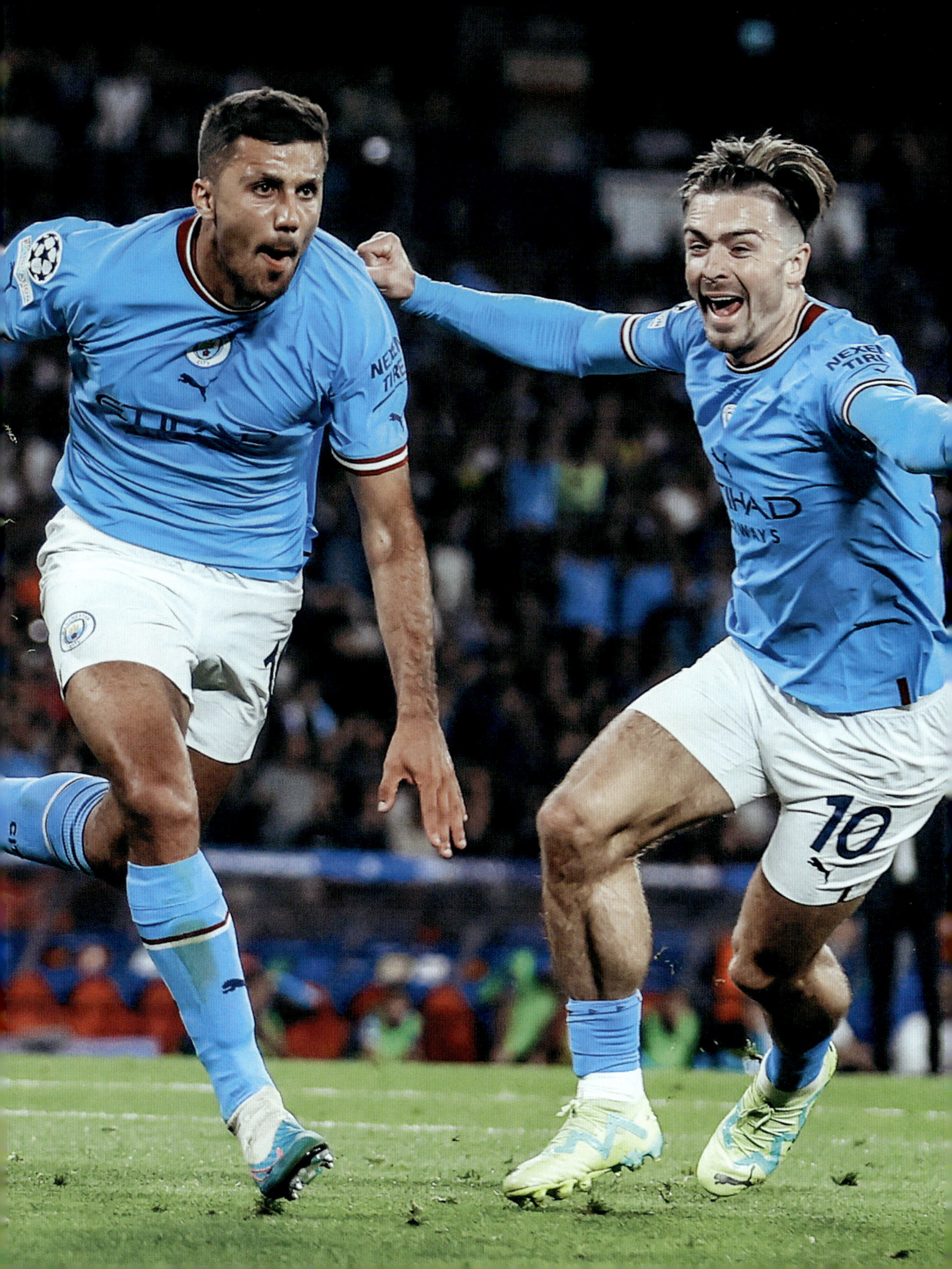
10

## TREBLE WINNERS

While City strived to settle into our trademark rhythm and flow, a disciplined and superbly drilled Inter served notice that they were far from there to simply make up the numbers.

And when – just as in the 2021 final - Kevin De Bruyne was forced off the field through injury, this time with a hamstring complaint, many fans could have been forgiven for fearing that lightning was about to strike twice.

City and Pep were not to be denied, however.

With Phil Foden summoned on in place of KDB towards the end of the first half, space and opportunities – slowly but surely – came City's way in what was a nerve-shredding, emotionally draining affair.

Masters of the game of patience, City's moment of ultimate deliverance finally arrived with 22 minutes remaining on the clock.

An inviting Manuel Akanji through ball gave Bernardo Silva just enough time and space on the right side of the Inter box to fire in a quickfire cross.

The ball was deflected back to the waiting Rodri driving into the box and from 16 yards he delivered the sweetest, most important strike of his career, arcing the ball beyond Inter keeper Andre Onana and the Italian's defence into the right edge of the net.

Even then, however, the deal wasn't sealed.

After Foden had seen Onana deny his close-range shot which would have doubled the advantage, City then had to withstand a ferocious late Inter assault as the tension proved unbearable.

First Federico Dimarco's header bounced off the bar before Romelu Lukaku then inadvertently blocked his goalbound follow-up.

And with time all but up, Ederson then made a stunning late save to deny Lukaku.

City, though, were not to be denied and after years of blood, sweat, toil and tears, we were finally and deservedly crowned champions of Europe, and with it Treble winners.

The celebrations went on long and loud into the

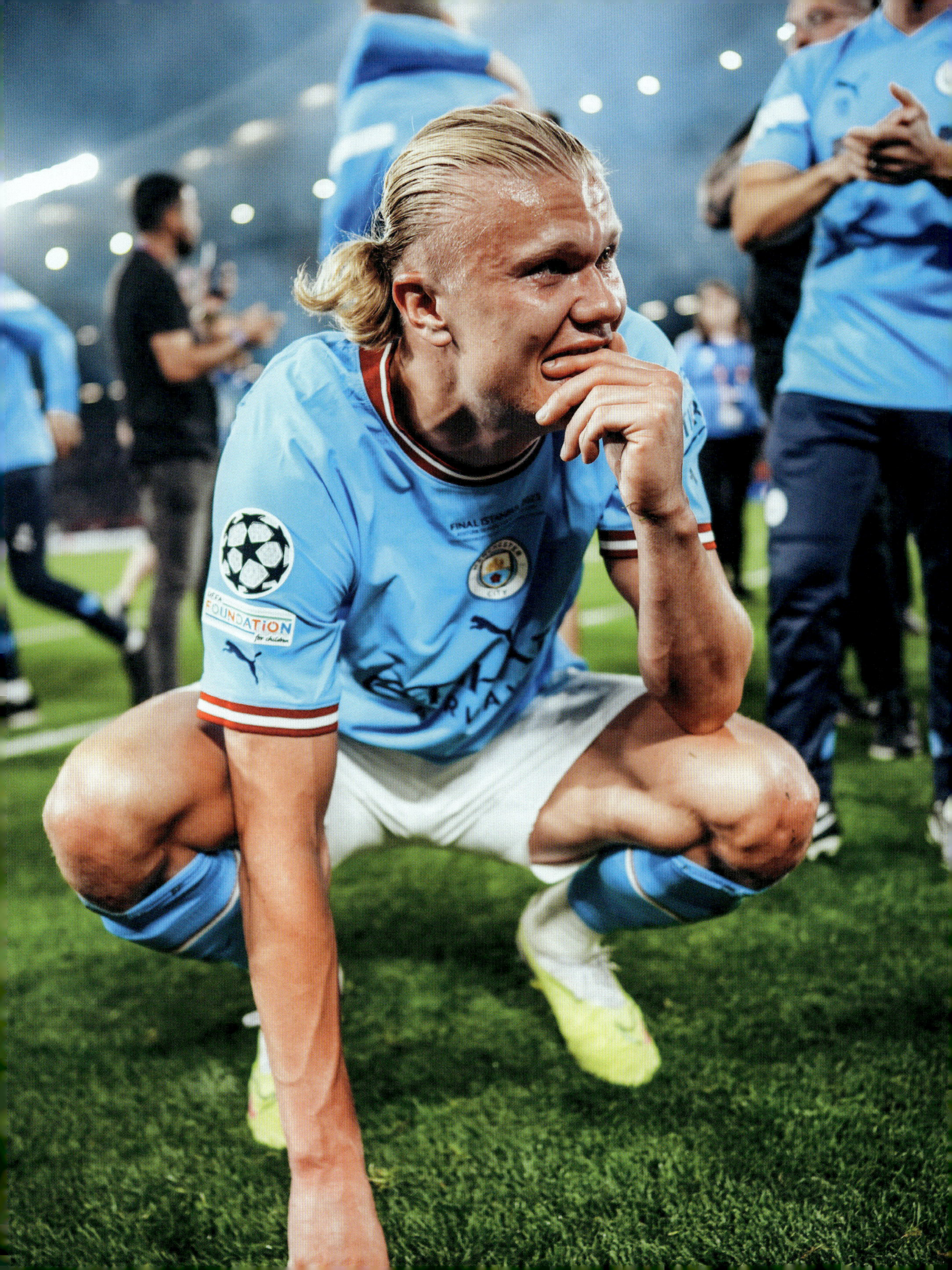
FOUNDATION

## TREBLE WINNERS

Istanbul night as the players, staff and their families joyously drank in the moment sharing it with the thousands of ecstatic City fans who had made the journey out to Turkey to bear witness to this most momentous of evenings.

Given the two-hour time zone difference between Manchester and Istanbul, it meant that by the time a weary Guardiola finally made his way into the post-match press conference, it was 1.25am Turkish time.

A third Champions League success as a manager meant that City's incredible leader had stamped his own place in the record books too, Pep having become the first boss to win two Trebles, following his feat with Barcelona in 2009.

Not surprisingly, after the most relentless, lengthy and dramatic campaign of his glorious career, the boss looked both physically and emotionally drained as he tried to take stock of the sheer enormity of the achievement.

But there was no disguising Pep's enormous feeling of pride as he hailed his history makers...not to mention sense of huge professional satisfaction.

"I am tired, calm, satisfied of course. This trophy is so difficult to win. It's impossible," Guardiola reflected after the final whistle.

"Sometimes it looks like this competition this year, this final was written in the stars.

"The goal, the chances they had. Ederson's save where in extra time you could lose the game.

"I will be the same person and we will be the same team and we will be the same club. Today was our year, and of course we are incredibly satisfied to achieve something unique, the Treble for this club.

"The feeling I have right now is we leave the Champions League and give credit to the five Premier Leagues. In seven years, two FA Cups, four Carabao Cups, Community Shields.

"That gives credit to what we have done. We have to win Europe to be considered one of the really good teams and we won it.

"Suffering, you could expect it because Inter is an exceptional team.

"Sometimes you need this type of luck that in the past, against Tottenham and in other games, the final against Chelsea, we didn't have it.

"Today we had it."

And rather than marking the end of the journey, in trademark fashion Guardiola also spoke in that moment of ultimate achievement how he wanted this to mark merely the first chapter of City's European successes.

"Now we have the first and the people can say 'Manchester City have already the first Champions League'. But I don't want after one Champions League to disappear," Pep asserted.

"So, we have to work harder in the next few years, next season and be there.

"There are teams who win the Champions League

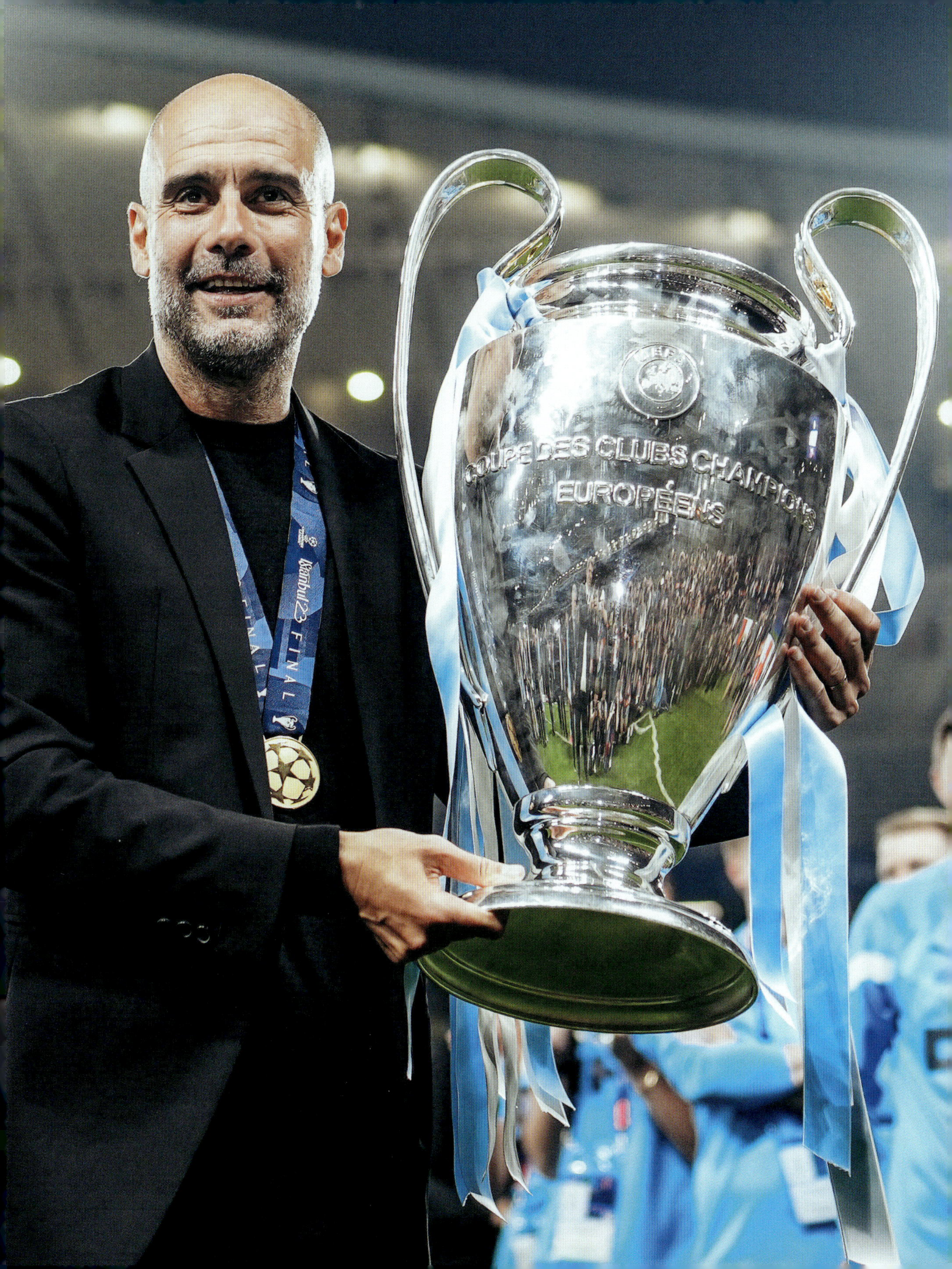
COUPE DES CLUBS CHAMPIONS
EUROPÉENS

EDERSON
ORTEGA MORENO
18
COUPE DES CLUBS CHAMPIONS EUROPÉENS

THE STORY OF THE CHAMPIONS LEAGUE

after one or two seasons and disappear. We have to avoid it.

"Knowing where we've been, this is not going to happen. But at the same time I have to admit it is a big relief for the club, and for everyone we have this trophy."

It was somehow fitting, too, that it was Istanbul that provided the backdrop for City's first-ever Champions League win.

After all it was that same evocative, exotic and enticing cultural melting pot where two continents collide that had played host to our first game in the European Cup way back in 1968.

Beforehand, outspoken coach Malcolm Allison had famously declared his exciting City side would go on to terrify Europe.

Instead, a star-studded squad containing the fabled trinity of Francis Lee, Mike Summerbee and Colin Bell, suffered a shock 2-1 first-round aggregate loss to Fenerbahce.

Fifty-five years later, on a night where the stars truly did align, City more than atoned for that result and all the trials and tribulations in the ensuing five-and-a-half decades.

Champions of Europe, Treble winners, history makers.

Pep Guardiola and his fabulous Manchester City know their place amongst the pantheon of football's greatest-ever teams is now secure.

For eternity.

**CITY:** Ederson, Akanji, Stones (Walker 82), Dias, Ake, Rodrigo, Gundogan (c), De Bruyne (Foden 36), Bernardo, Grealish, Haaland
**Subs not used:** Ortega Moreno, Carson, Phillips, Laporte, Alvarez, Gomez, Mahrez, Perrone, Palmer, Lewis

www.mancity.com 219

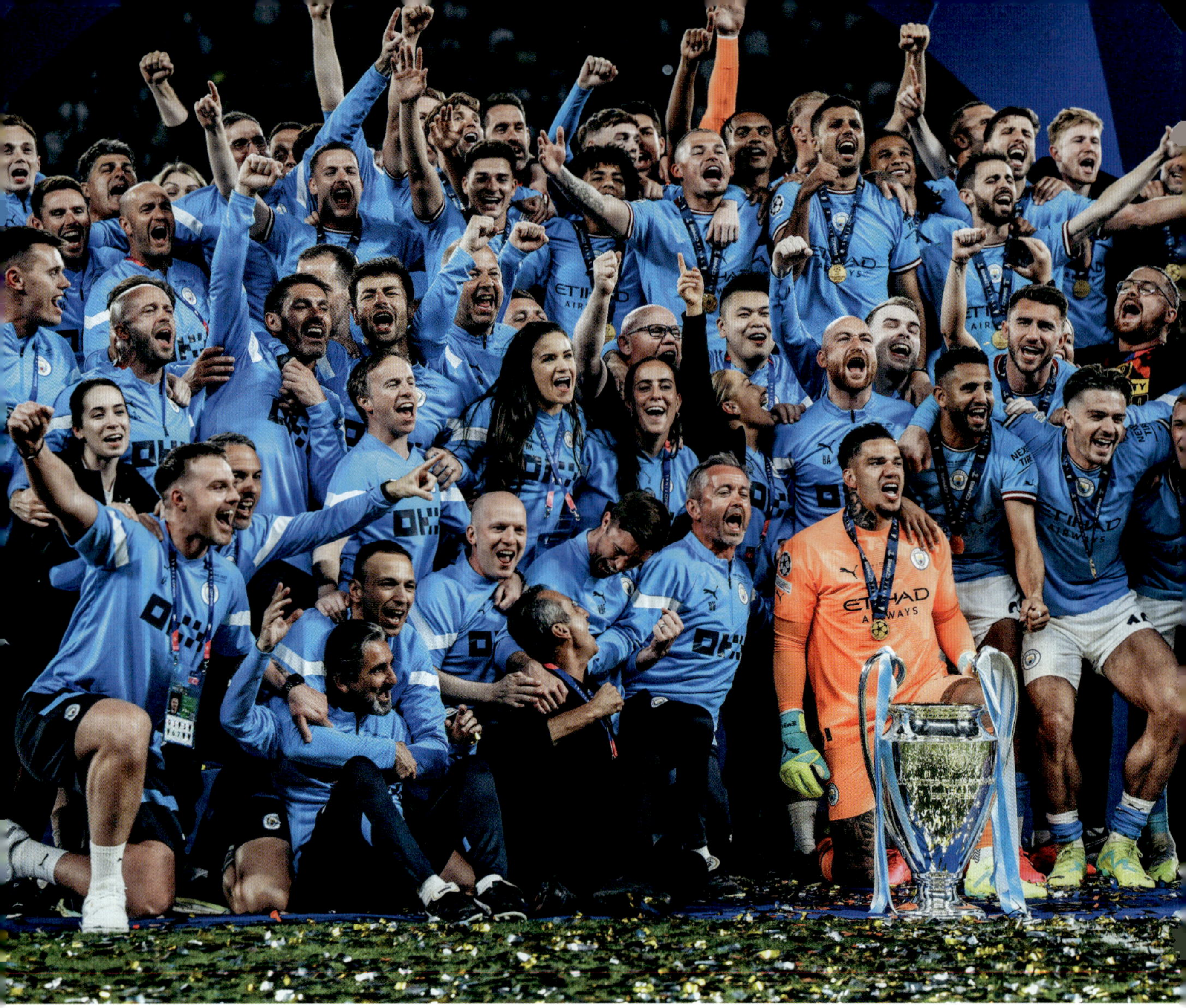
ETIHAD
AIRWAYS

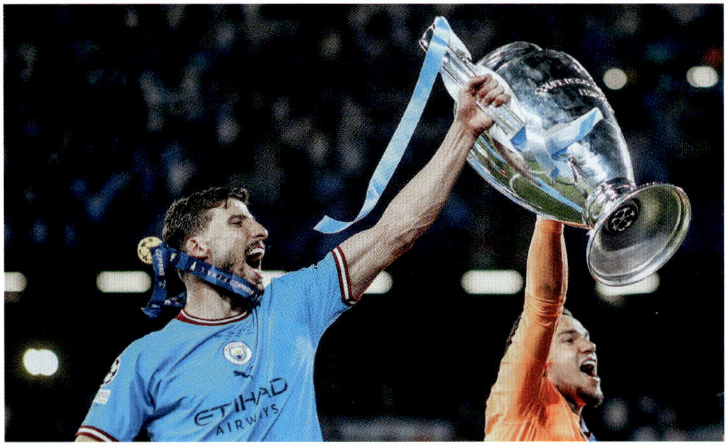
ETIHAD
AIRWAYS

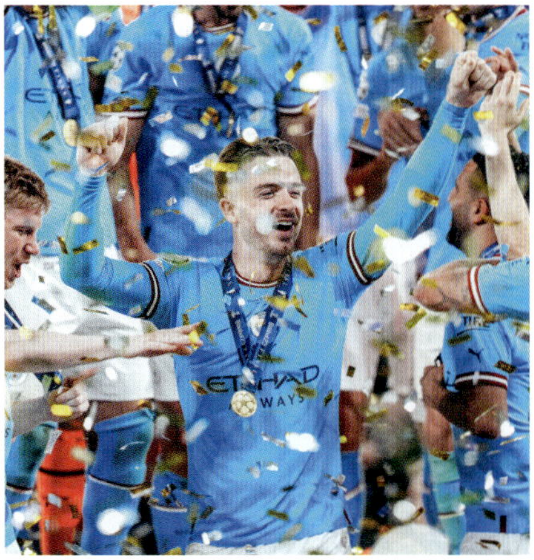

THE STORY OF THE CHAMPIONS LEAGUE

www.mancity.com 221

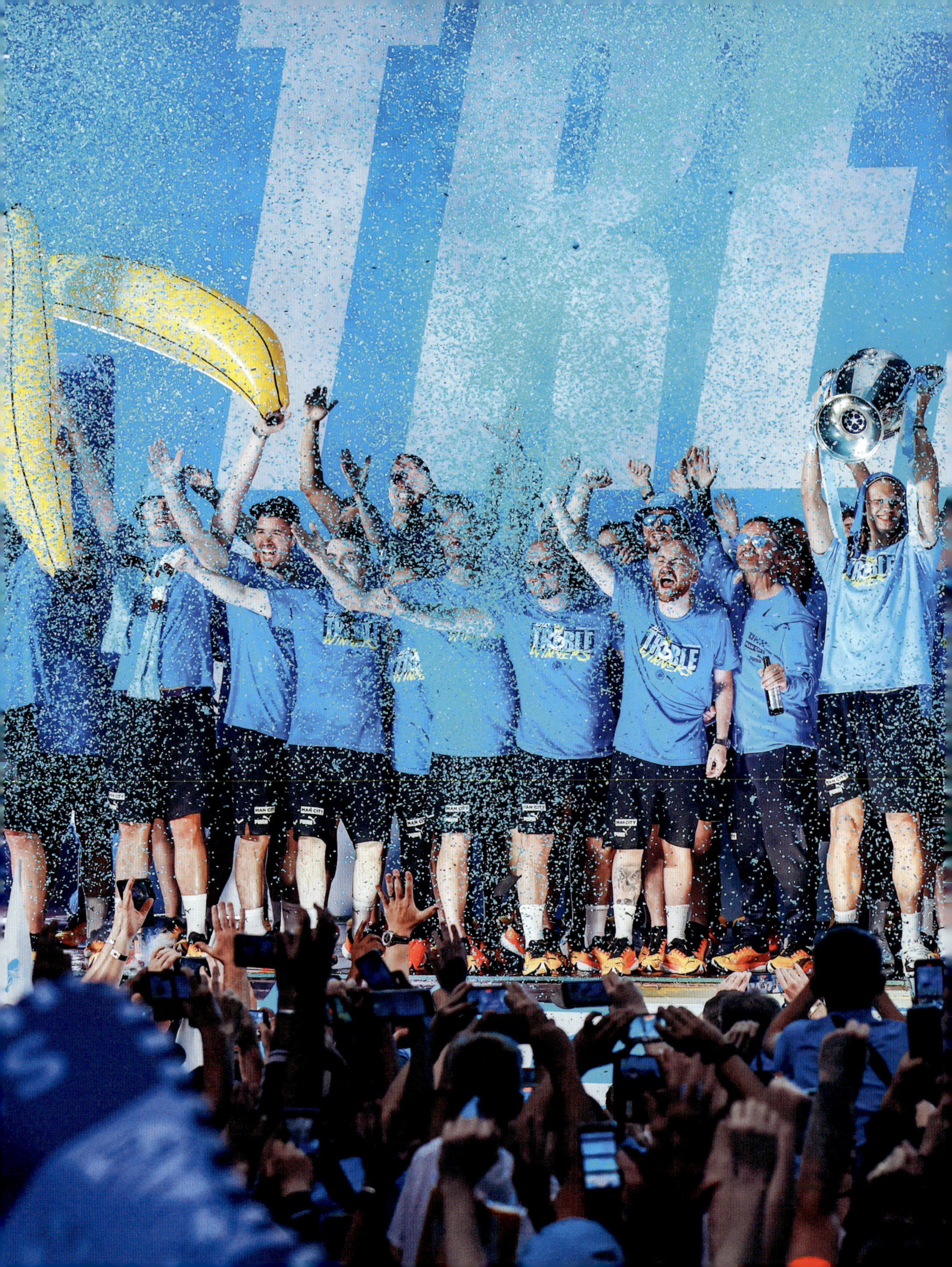
TREBLE
WINNERS
MAN CITY

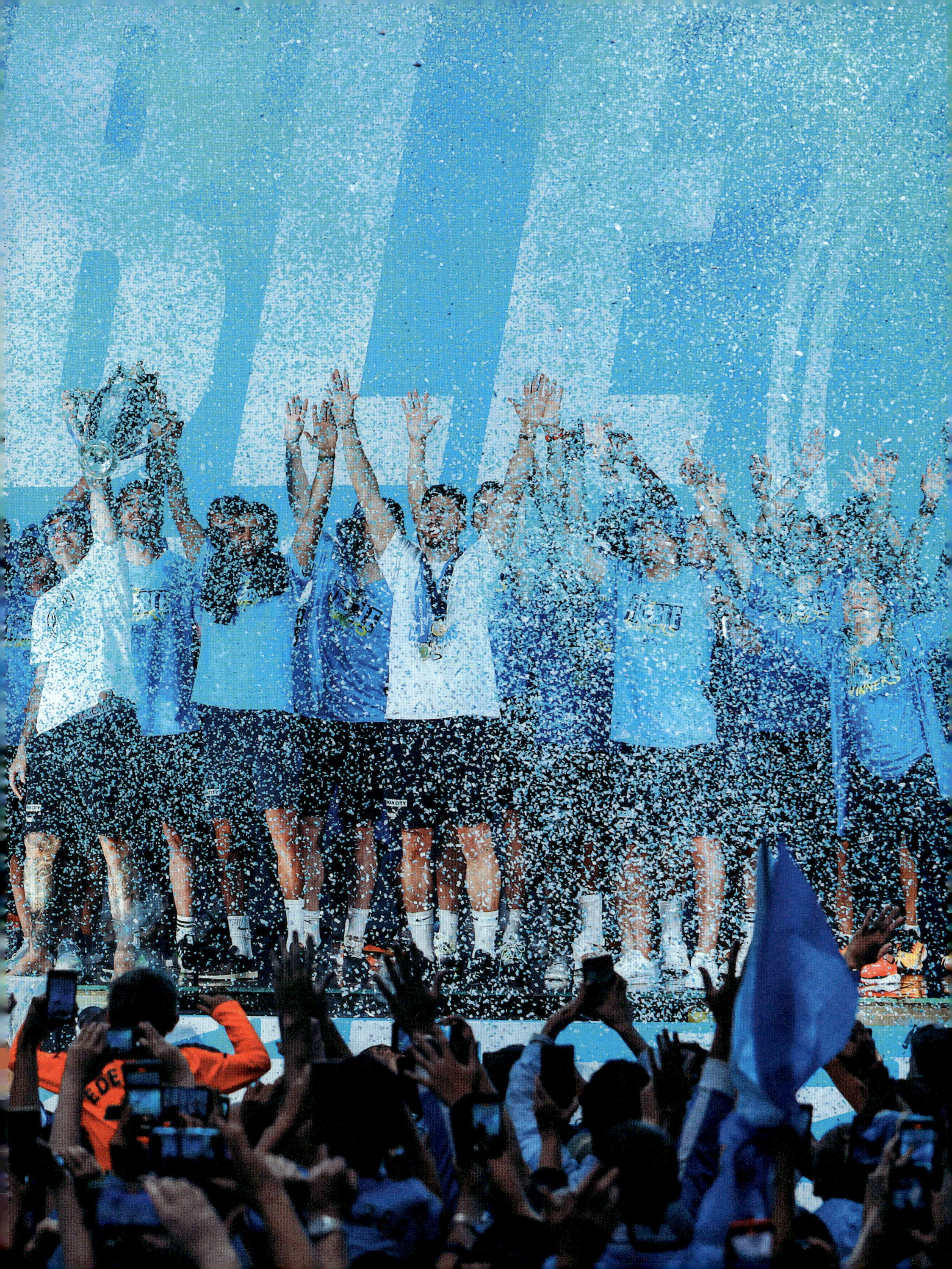

TREBLE HEROES

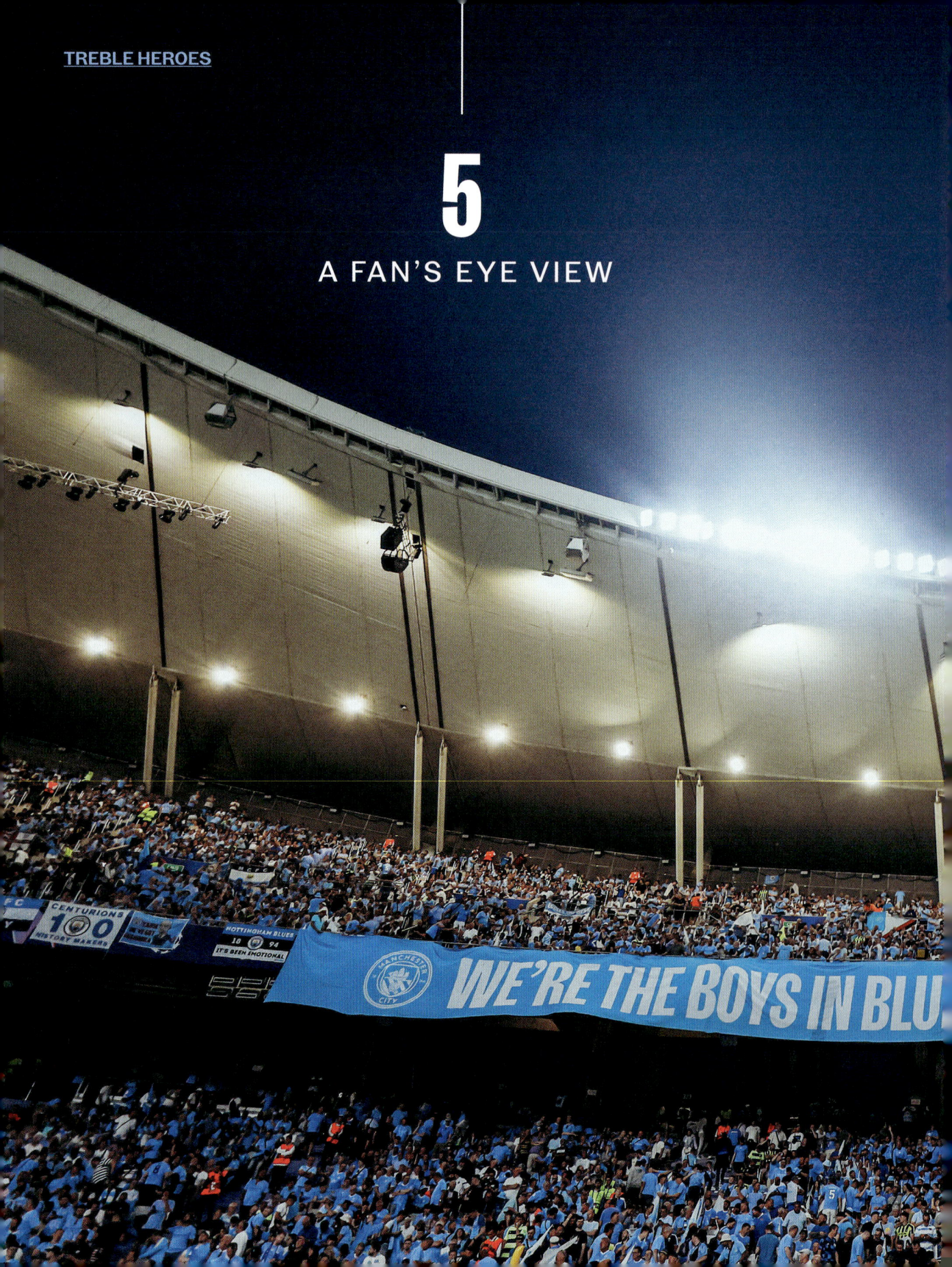

# 5
## A FAN'S EYE VIEW

# 48 HOURS IN ISTANBUL

by Jack Mumford

## TREBLE HEROES

"Woah, we're the boys in blue. Woah, coming after you!"

That was the soundtrack to potentially the greatest weekend of my life.

And the song rang true from arrival at Manchester Airport on Friday until touching back down in the north west of England on Sunday morning.

Just like Wembley a week earlier, thousands were carried along on a wave of blue shirts, bucket hats and sunburnt faces to a defining moment in Manchester City's history.

The boys in blue, with the best defence in Europe, were on a mission to be Treble winners and there was a real air of confidence that this was our time.

It was nothing like arrogance. You'll be hard-pressed to find a City fan heading into a major final that isn't consumed by doubt.

However, the earlier Premier League and FA Cup successes, our dominant run to the final against giants of the European game like Bayern Munich and Real Madrid, and everything Pep Guardiola has achieved at City, meant the thousands landing in the Turkish metropolis dared to dream.

Metropolis is perhaps not a sufficient word for the city that more than 15 million people call home.

Straddling the continents of Europe and Asia on either side of the Bosphorus and a vital stop on the old Silk Road, Istanbul has been a stronghold of the Roman, Byzantine and Ottoman empires at different points during the last millennium.

That history still lives and breathes around every corner, while the old centre of Istanbul remains a UNESCO World Heritage Site.

Phenomenal mosques dominate the skyline and the narrow streets transport you back to a different time. It was down many of these winding roads, in the bars and kebab houses, that City fans could be found on Friday night and Saturday afternoon.

The chanting was continuous and the mixing of City and Inter fans friendly throughout.

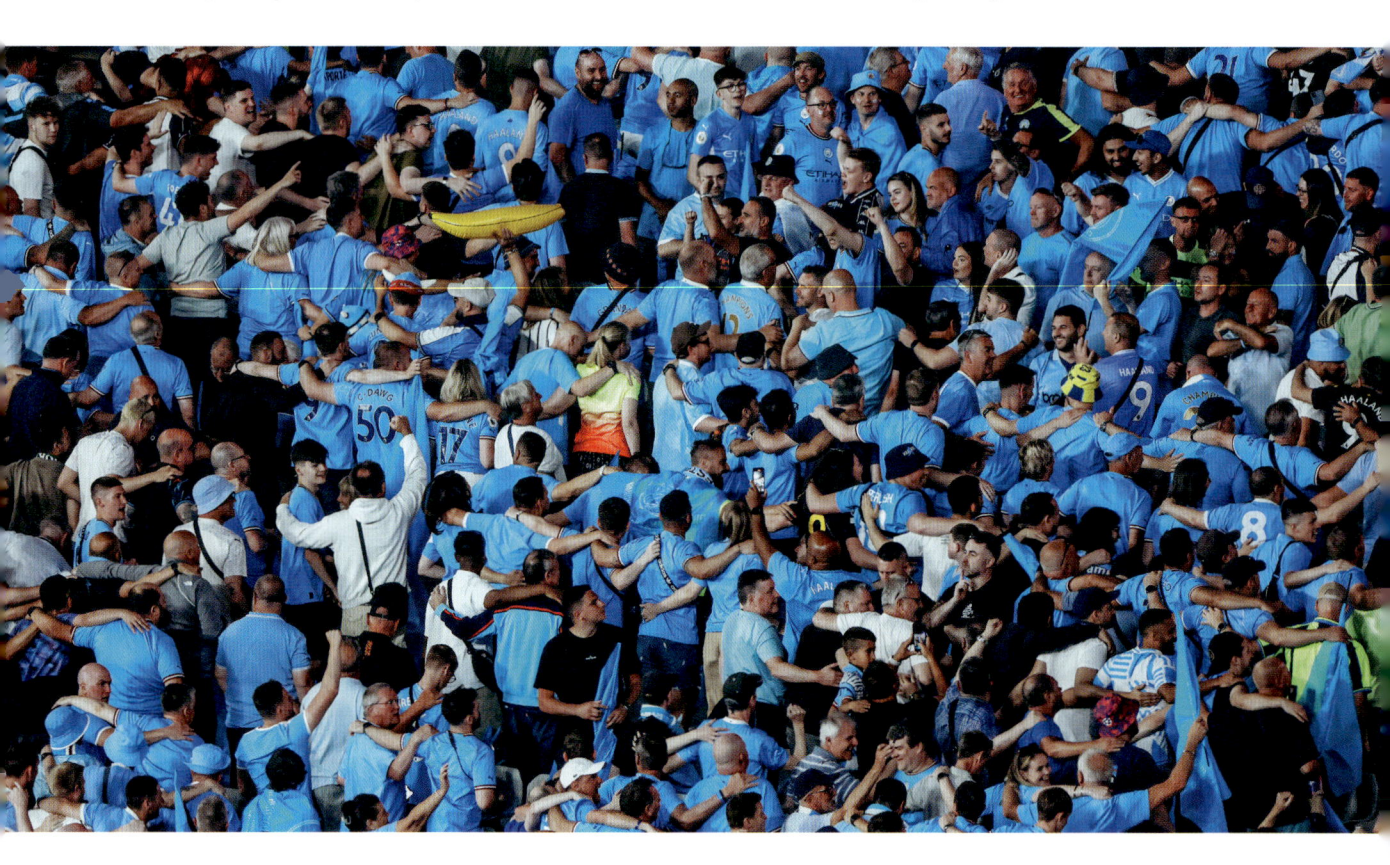

48 HOURS IN ISTANBUL

www.mancity.com 227

228 www.mancity.com

## 48 HOURS IN ISTANBUL

Local advice was to head to the Ataturk Olympic Stadium early, and it proved wise.

Although we moved at a snail's pace along the 16 miles from the official coach pick-up point in Yenikapi to the ground itself, spirits were not dampened upon arrival.

Out in the hills, the Ataturk's unique design contrasted with the countryside behind it.

Once through the turnstiles, the open-air space behind the stands provided a panorama of the stage on which history would be made.

Down in the seating areas, Blues gathered much earlier than usual to soak in the surroundings and welcome the team out to warm up.

Although kick-off was not until 10pm local time, shorts with City shirts old and new were the order of the day.

Blue Moon sounded around the ground 20 minutes out before UEFA's pre-match show started in earnest.

Then the game itself. A tense affair from the word go, every whisper of an opening sparked shrieks of anticipation or terror, depending on which side was attacking.

Kevin De Bruyne sat down, clearly unable to continue, and all around me groaned. Surely such a special season couldn't end in disappointment?

While the nerves were palpable in the stands, the players had settled into a rhythm early in the second half. All could see that Inter's defenders were struggling to close us down with the same voracity they had before the break.

So when Manuel Akanji stepped forward at the midway point of the second period, he found plenty of space to wander into. His pass through to Bernardo Silva had everyone clamouring for the best vantage point.

The Portuguese winger's half-blocked cross rolled into an empty space and the 20,000 City fans fell silent.

www.mancity.com 229

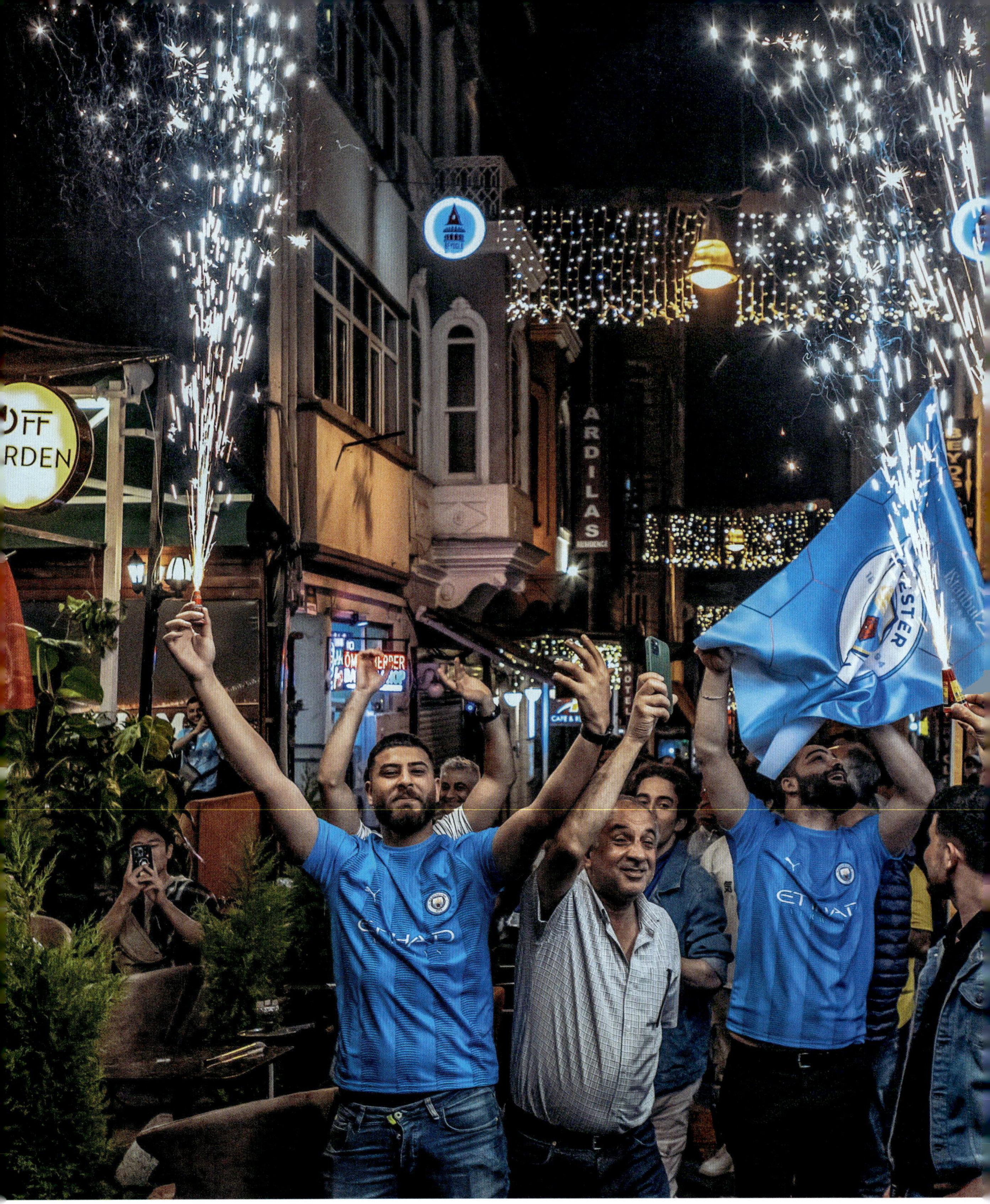
ARDILAS
ETIHAD

**48 HOURS IN ISTANBUL**

Rodrigo stepped on to it and there was an audible intake of breath. In a flash, the ball hit the back of the net and the crowd erupted.

By the time the match kicked off again, fans were strewn across each other in all directions.

The next 25 minutes or so was a living hell. Every Inter attack made my stomach sink and every Ederson save made my legs weak with relief.

With all of this happening at the other end of the pitch, there was a delay between match action and City fan reaction.

When the Brazilian made his final save of the night, it was the raised arms of City's players, not the referee's whistle, that triggered a collective release of emotion from all in the stands.

The remainder of the evening was an out-of-body experience. Players and staff celebrated on the pitch, Ilkay Gundogan lifted the trophy, thousands flooded out of the ground in a state of wonder and City were champions of Europe.

At moments like that, it's hard not to reflect on the journey to this point.

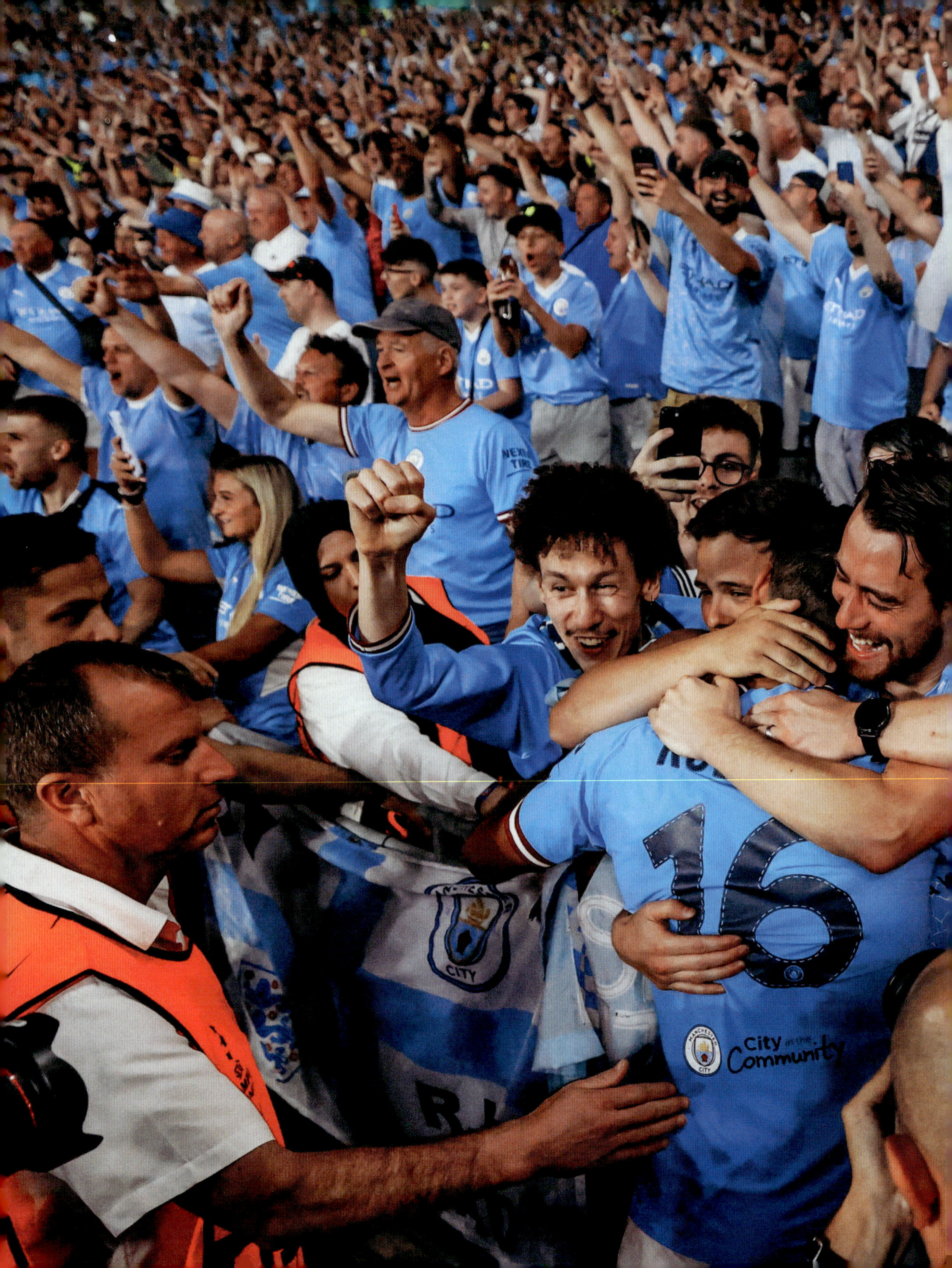
16
City in the Community
CITY

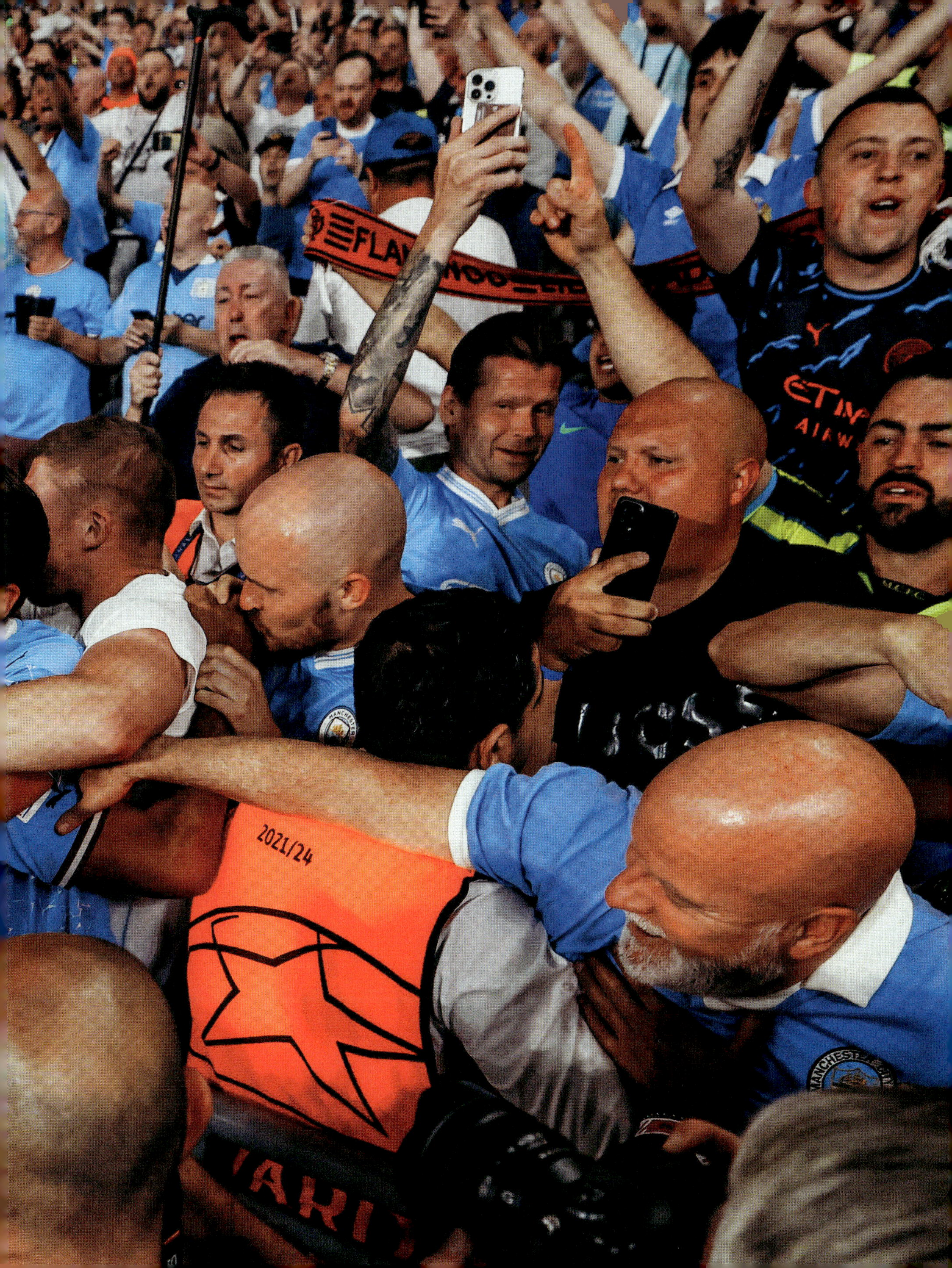
2021/24

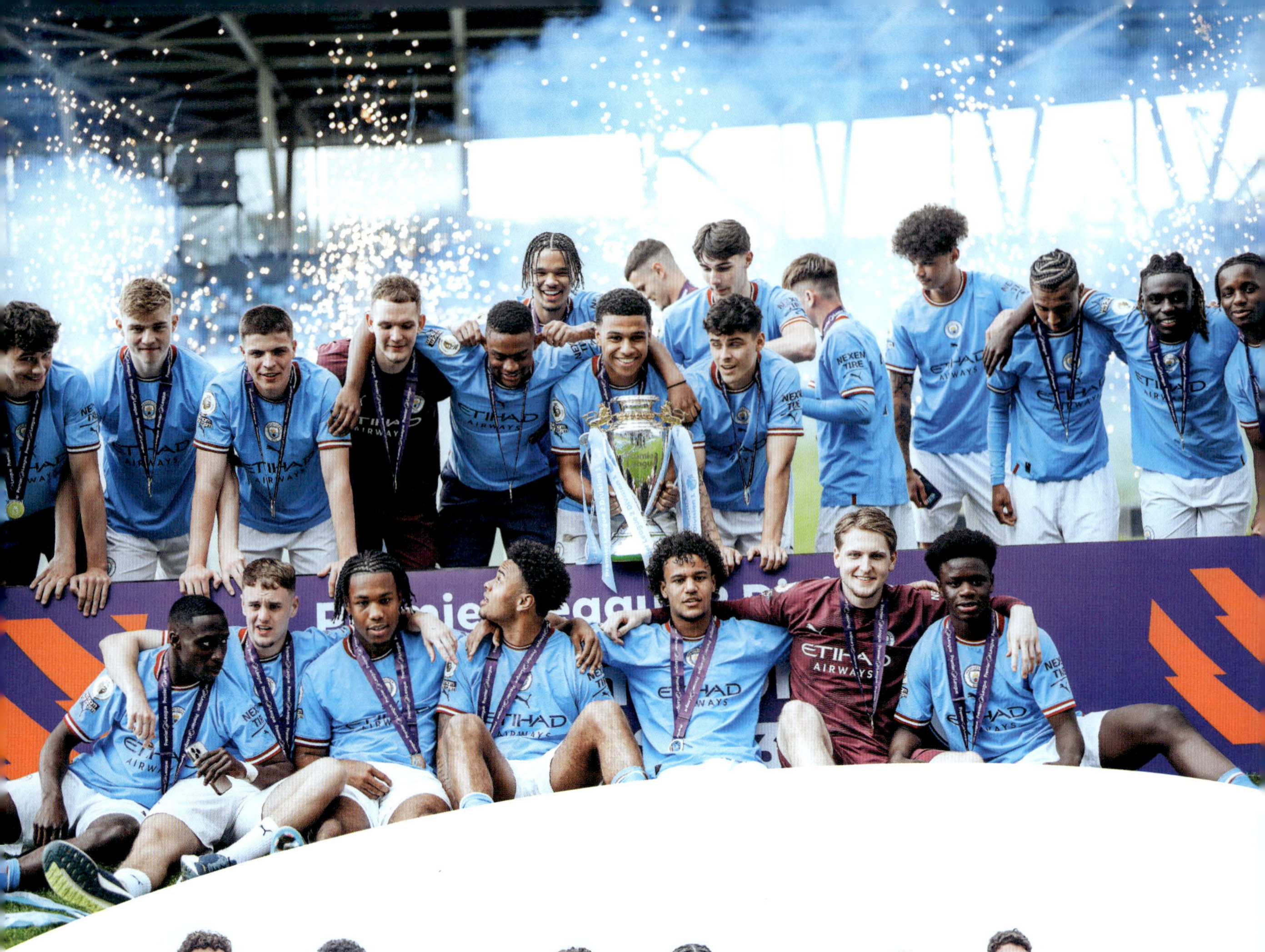
ETIHAD
AIRWAYS

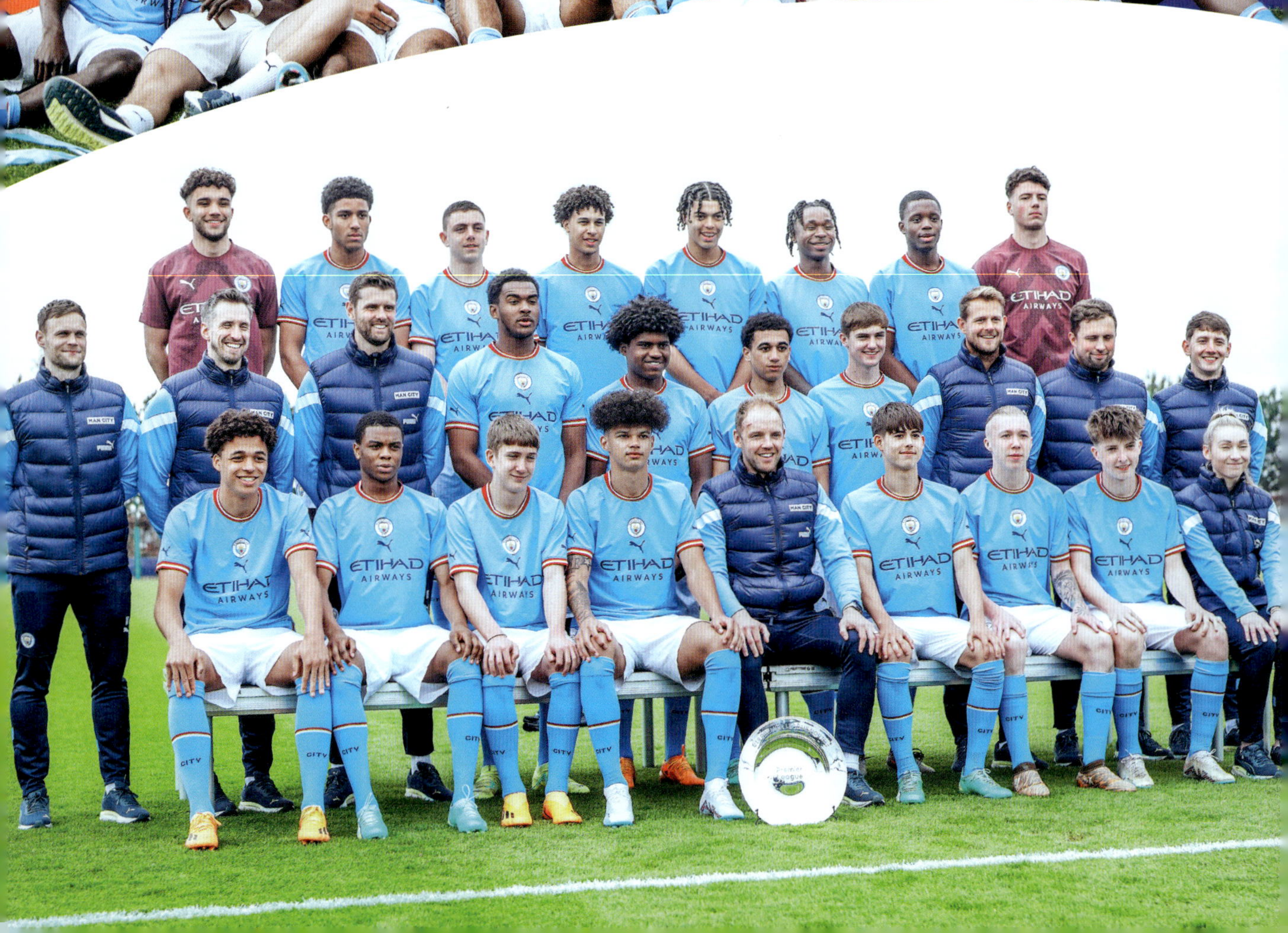
ETIHAD
AIRWAYS

# 6

## THE ACADEMY

# TREBLE
# TREBLE

**Wherever you looked across Manchester City during the momentous 2022/23 campaign, Treble was the defining word.**

For while Pep Guardiola's side took their rightful place amongst the all-time giants of the English and European game by claiming the ultimate Treble of Champions League, Premier League and FA Cup, the club's famed Academy also re-wrote the record books by securing two historic hat-tricks of their own.

At both Elite Development Squad and Under-18s level it was another quite extraordinary season by any measure.

Brian Barry-Murphy's exciting Under-21s arguably rose to even greater heights on the way to securing an unprecedented third consecutive Premier League 2 title – an achievement no side had ever managed before.

That feat was then mirrored by Ben Wilkinson's Under-18s who, after edging past Sunderland to secure a fourth straight regional title, overcame West Ham in a titanic national final held at the Etihad Stadium to claim a hat-trick of national crowns – again a Premier League first.

It represents a quite staggering and unprecedented haul of silverware.

However, it was the manner of our success that was arguably even more eye-catching – and satisfying.

Adhering to the fundamental core values of a beautiful brand of possession-based, attacking football that underpinned the approach of Guardiola's first team, City's Academy garnered widespread and deserved praise for the way we secured our latest successes.

At both Under-21 and Under-18 level, as well as filtering further down the age ranges, the City youngsters belied their youth by perfecting a blend of bewitching, beguiling and quite beautiful football.

TREBLE WINNERS

# ELITE DEVELOPMENT SQUAD

Appropriately enough, City's Elite Development Squad harnessed style alongside real substance in carving their names into the history books by sealing that third consecutive Premier League 2 title.

Brian Barry-Murphy's supremely talented group once again perfected the fiendish art of making the difficult look easy as we became the first side to ever win three straight PL2 crowns.

It was a memorable success built on City's overarching principles of a beguiling brand of football allied to a ferocious work ethic, relentless hunger to improve and all underpinned by a focus on the collective rather than the individual.

It was yet another magnificent achievement for our youngsters and one that capped a stunning second season at the helm for Barry-Murphy.

Appointed to the role in the summer of 2021 in succession to Enzo Maresca after our maiden PL2 title success in 2020/21, City's Under-21s have gone on to thrive under the former Rochdale manager's inspired leadership.

Our brand of exciting, possession-based attacking football saw the EDS squad motor on from strength to strength as the season progressed.

In his two years at the helm, Barry-Murphy has seen many of his players go on to make their first-team debuts, as well as further their football education by regularly training with Guardiola's squad.

Furthermore, three members of the EDS side – Northern Ireland's Shea Charles, Thomas Galvez of Finland and Australia's Alex Robertson – have all been capped at senior international level by their countries over the course of the past 12 months.

It was a new-look EDS squad that embarked upon the 2022/23 campaign, with several of the mainstays of the group which lifted the 2021/22 title either having left for new challenges elsewhere or departed on loan.

As a result, several members of last season's all-conquering Under-18s cohort were fast-tracked up to work alongside Barry-Murphy and his coaching team.

But though it may have been an even more youthful and largely inexperienced squad, the talent and technique that have been the bedrock of City's Academy set-up were evident from the get-go.

Having benefitted from the advice and input of John Stones, Ilkay Gundogan and Phil Foden, who had all accompanied the squad on a successful pre-season tour to Croatia, our Under-21s promptly hit the ground running with a superb 3-0 success at Liverpool on the opening day of the season.

That was the precursor to an impressive – and intense – run of fixtures which took the Under-21s through until the break for the World Cup finals in early November.

Barry-Murphy's side shoe-horned in 20 games in just over three months across the league, EFL Trophy and UEFA Youth League.

Though October saw us slip to losses at home to Blackburn and away to Everton, those twin setbacks proved the exception rather than the rule in the league, with City's class and consistency already earmarking us out as the side to beat once more.

And a quite remarkable 6-1 demolition derby success away at Manchester United in early November ensured we went into the World Cup break on a huge high.

Effervescent Portuguese winger Carlos Borges claimed his third hat-trick of the season at Leigh Sports Village in a campaign that would eventually net 29 goals in total and see him voted PL2 Player of the Season. It was the third straight year a City youngster had been handed the prize, with Borges following in the footsteps of previous winners James McAtee and Liam Delap.

Our success wasn't restricted to the league either.

## THE ACADEMY

Carlos Borges was named PL2 Player of the Season after netting 29 goals

*"It's not the winning that has impressed me – it's the way we have done it. The players and all the staff deserve to be congratulated on such a magnificent achievement"*

A superb UEFA Youth League group campaign saw the City youngsters go undefeated as we topped Group G to qualify for the knockout stages for the first time in four years, a stunning 5-1 win away at Sevilla establishing the template for our European progress.

And though our EFL Trophy hopes ended in the lottery of a penalty shootout defeat at Grimsby after a 1-1 draw, nothing could detract from the promise and panache of a superb 3-1 win away at a hugely experienced Derby earlier in the group stages.

A subsequent winter training camp in Agadir, Morocco, also proved a real catalyst in terms of further fostering and harnessing the already tight spirit and camaraderie within the Under-21s before many of the group, along with Barry-Murphy and his coaching staff, accompanied City's first team on a December warm-weather trip to Abu Dhabi.

Refreshed and refocused after those twin overseas trips, City regrouped in January eager to mirror the way our two earlier title triumphs had gathered New Year momentum in 2021 and 2022.

City more than answered the call.

Our first game back after a two-month break saw Barry-Murphy's side crush previously unbeaten league leaders Arsenal 6-0 at the Academy Stadium in a quite magnificent display.

The win saw us leapfrog the Gunners into top spot and from that point in, our Under-21s never looked back.

In the league, we put together a 10-game unbeaten run, featuring a 5-0 rout of high-flying Crystal Palace

www.mancity.com 237

## TREBLE WINNERS

in southeast London, a 6-0 home derby victory over Manchester United that neatly bookended our win earlier in the season, and a similarly impressive 5-1 triumph at West Ham.

By the time we had despatched Chelsea 3-1 at the Academy Stadium, that third title win was within our grasp.

And, appropriately enough, we sealed the deal in emphatic fashion, clinching the title with a dominant 3-0 success away at Blackburn Rovers in late April on a memorable weekend that also saw our youngsters claim the U18 Premier League North crown and City's first team reach the FA Cup final.

The only setback came in Europe in late February when, in front of a partisan 15,000 strong crowd in Croatia, we exited the UEFA Youth League 2-1 to Hajduk Split at the last-16 stage.

City could and arguably should have emerged victorious that afternoon but both Barry-Murphy and midfield playmaker Oscar Bobb, who enjoyed another superb campaign overall, spoke afterwards about how the lessons learned from that setback would only stand the players in good stead looking to the future.

In regards to our latest league success, on every metric City proved a class apart.

Our title triumph has also proved a real collective effort with every member of Barry-Murphy's squad making their own vital contribution to the cause, with 20 players either scoring or providing an assist.

Not surprisingly, the head coach was full of praise for his young charges as he looked back on a memorable 12 months.

"I said to the players it's not the winning that has impressed me – it's the way we have done it," Barry-Murphy asserted as he reflected on another season to savour.

"Winning the title again at Blackburn was an amazing day for the players and fitting reward for the work they have put in across the season.

"I have just been a big fan of the way we have played for much of the season.

"To play with such style in such an important game, when we won the title at Blackburn, was so impressive and some of our play that day was exhilarating.

"The players and all the staff deserve to be congratulated on such a magnificent achievement."

As Brian declared, it was a campaign that will live long in the collective memory.

And one that again saw the players demonstrate the very best of Manchester City.

**Party time in the dressing room after winning the title at Blackburn**

*Emilio Lawrence scored in the 8-0 win over Wolves, one of many thumping triumphs for our U18s*

# UNDER 18s

**In what was a Premier League Under-18 campaign of Grand National proportions, it was only fitting that Ben Wilkinson's Manchester City side once again emerged as the ultimate thoroughbreds.**

Taken at face value, one could be forgiven for thinking that a third successive and unprecedented National title merely represented business as usual as far as City were concerned.

However, this latest league success was anything but.

At regional level, Wilkinson's young charges were pushed all the way to the finishing line by a resolute and resilient Sunderland in what proved a thrilling and compelling battle for Under-18 North supremacy that went all the way to the penultimate weekend of the season.

That set the scene for a pulsating and eagerly awaited National showdown with a West Ham side that had married FA Youth Cup glory alongside their Southern title success.

Across 120 pulsating, pressure-filled minutes at the Etihad, the two best sides in England went toe to toe with Justin Oboavwoduo's second-half header deservedly drawing City level after the Hammers had taken a 30th minute lead. And with the rain lashing down at a spellbound Etihad, Oboavwoduo struck again on 102 minutes to compete a stunning turnaround and seal a historic third successive National title for the club.

The fact that City once again emerged victorious was not only a testament to the group's talent and technique.

It was also a resounding demonstration of the grit and guile that goes alongside raw talent in terms of the demands and disciplines that underpin City's Academy.

With several members of last season's national title-winning squad having been elevated up into our Under-21s, it meant an even younger look to this season's City group when the campaign kicked off.

City, though, soon demonstrated the same desire and drive that had characterised our three previous regional title triumphs.

After an opening day 2-2 draw away at Newcastle United, our Under-18s swiftly gained traction and momentum. A thrilling 4-3 win away at Liverpool was followed in October by successive 6-2 and 5-0 victories at home to Leeds and Blackburn respectively.

www.mancity.com 239

## TREBLE WINNERS

Justin Oboavwoduo (below) was one of the key players for U18s lead coach Ben Wilkinson (right)

*"We are very pleased with the way the season has gone but we always look at it that there is room for improvement. That, after all, is the essence of what this club stands for"*

The sole league setback was a 3-2 derby defeat to Manchester United – but City would ensure we gained revenge on our nearest neighbours later in the campaign.

In the Cup competitions, meanwhile, the autumn and winter were full of encouraging omens as we progressed through the group stages of the Under-18 Premier League Cup with aplomb and also motored through the gears in the early rounds of the FA Youth Cup.

Despite that encouraging first half of the campaign, however, for Wilkinson and his coaching staff the belief was that City had only scratched at the surface of our potential, with the head coach challenging the players to up the ante once we regrouped after the Christmas and New Year break.

It was Wilkinson's contention that City needed to harness our hunger, desire and work rate to even greater heights if we were to prevail.

"We asked all the players for a greater level of consistency at Christmas and greater maturity and understanding of what we are after," Wilkinson revealed.

To an individual, the group more than answered the call. From the 7 January restart, City embarked on a quite magnificent run of 13 consecutive league victories, the last of which was a 4-2 home win over Sunderland – a result which saw us overhaul the Wearsiders to claim the crown in quite fitting style.

Along the way there were several memorable and thumping triumphs including an eight-goal haul against Wolves, six strikes against Leeds United and 5-0 victories over Blackburn Rovers and Nottingham Forest.

City also served up more than a measure of revenge for that earlier derby defeat, gaining ample satisfaction with a crucial and deserved 3-1 win away at United.

Furthermore, skipper Nico O'Reilly scored two contenders for goal of the season, the first an outrageous injury-time scorpion kick which sealed a dramatic 2-1 win at Middlesbrough, before he then executed a quite breathtaking and audacious long-range chip in that victory at United.

Boasting the most potent attack and the steeliest defence in the Premier League North, few could deny we once again proved deserved regional champions.

And it set the scene for that dramatic and glorious

denouement with the Hammers' juniors.

The only twinges of regret for our Under-18s came in our exits from the Premier League Cup and FA Youth Cup at the quarter-final and semi-final stages respectively.

In both games – a 1-0 home loss to Spurs in the PL Cup and agonising 2-1 extra-time defeat away at Arsenal in the Youth Cup – Wilkinson's side found themselves reduced to 10 men early in the first half.

Despite that numerical impediment, in both games City could count ourselves desperately unlucky not to prevail.

"There have been so many positives but, inevitably, there have been a couple of bumps along the way," Ben reflected.

"In terms of the FA Youth Cup and Premier League Cup, we were a little bit disappointed that in both games we went down to 10 men in the first half and still could have won both games.

"So, there is still loads of learning as everyone has had their own individual journey. Some have flown since day one, others have had to navigate bumps in the road.

"Some will come out thinking they have had a great year; some may be a little disappointed, but their year may be next year.

"Looking at the bigger picture we are very pleased with the way the season has gone but we always look at it that there is room for improvement.

"That, after all, is the essence of what this club stands for and represents."

www.mancity.com 241

**LISTEN UP:**
Erling Haaland takes in his first City team talk from Pep Guardiola ahead of the Community Shield

## 7
### FIRST TEAM ON FILM

# BEHIND THE SCENES

**City were sensational on the pitch across 2022/23 – and the club's behind-the-scenes access was much the same too.**

The embedded first team film unit were with the players and staff every step of the way as they secured the Treble, capturing some incredible footage on their 4K cinema cameras.

To give you a flavour of what it's like to be up close and personal with the likes of Pep Guardiola, Erling Haaland and Jack Grealish, here are some exclusive digital stills taken from the video footage. They provide a true insight into what was a thrilling campaign.

## TREBLE WINNERS

**ALL EARS:**
Ilkay Gundogan, Erling Haaland and Jack Grealish wait for the boss to address them at half-time at West Ham, a game we eventually won 2-0

**PAYING THE PENALTY:**
Lorenzo Buenaventura listens intently as Ederson talks him through the decision to award a spot-kick against him in the 3-1 win at Arsenal

**TABLE TOPPER:**
Jack Grealish buzzing after the vital 3-1 victory at Arsenal, a result which returned us to the summit of the Premier League

BEHIND THE SCENES

**FOREST FRUSTRATION:**
Ilkay Gundogan can't hide his disappointment as he makes his way back to the dressing room following Nottingham Forest's late leveller at the City Ground

**RALLYING RUBEN:**
Ruben Dias hits the squad with an impassioned speech as they get set for the away game at Bournemouth

www.mancity.com 245

TREBLE WINNERS

**WATCHING BRIEF:**
Our away Champions League game against RB Leipzig in focus for City players and staff

BEHIND THE SCENES

**ON THE WAY BACK:**
Phil Foden returns to the CFA after recovering from appendix surgery

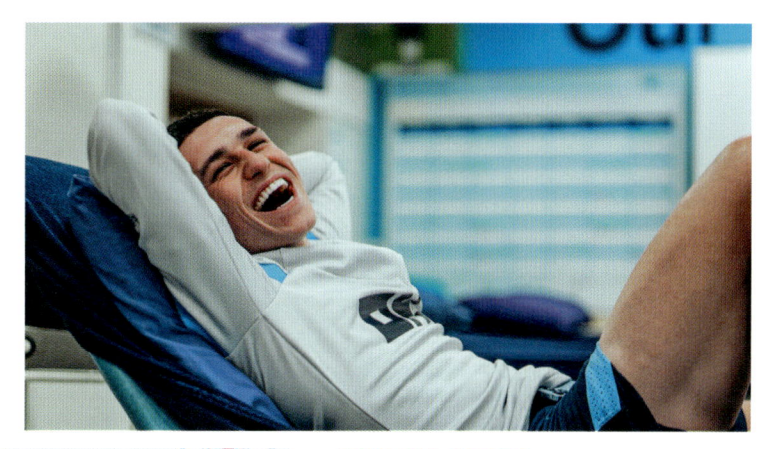

**SMILING SCOTT:**
Scott Carson waves to the cameras after an intense training session

**PREMIER LEAGUE GREATS:**
Pep Guardiola welcomes Thierry Henry to the CFA

www.mancity.com 247

TREBLE WINNERS

BEHIND THE SCENES

**BOSSING IT:**
When it comes to motivation, there's no one better in the game than Pep Guardiola

www.mancity.com 249

TREBLE WINNERS

**CENTRE OF ATTENTION:**
Aymeric Laporte keeps Jack Grealish amused as the pair prepare for action

**ALL SMILES:**
Ruben Dias enjoys a laugh off camera

BEHIND THE SCENES

## THE DEEP END:
Ilkay Gundogan takes a dip in the pool as he takes a break from action on the pitch

www.mancity.com 251

TREBLE WINNERS

**THE BOSS:**
Pep Guardiola deep in thought as he watches on in training

**SMILING STONES:**
John Stones takes a break from his phone to pose for the cameras

**IN STITCHES:**
Kyle Walker can't hold back as he enjoys the dressing room banter at the CFA

BEHIND THE SCENES

**GENTLEMAN JACK:**
Jack Grealish takes time out from training to talk to young fans at the CFA

**FOLLOWER OF FASHION:**
Kyle Walker gets set to give his verdict on Ruben Dias's gear as they talk fashion in the dressing room

www.mancity.com 253

TREBLE WINNERS

**QUALITY QUARTET:**
Kalvin Phillips, Erling Haaland, Manuel Akanji and Kevin De Bruyne enjoy some downtime in the dressing room

BEHIND THE SCENES

www.mancity.com 255

## TREBLE WINNERS

**GREEN FINGERS:**
Everything in the City garden is rosy as John Stones waters a Bonsai tree at the CFA

**DIFFERENT GRAVY:**
It's thirsty work as Jack Grealish enjoys a hot cup of Bovril

**SMILE SAYS IT ALL:**
Riyad Mahrez can't contain his delight as Arsenal are defeated by Nottingham Forest, securing the Premier League for City in the process

BEHIND THE SCENES

### PEP TALK:
With the Premier League secured, Pep Guardiola offers words of wisdom to the team ahead of the FA Cup final

### SLIDE AWAY:
Kitman Brandon Ashton flies across the dressing room floor as the team celebrate lifting the Premier League

www.mancity.com 257

TREBLE WINNERS

**YES BOSS:**
Pep Guardiola offers words of encouragement to Jack Grealish at half-time during the FA Cup final

BEHIND THE SCENES

**PHIL ON CLOUD NINE:**
Phil Foden can't believe it after watching Ilkay Gundogan opening the scoring after 12 seconds in the FA Cup final

**HEAD START:**
We've always said Ederson is head and shoulders above any goalkeeper in the game!

**DE BRUYNE DELIGHT:**
Kevin De Bruyne has a moment to reflect on the team's FA Cup final win over Manchester United at Wembley Stadium

www.mancity.com 259

TREBLE WINNERS

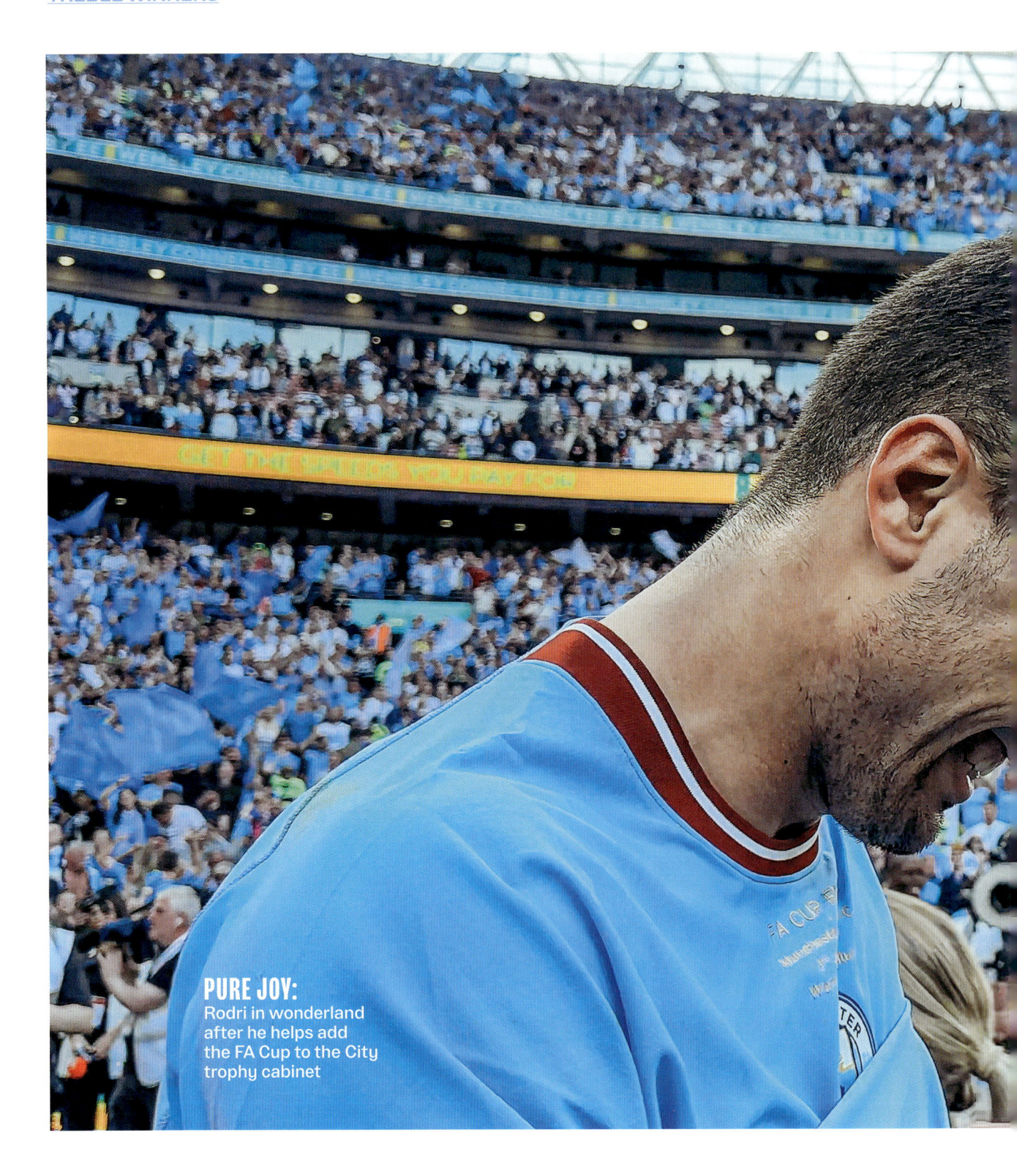

**PURE JOY:**
Rodri in wonderland after he helps add the FA Cup to the City trophy cabinet

BEHIND THE SCENES

www.mancity.com 261

TREBLE WINNERS

**EYE SPY:**
After having his eyes on the prize in the 90 minutes at Wembley, Ederson turns his attention to the crowd after the FA Cup final win over Manchester United

BEHIND THE SCENES

**FAN FERVOUR:**
Ederson, Phil Foden, Nathan Ake, Rico Lewis and Bernardo Silva celebrate in front of delighted supporters after our FA Cup win over Manchester United

**DOUBLE ACT:**
Good friends Erling Haaland and Jack Grealish pose with the FA Cup trophy after the 2-1 victory over Manchester United

www.mancity.com 263

TREBLE WINNERS

**CROWNING GLORY:**
Kevin De Bruyne lets his hair down in the Wembley Stadium dressing room after our FA Cup final victory

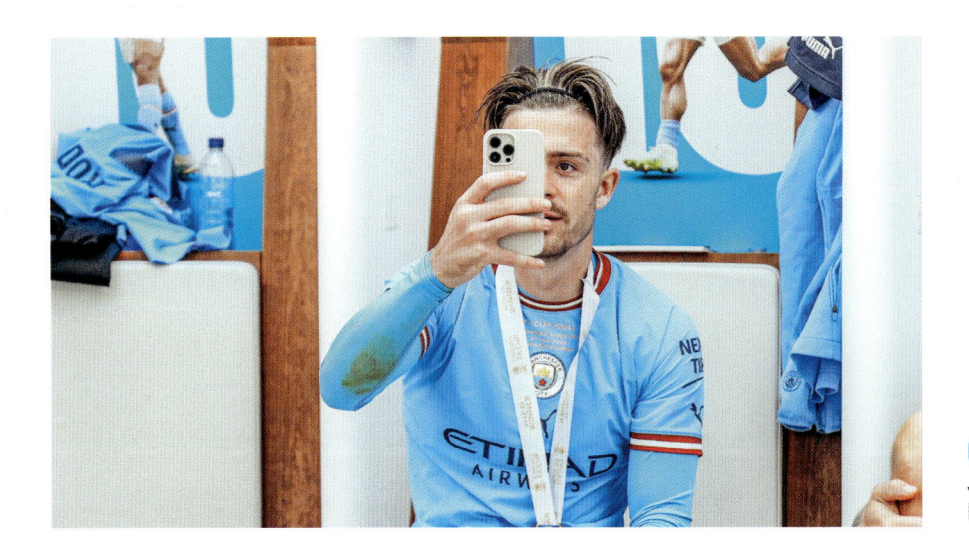

**CALL THE SHOTS:**
Just a quick call to say I'm an FA Cup winner

BEHIND THE SCENES

### CALM AFTER THE STORM:
Manager Pep Guardiola enjoys a moment of peace with the FA Cup trophy after our final win over Manchester United

### DRINK IT IN
Winning the FA Cup final is thirsty work for Ederson

TREBLE WINNERS

**BEHIND THE SCENES**

**CHILLING OUT:**
Erling Haaland and kitman Brandon Ashton take a breather from the big build-up ahead of the Champions League final

## TREBLE WINNERS

**RALLYING CALL:**
Captain Ilkay Gundogan offers motivational words to his team-mates ahead of the Champions League final

**TALKING TACTICS:**
Nathan Ake and Rodri discuss their responsibilities ahead of the Champions League final

**EMOTIONAL ENDING:**
Rodrigo can't contain his delight on the final whistle at the Ataturk Olympic Stadium as City win our first-ever Champions League trophy

268 www.mancity.com

BEHIND THE SCENES

**PITCH PERFECT:**
Jack Grealish can't quite believe he's a European champion as City players and staff celebrate on the pitch at the Ataturk Olympic Stadium

TREBLE WINNERS

**PIZZA THE ACTION:**
Jack Grealish samples some Italian cuisine as he poses with the Champions League trophy

BEHIND THE SCENES

**DRINK UP:**
Cheers to John Stones as he enjoys a beer in the aftermath of our Champions League final win over Inter

WINNERS
UEFA CHAMPIONS LEAGUE 2022/2023
DE BRUYNE
17
GREALISH
10
25
20
Istanbul 23
FINAL

# 8
## STATISTICS

# RECORDS & MILESTONES

**City are just the second English club to have won the ultimate Treble in the men's game.**

Pep Guardiola's side have been consistently attaining excellence throughout the Catalan's seven years at the Etihad Stadium.

There were the Centurions, the first and only side to reach 100 Premier League points, and the Fourmidables, named so after lifting all four domestic trophies in the same campaign.

However, with one of the rarest achievements in club football, a new height has been reached.

A third straight Premier League success was testament enough to our relentless will to win.

But it was topped off by victories in the first ever all-Manchester major final and then on that unforgettable night in Istanbul.

Here are some of records and milestones set by a very special City side…

TREBLE WINNERS

## OUR PLACE IN HISTORY

**It is only the tenth occasion a European side has won a Treble – when defined as the European Cup plus the nation's top-flight league title and leading cup competition.**

City join Celtic (1967), Ajax (1972), PSV Eindhoven (1988), Manchester United (1999), Barcelona (2009 and 2015), Inter Milan (2010) and Bayern Munich (2013 and 2020).

We are only the fifth club in the history of English football to win three top-flight titles in a row after Huddersfield Town (1924-1926), Arsenal (1933-1935), Liverpool (1982-1984) and Manchester United (1999-2001 & 2007-2009).

We start the 2023/24 campaign with the target of becoming the first club in history to win the English top flight four years in succession.

In terms of the Premier League since Guardiola's arrival, we have accrued 625 points – which is 50 better than the next best and 136 more than third best.

The trophies mean there is now 119 years between the club's first major trophy triumph (the 1904 FA Cup) and our last, which represents the second longest gap between wins in English football behind Liverpool's 121 years (1901-2022).

Our seventh FA Cup success means we have extended the record for the longest time between a club's first FA Cup win and most recent, having already held this honour following our 2019 success.

Ilkay Gundogan's first volley on that sunny Wembley day is now the speediest goal in FA Cup final history, coming after just 12.91 seconds.

**5**
City are only the fifth club in the history of English football to lift three top-flight titles in a row after Huddersfield (1924-1926), Arsenal (1933-1935), Liverpool (1982-1984) and Manchester United (1999-2001 & 2007-2009)

**12.91**
The time it took for Ilkay Gundogan to score at Wembley, the fastest in FA Cup final history

RECORDS & MILESTONES

## GUARDIOLA'S STANDING IN THE GAME

**The Champions League final also marked our manager's 300th win as City boss.**

Pep Guardiola is the driving force behind our incredible achievements of recent seasons and the mastermind that has taken us to the summit of European football.

His 300 victories as City boss have come in just 413 competitive fixtures, surpassing the previous English record, shared by former Arsenal manager Arsene Wenger and Liverpool boss Bob Paisley, by 102 matches.

Our 4-0 semi-final second leg victory over Real Madrid saw him become the quickest manager to achieve 100 Champions League wins.

The Catalan took just 160 matches as a boss in the competition to reach the total, faster than previous record holder Carlo Ancelotti, who took 180 games to get to three figures.

In fact, Guardiola is only the third manager to reach the landmark, with Sir Alex Ferguson the first to do it after 184 fixtures.

Already the most successful manager in City's history, he has now lifted 14 major honours with the club.

Having only been in England seven seasons, his five league titles makes him the joint-fourth most successful manager in English history, pulling level with the likes of Matt Busby and Tom Watson, who managed on these shores significantly longer than Guardiola has.

His third Champions League success places him joint-second in the list of the most successful managers in European Cup history – only one behind current record holder Ancelotti.

He boasts an astonishing win percentage of over 73% during his time at City since taking the reins ahead of the 2016/17 campaign.

During that time, we've found the net 1,015 times, at an average of just under 2.5 per match, conceding just 336 in the process.

It means that, under the Catalan's guidance, City boast a remarkable goal difference of +679.

**100**
Our 4-0 victory over Real Madrid in the semi-final second leg gave Pep Guardiola his 100th Champions League win, making him the quickest manager to reach the landmark

**OVER 73%**
Pep Guardiola's astonishing win percentage during his time at City

TREBLE WINNERS

**36**

The number of goals scored by Erling Haaland is the most in a Premier League season

## HAALAND'S SENSATIONAL START

**Erling Haaland's first season at Manchester City will be hard to match.**

The winner of the Premier League and Champions League Golden Boot has already surpassed many of the greatest goal scorers we have previously seen in English football in a number of ways.

He was selected as the Etihad Player of the Season, Premier League Player of the Season, Premier League Young Player of the Season and FWA Men's Footballer of the Year. He was also included in the Champions League Team of the Season.

The Norwegian's 36 Premier League strikes is the most in the history of the competition – edging out the 34 hit by Andrew Cole in 1993/94 and Alan Shearer in 1994/95 when the league comprised of 42 games.

In fact, his 52 goals across all competitions is the most ever scored by a player at a Premier League club.

His record of a goal every 77 minutes is the best of any player in Premier League history, while his tally of six hat-tricks in all competitions was as many as every other Premier League player combined last season.

It took him just 19 matches to reach four Premier League hat-tricks, eclipsing the previous record of Ruud van Nistelrooy, who took 65 games.

After 12 in this campaign, he now has 35 goals in 30 Champions League nights. Still just 22 at the end of the season, he was the youngest player and the quickest in terms of matches to hit 35 goals in Europe's elite competition.

## DE BRUYNE SMASHES ASSISTS RECORD

**With a cross for Haaland in the 4-1 win over Southampton in April, Kevin De Bruyne broke new ground for Premier League playmakers.**

The Belgian has consistently set the standards throughout Guardiola's time in Manchester, and is recognised by many as a true Premier League great.

This latest moment of genius saw him reach 100 Premier League assists in just 237 matches.

That is 56 games faster than previous quickest Cesc Fabregas, who took 293 fixtures to register 100 assists.

He is just the fifth player in the Premier League era to reach triple figures, after Ryan Giggs, Fabregas, Wayne Rooney and Frank Lampard.

### 28

The number of assists for Kevin De Bruyne across all competitions, putting him at the top of the charts for assists for any player in Europe's top-five leagues

**TREBLE WINNERS**

# CITY'S 2022/23 STATS BY COMPETITION

**Winning a Treble is the culmination of almost a year's hard graft.**

While the two finals and our decisive Premier League fixtures will live long in the memory, it was the collective effort throughout the season that put us in the position to enjoy those moments.

Pep Guardiola's City sides keep coming back for more, that's what has made us such a relentless winning machine under the guidance of the Catalan.

We have now lifted 14 major trophies since Guardiola arrived at the Etihad in 2016, comprising five Premier Leagues, four League Cups, two FA Cups, two Community Shields and that unforgettable Champions League victory.

Our 2022/23 campaign saw us set the standard in England and across Europe.

Here we explore the numbers behind that dominance...

**2.34**
Our points-per-game average in the Premier League

## A SEASON SUMMARY

Given our deep runs to FA Cup and Champions League success, City had to play a gruelling 61 games in 2022/23.

We won 44 of those, a figure which has only been reached six times by an English club. Four of those six occasions have all been achieved by a Guardiola City side.

Until the last day of the Premier League season, we had reached 25 consecutive games unbeaten across all competitions.

Across every game City played last season, we averaged 63.6% possession of the ball, completing 35,142 passes and plundering a whopping 151 goals in all competitions, just shy of 2.5 per game.

Rodrigo was our most used player throughout the campaign, appearing in 56 matches for a total of 4,478 minutes.

Only Ederson and Erling Haaland also registered more than 4,000 minutes on the pitch in total, while five players played at least 50 times.

RECORDS & MILESTONES

TREBLE WINNERS

**625**

Our total number of Premier League points in Pep Guardiola's time in charge. Liverpool have the next most, with 575

**96**

The number of goals we scored in the Premier League. We only failed to score in three league games

## PREMIER LEAGUE

City won 28 of our 38 games this season, totalling 84 of our 89 points – handing us a fantastic 73% win ratio.

Our points-per-game average stood at 2.34.

Our 89 points is the joint-ninth highest points tally for a Premier League campaign – a list we already feature three times on for our Centurions season in 2017/18, 98 points total in 2018/19 and 93 recorded in 2021/22.

That means across Guardiola's seven seasons in England we have totalled a staggering 625 points, ahead of Liverpool, who have gained 575 in that time.

We averaged a total of 65.2% possession in each Premier League match last term and we scored a whopping 94 goals across our 38 top-flight fixtures, averaging 2.47 goals per game.

Erling Haaland's sensational maiden season at the Etihad Stadium saw him score 36 league goals.

The Norwegian finished six ahead of Tottenham Hotspur's Harry Kane and made him the third City player to win the Golden Boot.

By doing so he set a new record for most goals in a single campaign, going beyond Alan Shearer and Andrew Cole's hauls of 34 in 1993/94 and 1994/95 respectively.

Kevin De Bruyne was awarded the Playmaker of the Year award for a third time and remains the only player to win it more than once.

He did so after contributing 16 assists – the most across the entirety of the division.

Our longest winning run of the campaign saw us record 12 successive triumphs, starting with a 4-1 away success at Bournemouth in February and ending with a 1-0 win over Chelsea at home in May.

RECORDS & MILESTONES

## FA CUP

This was the second time we completed a league and FA Cup double, following a similar achievement in 2018/19 when City also lifted the Carabao Cup to become the only club to win the domestic treble.

Our superb defensive form saw us reach the final without conceding but a first-half Manchester United penalty at Wembley meant we went 483 minutes before being breached.

Ilkay Gundogan's sensational volley to start the scoring was clocked at 12.91 seconds, making it the fastest goal in FA Cup final history.

It beat the previous record in a final held by Everton's Louis Saha, who scored after just 25 seconds in the 2009 final against Chelsea.

His second volley meant he became the first player to score twice from outside the box in a single FA Cup final since 1963.

In total, our 19 goals across six games was the best in the competition – with Wrexham and Grimsby Town's 15 the nearest.

Riyad Mahrez was our top scorer with five goals – largely thanks to City's first-ever Wembley hat-trick in the semi-final victory over Sheffield United. Kevin De Bruyne's four assists made him the joint-most creative player in the tournament.

Stefan Ortega Moreno's five clean sheets en route to the final meant he led that metric amongst all goalkeepers.

**30**

The number of FA Cup matches Pep Guardiola has won, making him our most successful manager in the competition

www.mancity.com 281

## TREBLE WINNERS

**32**
The number of goals we scored in the Champions League, the best in the tournament by six

**12**
The number of Champions League goals for Erling Haaland, equalling the best ever total by a player for an English club

**5**
Erling Haaland became just the third player to hit five goals in one match, against RB Leipzig at the Etihad

## CHAMPIONS LEAGUE

Coming 53 years after we won our only previous European trophy, the 1970 Cup Winners' Cup, City wrote the best moment in our history when it comes to continental football.

We won eight of our 13 matches in the competition, drawing the other five.

City's 32 goals across our 13 matches was the best in the tournament by six, coming from a total of 201 shots on goal.

Erling Haaland won the Golden Boot with 12 finishes, equalling the best-ever total by a player for an English club and setting the record for a City player.

He became only the third player to hit five in one match in the special Round of 16 defeat of RB Leipzig at the Etihad Stadium.

Kevin De Bruyne's seven assists was the most in the tournament, one ahead of Real Madrid winger Vinicius Junior.

The Blues conceded only five goals across the whole tournament. That's the best in the competition and made even more impressive when you take into account that City played the joint-most games.

Ederson played 11 of the matches, making 26 saves during that time, including vital interventions in the closing stages of the final. Our eight clean sheets was the joint best with finalists Inter.

City's 8,224 passes across our 13 games was the most in the competition. Rodrigo's 905 completed passes led the way, with 145 of those breaking the lines of the opposition.

RECORDS & MILESTONES

www.mancity.com 283

TREBLE WINNERS

# PREMIER LEAGUE

### August
| | | | | |
|---|---|---|---|---|
| 07.08.2022 | West Ham United | 0 | 2 | Manchester City |
| 13.08.2022 | Manchester City | 4 | 0 | Bournemouth |
| 21.08.2022 | Newcastle United | 3 | 3 | Manchester City |
| 27.08.2022 | Manchester City | 4 | 2 | Crystal Palace |
| 31.08.2022 | Manchester City | 6 | 0 | Nottingham Forest |

### September
| | | | | |
|---|---|---|---|---|
| 03.09.2022 | Aston Villa | 1 | 1 | Manchester City |
| 17.09.2022 | Wolves | 0 | 3 | Manchester City |

### October
| | | | | |
|---|---|---|---|---|
| 02.10.2022 | Manchester City | 6 | 3 | Manchester United |
| 08.10.2022 | Manchester City | 4 | 0 | Southampton |
| 16.10.2022 | Liverpool | 1 | 0 | Manchester City |
| 22.10.2022 | Manchester City | 3 | 1 | Brighton |
| 29.10.2022 | Leicester City | 0 | 1 | Manchester City |

### November
| | | | | |
|---|---|---|---|---|
| 05.11.2022 | Manchester City | 2 | 1 | Fulham |
| 12.11.2022 | Manchester City | 1 | 2 | Brentford |

### December
| | | | | |
|---|---|---|---|---|
| 28.12.2022 | Leeds United | 1 | 3 | Manchester City |
| 31.12.2022 | Manchester City | 1 | 1 | Everton |

### January
| | | | | |
|---|---|---|---|---|
| 05.01.2023 | Chelsea | 0 | 1 | Manchester City |
| 14.01.2023 | Manchester United | 2 | 1 | Manchester City |
| 19.01.2023 | Manchester City | 4 | 2 | Tottenham Hotspur |
| 22.01.2023 | Manchester City | 3 | 0 | Wolves |

### February
| | | | | |
|---|---|---|---|---|
| 05.02.2023 | Tottenham Hotspur | 1 | 0 | Manchester City |
| 12.02.2023 | Manchester City | 3 | 1 | Bournemouth |
| 15.02.2023 | Arsenal | 1 | 3 | Manchester City |
| 18.02.2023 | Nottingham Forest | 1 | 1 | Manchester City |
| 25.02.2023 | Bournemouth | 1 | 4 | Manchester City |

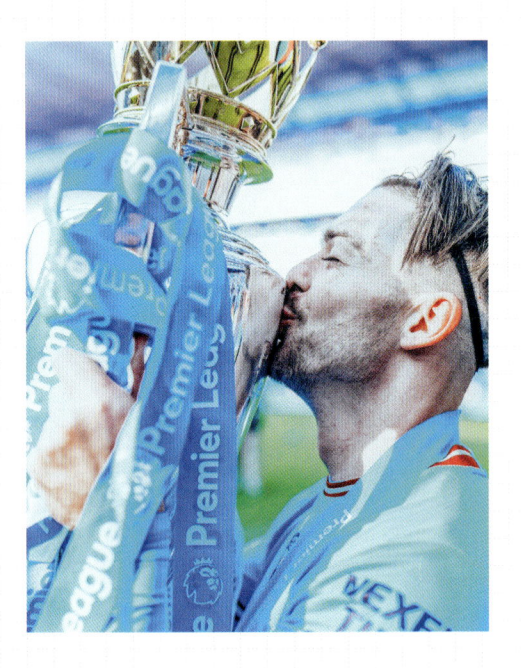

### March
| | | | | |
|---|---|---|---|---|
| 04.03.2023 | Manchester City | 2 | 0 | Newcastle United |
| 11.03.2023 | Crystal Palace | 0 | 1 | Manchester City |

### April
| | | | | |
|---|---|---|---|---|
| 01.04.2023 | Manchester City | 4 | 1 | Liverpool |
| 08.04.2023 | Southampton | 1 | 4 | Manchester City |
| 15.04.2023 | Manchester City | 3 | 1 | Leicester City |
| 26.04.2023 | Manchester City | 4 | 1 | Arsenal |
| 30.04.2023 | Fulham | 1 | 2 | Manchester City |

### May
| | | | | |
|---|---|---|---|---|
| 03.05.2023 | Manchester City | 3 | 0 | West Ham United |
| 06.05.2023 | Manchester City | 2 | 1 | Leeds United |
| 14.05.2023 | Everton | 0 | 3 | Manchester City |
| 21.05.2023 | Manchester City | 1 | 0 | Chelsea |
| 24.05.2023 | Brighton | 1 | 1 | Manchester City |
| 28.05.2023 | Brentford | 1 | 0 | Manchester City |

## RECORDS & MILESTONES

| | | P | **HOME** W | D | L | F | A | **AWAY** W | D | L | F | A | GD | PTS |
|---|---|---|---|---|---|---|---|---|---|---|---|---|---|---|
| 1 | Manchester City | 38 | 17 | 1 | 1 | 60 | 17 | 11 | 4 | 4 | 34 | 16 | +61 | 89 (C) |
| 2 | Arsenal | 38 | 14 | 3 | 2 | 53 | 25 | 12 | 3 | 4 | 35 | 18 | +45 | 84 |
| 3 | Manchester United | 38 | 15 | 3 | 1 | 36 | 10 | 8 | 3 | 8 | 22 | 33 | +15 | 75 |
| 4 | Newcastle United | 38 | 11 | 6 | 2 | 36 | 14 | 8 | 8 | 3 | 32 | 19 | +35 | 71 |
| 5 | Liverpool | 38 | 13 | 5 | 1 | 46 | 17 | 6 | 5 | 8 | 29 | 30 | +28 | 67 |
| 6 | Brighton & Hove Albion | 38 | 10 | 4 | 5 | 37 | 21 | 8 | 4 | 7 | 35 | 32 | +19 | 62 |
| 7 | Aston Villa | 38 | 12 | 2 | 5 | 33 | 21 | 6 | 5 | 8 | 18 | 25 | +5 | 61 |
| 8 | Tottenham Hotspur | 38 | 12 | 1 | 6 | 37 | 25 | 6 | 5 | 8 | 33 | 38 | +7 | 60 |
| 9 | Brentford | 38 | 10 | 7 | 2 | 35 | 18 | 5 | 7 | 7 | 23 | 28 | +12 | 59 |
| 10 | Fulham | 38 | 8 | 5 | 6 | 31 | 29 | 7 | 2 | 10 | 24 | 24 | +2 | 52 |
| 11 | Crystal Palace | 38 | 7 | 7 | 5 | 21 | 23 | 4 | 5 | 10 | 19 | 26 | -9 | 45 |
| 12 | Chelsea | 38 | 6 | 7 | 6 | 20 | 19 | 5 | 4 | 10 | 18 | 28 | -9 | 44 |
| 13 | Wolverhampton Wanderers | 38 | 9 | 3 | 7 | 19 | 20 | 2 | 5 | 12 | 12 | 38 | -27 | 41 |
| 14 | West Ham United | 38 | 8 | 4 | 7 | 26 | 24 | 3 | 3 | 13 | 16 | 31 | -13 | 40 |
| 15 | Bournemouth | 38 | 6 | 4 | 9 | 20 | 28 | 5 | 2 | 12 | 17 | 43 | -34 | 39 |
| 16 | Nottingham Forest | 38 | 8 | 6 | 5 | 27 | 24 | 1 | 5 | 13 | 11 | 44 | -30 | 38 |
| 17 | Everton | 38 | 6 | 3 | 10 | 16 | 27 | 2 | 9 | 8 | 18 | 30 | -23 | 36 |
| 18 | Leicester City | 38 | 5 | 4 | 10 | 23 | 27 | 4 | 3 | 12 | 28 | 41 | -17 | 34 (R) |
| 19 | Leeds United | 38 | 5 | 7 | 7 | 26 | 37 | 2 | 3 | 14 | 22 | 41 | -30 | 31 (R) |
| 20 | Southampton | 38 | 2 | 5 | 12 | 19 | 37 | 4 | 2 | 13 | 17 | 36 | -37 | 25 (R) |

### PREMIER LEAGUE APPEARANCES

| | | | | |
|---|---|---|---|---|
| Rodrigo | 36 | Ruben Dias | 26 |
| Ederson | 35 | Nathan Ake | 26 |
| Erling Haaland | 35 | John Stones | 23 |
| Bernardo Silva | 34 | Joao Cancelo | 17 |
| Kevin De Bruyne | 32 | Rico Lewis | 14 |
| Phil Foden | 32 | Cole Palmer | 14 |
| Ilkay Gundogan | 31 | Sergio Gomez | 12 |
| Julian Alvarez | 31 | Aymeric Laporte | 12 |
| Riyad Mahrez | 30 | Kalvin Phillips | 12 |
| Manuel Akanji | 29 | Stefan Ortega | 3 |
| Jack Grealish | 28 | Maximo Perrone | 1 |
| Kyle Walker | 27 | Shea Charles | 1 |

### PREMIER LEAGUE GOALS

| | |
|---|---|
| Erling Haaland | 36 |
| Phil Foden | 11 |
| Julian Alvarez | 9 |
| Ilkay Gundogan | 8 |
| Kevin De Bruyne | 7 |
| Riyad Mahrez | 5 |
| Jack Grealish | 5 |
| Bernardo Silva | 4 |
| Rodrigo | 2 |
| John Stones | 2 |
| Joao Cancelo | 2 |
| Nathan Ake | 1 |

TREBLE WINNERS

# CHAMPIONS LEAGUE

| GROUP G | P | W | D | L | F | A | GD | PTS |
|---|---|---|---|---|---|---|---|---|
| Manchester City | 6 | 4 | 2 | 0 | 14 | 2 | 12 | 14 |
| Borussia Dortmund | 6 | 2 | 3 | 1 | 10 | 5 | 5 | 9 |
| Sevilla | 6 | 1 | 2 | 3 | 6 | 12 | -6 | 5 |
| FC Copenhagen | 6 | 0 | 3 | 3 | 1 | 12 | -11 | 3 |

| Date | Home | | | Away |
|---|---|---|---|---|
| **Group stage matchday 1** | | | | |
| 06.09.2022 | Sevilla | 0 | 4 | Manchester City |
| **Group stage matchday 2** | | | | |
| 14.09.2022 | Manchester City | 2 | 1 | Borussia Dortmund |
| **Group stage matchday 3** | | | | |
| 05.10.2022 | Manchester City | 5 | 0 | FC Copenhagen |
| **Group stage matchday 4** | | | | |
| 11.10.2022 | FC Copenhagen | 0 | 0 | Manchester City |
| **Group stage matchday 5** | | | | |
| 25.10.2022 | Borussia Dortmund | 0 | 0 | Manchester City |
| **Group stage matchday 6** | | | | |
| 02.11.2022 | Manchester City | 3 | 1 | Sevilla |
| **Round of 16 First Leg** | | | | |
| 22.02.2023 | RB Leipzig | 1 | 1 | Manchester City |
| **Round of 16 Second Leg** | | | | |
| 14.03.2023 | Manchester City | 7 | 0 | RB Leipzig |
| **Quarter Final First Leg** | | | | |
| 11.04.2023 | Manchester City | 3 | 0 | Bayern Munich |
| **Quarter Final Second Leg** | | | | |
| 19.04.2023 | Bayern Munich | 1 | 1 | Manchester City |
| **Semi Final First Leg** | | | | |
| 09.05.2023 | Real Madrid | 1 | 1 | Manchester City |
| **Semi Final Second Leg** | | | | |
| 17.05.2023 | Manchester City | 4 | 0 | Real Madrid |
| **Final** | | | | |
| 10.06.2023 | Manchester City | 1 | 0 | Inter |

## CHAMPIONS LEAGUE APPEARANCES

| | |
|---|---|
| Ilkay Gundogan | 13 |
| Jack Grealish | 13 |
| Bernardo Silva | 13 |
| Ruben Dias | 12 |
| Rodrigo | 12 |
| Ederson | 11 |
| Manuel Akanji | 11 |
| Erling Haaland | 11 |
| Julian Alvarez | 10 |
| Kevin De Bruyne | 10 |
| Riyad Mahrez | 9 |
| Phil Foden | 8 |
| Nathan Ake | 8 |
| John Stones | 8 |
| Joao Cancelo | 6 |
| Sergio Gomez | 5 |
| Kyle Walker | 5 |
| Cole Palmer | 4 |
| Aymeric Laporte | 4 |
| Kalvin Phillips | 3 |
| Stefan Ortega | 2 |
| Rico Lewis | 2 |
| Josh Wilson-Esbrand | 2 |

## CHAMPIONS LEAGUE GOALS

| | |
|---|---|
| Erling Haaland | 12 |
| Riyad Mahrez | 3 |
| Bernardo Silva | 3 |
| Julian Alvarez | 3 |
| Rodrigo | 2 |
| Kevin De Bruyne | 2 |
| Ilkay Gundogan | 1 |
| Ruben Dias | 1 |
| Rico Lewis | 1 |
| Manuel Akanji | 1 |
| Phil Foden | 1 |
| John Stones | 1 |

## RECORDS & MILESTONES

# FA CUP

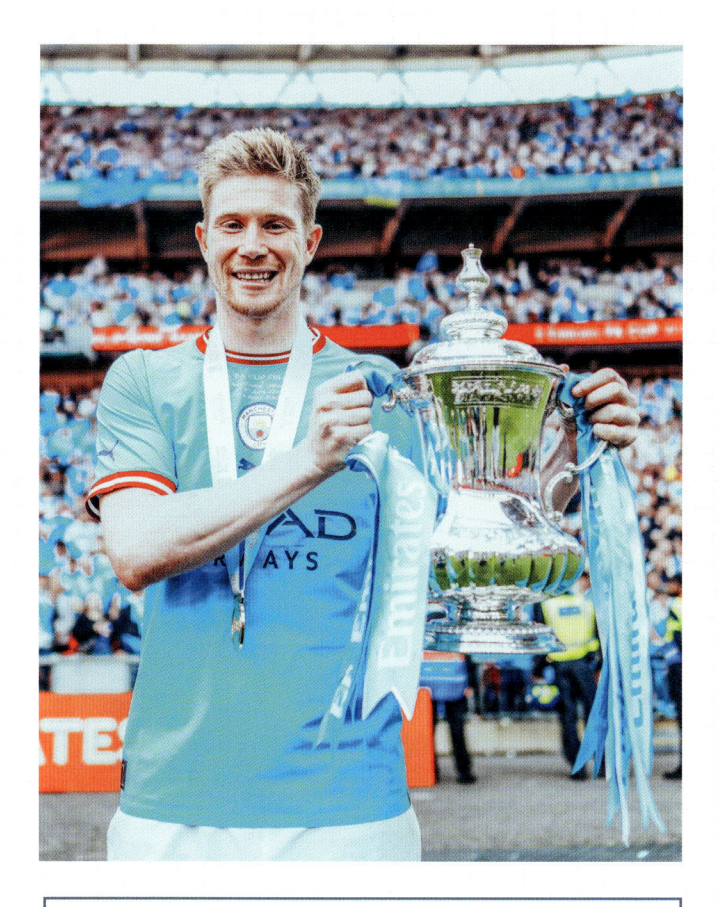

| | | | | |
|---|---|---|---|---|
| **Third Round** | | | | |
| 08.01.2023 | Manchester City | 4 | 0 | Chelsea |
| **Fourth Round** | | | | |
| 27.01.2023 | Manchester City | 1 | 0 | Arsenal |
| **Fifth Round** | | | | |
| 28.02.2023 | Bristol City | 0 | 3 | Manchester City |
| **Quarter-Final** | | | | |
| 18.03.2023 | Manchester City | 6 | 0 | Burnley |
| **Semi-Final** | | | | |
| 22.04.2023 | Manchester City | 3 | 0 | Sheffield United |
| **Final** | | | | |
| 03.06.2023 | Manchester City | 2 | 1 | Manchester United |

## FA CUP APPEARANCES

| | | | | |
|---|---|---|---|---|
| Stefan Ortega | 6 | Rodrigo | 4 |
| Manuel Akanji | 6 | Erling Haaland | 4 |
| Kyle Walker | 5 | Cole Palmer | 4 |
| Riyad Mahrez | 5 | Sergio Gomez | 4 |
| Julian Alvarez | 5 | Ilkay Gundogan | 3 |
| Rico Lewis | 5 | Nathan Ake | 3 |
| Aymeric Laporte | 5 | Ruben Dias | 3 |
| Jack Grealish | 5 | John Stones | 2 |
| Bernardo Silva | 5 | Ederson | 1 |
| Phil Foden | 5 | Joao Cancelo | 1 |
| Kevin De Bruyne | 4 | Maximo Perrone | 1 |
| Kalvin Phillips | 4 | | |

## FA CUP GOALS

| | |
|---|---|
| Riyad Mahrez | 5 |
| Erling Haaland | 3 |
| Julian Alvarez | 3 |
| Phil Foden | 3 |
| Ilkay Gundogan | 2 |
| Kevin De Bruyne | 1 |
| Cole Palmer | 1 |
| Nathan Ake | 1 |

www.mancity.com 287